Released from DPL

PRE

HEMLOCK'S
CUP

OTHER BOOKS BY DONALD COX

HEMLOCK'S CUP

The Struggle for Death with Dignity

DONALD W. COX

Prometheus Books • Buffalo, New York

Published 1993 by Prometheus Books

97 96 95 94 93   5 4 3 2 1

Library of Congress Cataloging-in-Publication Data

Cox, Donald W. (Donald William), 1921–
    Hemlock's cup : the struggle for death with dignity / by Donald Cox.
    Includes bibliographical references and index.
    ISBN 0-87975-808-2 (cloth)
    1. Terminally ill. 2. Right to die. 3. Assisted suicide. I. Title.
R726.C677   1993
179'.7—dc20   93-20382
                                                              CIP

Printed in the United States of America on acid-free paper.

For Karen Ann Quinlan, Nancy Cruzan, Patti Rosier, Diane Trumbull, Janet Adkins, Sherri Miller, Marjorie Wantz, and all the other heroines and heroes involved in the struggle to legalize both passive and active euthanasia, so that others might benefit in the future.

Contents

8   CONTENTS

Part IV: The People Speak

Part V: A Question of Morality

Foreword

Almost every day, from somewhere in the United States, a dying patient places a telephone call to a staff member or volunteer of the Hemlock Society or another euthanasia group. These urgent calls request information about how life can be brought to a close in a nonviolent manner by and for persons suffering from ravaging terminal illnesses. In the vast majority of instances, the callers are patients suffering from cancer, heart disease, emphysema, AIDS, or some other gravely debilitating condition. Occasionally, it is a family member making the call at the patient's request. These are not calls about suicide as that term is usually understood; they are not tragic acts of depressed and desperate persons.

Typically, the callers have been ill for several years and are now experiencing a rapidly deteriorating quality of life. Such patients have usually discussed with family members their desire to die rather than suffer, but fear being rebuffed by their physicians and have therefore foregone asking the one person who might help most. Sometimes doctors reassure patients that the pain and suffering will be adequately managed, but with insufficient detail to be convincing or without guaranteeing sufficient control of the manner and timing of death by offering a prescription.

A caller may be reluctant at first to divulge identifying details without assurances that confidentiality be provided. Hemlock does not try to keep callers on the line while simultaneously reaching a suicide pre-

vention squad to intervene. The Society certainly urges anyone mentally distraught, but not terminally ill, to call one of the crisis agencies
located in most urban communities in the United States. But callers are
rarely in this category. They are most often dying patients who have
known the prolonged suffering of parents, spouses, or other loved ones.

Persons with AIDS, for example, have frequently witnessed the
death of a partner or friend whose immune system had similarly been
destroyed. These callers need little information about what awaits them
if their disease or condition remains unchecked. They have seen the
weight loss, intractable pain, incoherency, wasting, blindness and de-
mentia that so commonly accompany the long drawn-out process of
dying in the medico-technological environment of the contemporary
health care delivery system.

Often callers indicate that they are currently not subject to intense
physical suffering, but nevertheless do not wish the course of their dying to cancel out the sense of dignity they have always valued after having
led a long and good life. They may want some assurance that they will
be able to preclude losing control of their own dying. And they may
wish to prevent the expense of months of terminal care from consum-
ing the savings they have accumulated for the benefit of their spouses,
children, or grandchildren. I remember the retired physician's attitude
when faced with the choice between him having a few more months
of life or his grandchildren going to college; he said "Don't waste the
money on me; those kids are going to college." One retiree lamented
that the medical expenses for himself and his wife just about wiped him
out. He now feared that the cost of continued care for his cancer would
force his wife into welfare dependence after his death.

Terminally ill callers have often been thinking about death for a
long period of time. The decision to choose death over further deterioration is not necessarily the byproduct of a recent hopeless diagnosis. Nor is it the result of clinical depression, even though some degree
of depression is understandable for a person in declining health. When
asked what method of suicide they are considering, callers often reveal
that they have access to a firearm, even though at the same time they
are repulsed by the thought of discovery afterwards by the family. It
is partly out of a desire to spare the anguish of family members that
patients usually seek information and access to medicines that can offer
a more palatable and tranquil, if not natural, death. Still, a large per-

centage of the handgun deaths in this country are suicides by terminally ill elderly patients who found no other means to their goal.

Many Americans mistakenly believe that the Hemlock Society can provide the means of death to members who are in such a situation. We may be asked for the "special formula" or the "black pill" which will bring a quick and painless end to their suffering. Callers may also believe that someone from the society can be with them at the end to assure that their dying is not interrupted or otherwise botched. They are often disappointed to learn that the society can neither make legal drugs available nor actively participate in their intentional deaths. Hemlock's primary mission is to raise American consciousness about an increasingly common and difficult situation, and its publications have been forthright in describing circumstances that we all may face. To help people trapped in such dilemmas, Hemlock offers information about medicants that bring about death in a humane manner. But the key to access to these medications still lies with the physicians who have a monopoly on the prescriptive authority for barbituates, opioids, and other legal pharmaceutical drugs. For many this is the most moral and humane course open to them.

As a result, callers are typically urged to open communication with their physician about their concerns and plans, even at the risk of alienating their doctors. They may find it necessary to seek other physicians who will be more sympathetic and cooperative, and we assure them that there are many, even if we cannot suggest them. We often hear of doctors who have prescribed quantities of barbituates or morphine adequate to bring about death, but who were very oblique in instructing their patients on how the drug must be used. One doctor said, "You should take one of these every twelve hours; if you take thirty, it will kill you." A doctor may realize that if he refuses to prescribe the drugs usable for self-deliverance, the only alternatives are a violent death through some other means or continued torture.

When the prescription drugs are made available, the actual process of dying may take a far longer period of time than is expected. Even with the strongest drugs, some patients slip away only after eight to twenty-four hours have passed, a very difficult trial for anyone present during this period. Terminally ill patients frequently develop high tolerance to morphine and dilaudid and fail to succumb to doses which would be fatal to the ordinary person. These patients may return to consciousness after a long, deep sleep, usually with a profound disappointment. They may also regurgitate part of the prescribed medication, with a consequent loss of lethal effect.

In these circumstances, it is understandable when distraught family members or close friends take matters into their own hands and resort to drastic measures to be sure that the patient dies as he or she desired. As a last resort, a son may feel compelled to suffocate his mother or father with a pillow or plastic bag rather than allow the suicide to fail. Several people have described in impassioned detail their anguish and fears as well as the legal complications they envisioned. If the death results from a "mercy killing" with a gun used by someone other than the patient, it must be expected that a prosecution for homicide or manslaughter will result. It is unfair to place people in such profound moral and emotional dilemmas, but this is precisely what our present laws do.

Since its founding in 1980, the Hemlock Society has called for legislation which would permit a willing physician to help a terminally ill patient to die when that patient has clearly decided that the cost of continued life outweighs any benefits remaining. At this time, twenty-seven states in the United States have specific statutes making assisted suicide a crime, even in situations where death is the only outcome that makes reasonable sense from a medical or ethical point of view. In the other states, doctors who assist patients in the manner prescribed here are likely to be prosecuted for homicide. Efforts in several states to change these restrictions, either through bills introduced by legislators or through voter referenda, have yet to be successful. Articles in medical journals as well as in the public press have documented that physician-assisted dying is common medical practice, but it is carried out in clandestine circumstances, so the actual frequency is hidden from researchers.

As one who has on many occasions been the recipient of the telephone calls described here and has sometimes been the last person to speak with a suffering patient before death occurs, I see the need for an account of the progress toward legislation of the right to choose death. *Hemlock's Cup* by Dr. Don Cox, the president of the Hemlock Society of the Delaware Valley, comes just at the right time.

Thousands of dying patients in America would be comforted to know that, if and when their suffering becomes intolerable, a humane alternative is available to them. Many of us believe that it is inevitable that such an arrangement will come; there are simply too many patients who do not wish to languish in such hopeless situations and will take the measures to preclude such pointless suffering, not to mention the many physicians who believe that the current level of suffering is barbaric. The only question now is: how soon will this occur? One of the great unresolved issues of our society, as we strive to be more caring and humane, is how to make some provision for intentionality in dying as a voluntary option for terminal patients.

We expect that our children and grandchildren will look back at this present time as a period when anachronistic attitudes mindlessly prolonged the relentless process of dying for far too many suffering people. Of course, there will be those patients and physicians who choose to fight against death to the very natural end. But there will be others who elect to bow to the inevitable and ask for an easeful death.

Doctors will soon have more miraculous tools to work with than the high-tech medical weaponry of today. Physicians should be allowed to forego the use of high-tech weapons on patients who so choose, to permit them to meet the end of life with peace and dignity. Wherever possible, death should be the blessing of a final benediction.

How soon such an enlightened alternative comes into being depends upon the courage of America's physicians, judges, and elected officials. They should agree to expand the rights of dying patients to make their own final choices in life.

RALPH MERO, Unitarian
Minister and former Northwest
Regional Director of the National
Hemlock Society, Seattle, Washington

Acknowledgments

Without the help of the following people, this book would never have been written: Derek Humphry, the Founder and President of the National Hemlock Society, who encouraged me to go ahead with the project when the idea for such a book was still incubating; Ralph Mero, the Director of Initiative #119 in Washington, who wrote the Foreword and counseled me on the behind-the-scenes struggles of his followers to help make his state the first in the nation to legalize euthanasia; the Hemlock Society of the Delaware Valley and its leader, Dr. Arlyn Miller, for sending me to Denver in November 1991 as a delegate to the annual convention of Hemlock; Rosemary Hogan, a word-processor operator extraordinaire, who somehow was able to make sense out of my hieroglyphics; my daughter, Heather, who acted as an intermediary to help to get my rough draft of eighteen chapters into the right hands; Ernest Jones, who helped me with the indexing; Nan and Walt Billings, the twin leaders of the Suncoast Hemlock Society in Florida for their advice; the late Edward Holten-Schmidt, a *Readers Digest* editor who taught me how "to tell the story" in a proper sequence; Mark Hall, my perceptive and meticulous editor, whose eagle eye caught many oversights on my part; and many more who can't be mentioned by name for discretionary reasons.

Part of this book is theirs, and I deeply appreciate all their assistance.

Donald W. Cox, President, The Hemlock Society of the Delaware Valley
Philadelphia, December 1992

Introduction

The hope of democracy is that eventually the people will wobble straight.
—Abraham Lincoln

A quarter century ago, my family and I kept a vigil at the bedside of my ninety-year-old father, who was lying in a comatose state inside an oxygen tent. He was hooked up to several intravenous (I.V.) tubes to keep him alive, even though his case had been diagnosed as terminal by his doctor. He had been a resident of a nursing home for two years, where he had survived in a vegetative state, suffering from senility, incontinence, and in the end, pneumonia.

It was December and my father's doctor, who ran the nursing home (and was later indicted for ripping off Medicare to the tune of over $100,000 in illegal government billings), told our family: "I'm trying to keep him alive through Christmas, so you can all enjoy your Yuletide holiday." In reality, we did not enjoy the anguished period of sweating out our father's fate. On the day after Christmas, he finally expired peacefully in a coma, suffering the ravages of a 105-degree fever.

There was no activist right-to-die organization like the Hemlock Society in the late sixties, which might help survivors to hasten the end of such terminal cases by either passive doctor-assisted suicide (asking the attending physician to turn off the I.V. tubes and respirators), or by some active means such as speeding up death with a lethal drug given orally or intravenously.

But those days are now past with the advent of living wills and powers of attorney, which have been legalized in most states. High-tech medical procedures, which can prolong the lives of terminally ill patients, have put the practitioners of medicine in a Catch-22 situation. Doctors who take the Hippocratic Oath at the beginning of their careers, promising to do all that they can to prolong life and to heal their patients, are now faced with the specter of being sued for malpractice, being fined, going to jail, and losing their licenses if they are caught assisting a patient to end his or her life prematurely.

The Four Major Medical Controversies of the '90s

In the last decade of the twentieth century, four interrelated medical problems loom on the horizon to challenge the medical profession, our politicians, and the people, who are the consumers. The paramount issue is a national health plan and cradle-to-the-grave insurance, which dramatically took center stage with the November 1991 election of the underdog Pennsylvania Democrat Harris Wofford to the U.S. Senate in his upset victory over the favored Republican, former Governor Dick Thornburgh. This "message to Washington" on the crying need for some form of health insurance for all—particularly the 40 million Americans who do not possess any such medical security—had long been overdue in the nation's capital. After all, we are one of the last two civilized nations on this planet (along with South Africa) not to have some kind of health insurance for all of its citizens.

Beneath this leaky umbrella problem, three additional major health concerns plague the body politic: one at the beginning of life, one in mid-life, and the last at the end of life. The first is abortion; the second is AIDS, which exploded on the American scene in full force on November 7, 1991, with the confession of basketball superstar Earvin "Magic" Johnson that he was HIV positive; and the third is the growing issue of doctor-assisted suicide (death with dignity) for the terminally ill.

Although this volume will be mainly focussed on the latter issue, separate chapters will be focussed on the first two to show their inter-relationship with the third. The common threads of *privacy* and *freedom of choice* hold them all together as the nation struggles to find a resolution for these three medical issues which are dividing the country.

The controversial, contemporary issue of doctor-assisted death has brought the question of *how* people will die in the '90s and beyond to the forefront. Headline-making stories have appeared on the last days of incurable and comatose patients like Karen Ann Quinlan and Nancy Cruzan; on the deaths of over a dozen terminally ill men and women in 1990, 1991, 1992, and 1993 by means of Dr. Jack Kevorkian's "suicide machine"; and on Proposition #119, which was placed on the state of Washington's ballot in November 1991. Such publicity has made us aware that this relatively recent medical problem, which asserts itself in mid-life and particularly at the end of life, needs an answer.

Individuals should have the right to die with dignity at the time and manner of their choice, but they also have a right to live. Seeking a proper balance between the two extremes is obviously a profound ethical problem for loved ones and medical specialists searching for a rational middle ground to resolve the fate of an incurably ill family member. The miracles of modern medical technology, with its ability to prolong the lives of brain-dead patients, have created an ethical dilemma which needs to be addressed. Medical doctors, who were formerly concerned with both caring and curing their patients, have become so enmeshed in the latter part of their twin goals that many of them have forgotten about the caring aspect of their profession.

This book attempts to explore the controversies surrounding the proper caring of the incurables in our society. In ancient China, the custom of treating the old and senile members of society was for their younger family members to take them out into the woods with a basket of fruit and food, bid them goodbye, and leave them to the forces of nature to take over the dying process. But our modern society considers that approach cruel and inhumane.

Abandoning the Elderly: in the U.S.A. of All Places

Even though the abandonment of terminal, elderly citizens as practiced in ancient China would be abhorred in modern civilization, a new kind of abandonment, colloquially known as "Granny Dumping," has suddenly resurfaced in the past fifteen years in this country. The story of eighty-two-year-old John Kingery, who suffered from Alzheimer's Disease, made national and international headlines after he was found on March 25, 1992, clutching a teddy bear, slumped in a wheelchair, and holding a bag of diapers, near the rest room of a dog-racing track in Coer D'Alene, Idaho (Associated Press, 1992). This helpless man had a typed note pinned to his chest, identifying him as "John King." He was wearing bedroom slippers and a sweatshirt that said: "Proud to be an American." He did not even know his own name and had been left on society's doorstep by his daughter, Sue Gifford, of Portland, Oregon, who had checked him out of an area nursing home ten days before. She and her family were no longer able to pay the nursing-home costs which were sapping the family's finances, so she made a desperate move to solve the problem.

One resident of Idaho, who, like his neighbors, was shocked when the incident involving the abandonment of John Kingery surfaced, expressed both outrage and a dose of understanding: "I can sympathize with the financial strain," said John Cooper, "But to take somebody out and drop them off like misplaced luggage—that's terrible." (Ibid.)

The American College of Emergency Physicians has recently surveyed the nation's hospitals and concluded that up to 70,000 elderly parents were abandoned in 1991 alone, by family members who were either unable or unwilling to care for them any longer. This trend will be exacerbated in the next thirty years when the number of Americans over the age of eighty-five is expected to grow fivefold, to a population surpassing 15 million. At the same time, the number of people suffering from Alzheimer's Disease is expected to triple from 4 million in 1992 to 12 million by 2020, according to government medical estimates.

It is worth noting that in the 1991 Congressional session, Senator Bill Bradley (Dem. N.J.) introduced a bill that would provide payments to families to provide adult daycare, so that adult children could get a respite from the pressures of raising their own children and taking care of elderly parents. Up to 1.5 million parents would qualify for such help, said Bradley. But no action had been taken on his proposed bill by July 1992.

Fallout from a Book

In one sense, this book is about another book—*Final Exit* by Derek Humphry, the founder of the Hemlock Society—and about the extraordinary rocketing of its sales from an obscure place in the pack of the thousands of books published each year in the United States, to a unique place at the pinnacle of the 1991 season.

How and *why* this phenomenon occurred and the growth of the death-with-dignity movement will be analyzed in the following chapters, along with a periphery of allied topics—like AIDS and abortion—to properly frame the answers to the above questions.

The Legacy of Socrates

As the leading right-to-die organization in America, the Hemlock Society takes its name from a historical event that occurred about 2900 years ago.

In 400 B.C. Athens was the center of philosophical thought in the then known Western world. That capital of ancient Greece was the home of an idle stonemason named Socrates. He was not a philosopher by training, but found himself drifting about his beloved city attaching himself mainly to a circle of rich young men and entangling the citizens in arguments over the issues of "justice," "piety," and "bravery." He sought ways to guide the intellectual and moral improvement of the populace.

Since Socrates was so highly skilled as a debater, he usually made his audiences look foolish. As the local gadfly, he was soon accused of propagating religious heresies. Finally, in 399 B.C., various victims of his dialogues accused him of corrupting the city's youth and introducing the city to the worship of new deities. Socrates was made the scapegoat of their venom and was put on trial. He was found guilty, condemned, and forced to commit suicide by drinking a cup of poison hemlock.[1]

In ancient Greece, the root of the hemlock was used for rational

---

1. It is important to note that while members of the modern Hemlock Society in the United States believe in the voluntary, free choice of ending one's life with the aid of a living will and a lethal drug prescription, the execution of Socrates was an involuntary act.

suicide, which was acceptable in Greco-Roman societies under certain conditions. (In Western literature, the term "drink the cup of Hemlock" has, through Shakespeare and others, come to mean the way to rational suicide.)

Socrates left future generations with several legacies, one of which was his changing the main concern of the evolving philosophy of the time from being centered on physics to that of ethics. He developed the now well-known Socratic method of using questions and answers to solve problems, which became rooted in succeeding generations of educators. Socrates also contributed to the discipline of logic by forming a circle of devoted disciples to propagate his teachings. Unfortunately, his death turned many of his devotees away from the flowering of democracy in Greece, which was to prevail in Athens for the next four centuries.

The Doctors' Dilemma: Is the Hippocratic Oath Still Valid?

Besides the legacy of Socrates, there is another medical inheritance from ancient Greece. Unfortunately, this one has become a millstone around the necks of patients and their families seeking medical assistance to end the suffering of their loved ones. The taking of the Hippocratic Oath by medical doctors at their graduation exercises has created an ethical dilemma for doctors who now must often make difficult decisions in the last stages of terminal illness. Some physicians, particularly the older ones in our society, have been known to say, when asked to assist an incurable patient to hasten his or her death: "I can't. It is contrary to my Hippocratic Oath." The strict adherence to this oath has often prolonged the life but also the suffering of an incurable patient.

Such doctors' feelings reflect a misinterpretation of the original Hippocratic Oath and its relevance to the peculiar conditions that doctors now face in the last decade of the twentieth century. Rapid advances in medical technology and in social philosophy (as reflected in recent Roper and Gallup Polls) on the issue of euthanasia have called into question the original intent of the Hippocratic Oath and the current interpretation of medical ethics.

Gregory Pence wrote in his recent book, *Classic Cases of Medical Ethics* (1990):

The common view of Hippocrates as forbidding killing by physicians was shattered in 1931 by Ludwig Edelstein, who considered Hippocrates as a follower of the mystic Pythagoras . . . who worshipped numbers as divine and who believed that all life was sacred. According to Edelstein, "Hippocrates was not at all representative of ancient Greek physicians."

Dr. Pence's translation from the Greek of the original Hippocratic Oath and Covenant reads as follows:

I swear by Apollo, Physician, and Asclepius and Panacea and all the gods and godesses, that I will fulfill according to my ability and judgment this Oath and Covenant. . . .

I will apply dietetic measures. . . .

I will neither give a deadly drug to anybody if asked for it.

To a woman I will not give an abortive remedy.

I will not use the knife. . . .

Whatever houses I visit, I will come for the benefit of the sick, free of all intentional injustices . . . or mischief . . . or sexual relations. . . .

What I may see or hear in the course of the treatment, I will keep to myself. . . .

If I fulfill and do not violate this Oath, it may be granted to me to enjoy life and art, being honored by fame . . . and if I transgress it and swear falsely, may the opposite of this be my lot.

Today, as Dr. Pence points out in his timely book, few medical schools give the "real oath, e.g., swearing never to perform abortions, never to kill patients who request death, and not to do surgery (with a knife)." Furthermore, many ancient Greek physicians disagreed with Hippocrates, thinking that life had certain limitations, after which life could end. Medical meetings over the succeeding centuries around the world have given stark evidence of the violation of almost every one of these so-called injunctions to doctors.

And so we are faced with the modern doctor's dilemma in our society—to prolong the life beyond a reasonable point or to assist the dying of those who are cancer-ridden, in great pain, brain dead, suffering from the final stages of AIDS, or in a comatose state.

Part I: The Door Reopens

Darkling I listen; and, for many a time
I have been half in love with easeful death,
Call'd him soft names in many mused rhyme;
To take into the air my quiet breath;
Now more than ever seems it rich to die,
To cease upon the midnight with no pain.

—John Keats, "Ode to a Nightingale"

1

The Dramatic Entrance of
Final Exit to Center Stage

There is a deep-seated fear of high-tech medicine in America, of being locked into machines and losing control of their own lives. . . . Let's make no mistake. Something is going on, whether you like it or not, with a growing segment of the American populace wanting the right to end their own lives if they are terminally ill or injured.
> —Derek Humphry, the Founder of the Hemlock Society,
> in a speech delivered in Colorado Springs, Colorado,
> on November 14, 1991

Who would have ever dreamed that the number-one best-selling nonfiction book for much of 1991 would be a book about death? Few Americans had ever heard of *Final Exit* before midsummer, when its sudden popularity proved that it was a book whose time had come. A crisis had been lurking under the surface of the American health delivery system and few politicians and medical professionals were addressing the problem, until a journalist from Great Britain who had personally suffered a family medical tragedy offered an insight into the people's and the doctors' dilemmas.

Why and How *Final Exit* Became a Best-Seller Overnight

After its quiet publication in early March 1991, *Final Exit* was just another obscure book jamming the shelves of the nation's bookstores, with little advertising and promotion to help its sales. And then, suddenly, on August 18, it appeared in the number-one spot on the *New York Times Book Review*'s "Advice and How-to List," and it also gained the top spot on *Publishers Weekly*'s nonfiction list of best-sellers for that week. A preview of this meteoric rise appeared in a front-page story in the *Times* on August 9.

This phenomenon was a rarity in the book business, since most best-sellers usually appear on the bottom of the list of these authoritative journals and then slowly wend their way up the ladder gradually over a matter of weeks. *Final Exit,* however, leaped to the top of the list from nowhere in late August, remained at the top of the *Times*' Advice List for the next four months, and continued to be among the best-sellers listed by *Publishers Weekly* during the same period. By September it was the best-selling book of all types in the U.S. and became the fifth highest best-seller for all of 1991. Why did it happen?

First of all, the book satisfied a growing need of the book-buying public for a medical "recipe" volume that spelled out rational and painless alternatives to painful, prolonged deaths. It also provided information on steps to achieve active euthanasia, beyond the passive euthanasia techniques of removing I.V. tubes and respirators from terminally ill patients.

The book was authored by Derek Humphry, the executive director of the Hemlock Society, a national, activist euthanasia-educational organization anchored in Eugene, Oregon, which advises members (who are mainly senior citizens and AIDS victims) on how to commit suicide nonviolently. Humphry had been a writer for the *London Times* and later for the *Los Angeles Times,* where he practiced the art of advocacy journalism. He had previously published two best-sellers—*Let Me Die Before I Wake* in 1981 (a passive-euthanasia companion to *Final Exit*) and *Jean's Way,* the story of his late wife's last days of suffering from an incurable cancer. He had helped Jean to die peacefully by giving her a cup of coffee laced with a doctor-prescribed overdose of sleeping pills.

After hundreds of his readers wrote to Humphry about how much his earlier books had helped to give them the courage to assist their incurable relatives to die, Derek felt a decade later that the "time was ripe for publishing an updated, responsible suicide manual." He was concerned with the cruel fate of the 1.3 million Americans who die annually in hospitals and the hundreds of thousands in nursing homes, many of whom are hooked up to life-supporting tubes and machines long after they have been declared brain dead or have declined into a vegetative state.

Final Exit has a foreword by Betty Rollin, a TV journalist who had previously described her own mother's suicide in her book *Last Wish,* published in 1987. After the book came out, Rollin received hundreds of letters. "Among the saddest," she said, "were those from people—or the close relatives of people—who have tried to die, failed, and suffered even more. Many of those people sought help—from physicians or family—but were denied it because, although suicide is legal, doctor assisted suicide is not." She added, in her introduction to the book, "Until there is a law which would allow physicians to help people who want a final exit, here is Derek Humphry's book, fittingly named, to guide them."

What is *Final Exit* All About?

What Humphry sought in his slim 44,000-word volume was to provide a viable, active-euthanasia manual as a successor to *Let Me Die Before I Wake,* which was devoted to explaining euthanasia through the case-history format. Humphry reprinted Hemlock's well-known Drug Dosage Table in *Final Exit* and opened new territories in the field of euthanasia by giving guidance to nurses and physicians about helping their incurable patients to die. Humphry commented before publication: "I have poured everything I have learned about my fifteen years working in the subject into this new book."

He explained the difference between the two companion books this way: "*Final Exit* could be said to deal with the 'nuts and bolts' of voluntary euthanasia, while [the still popular] *Let Me Die Before I Wake* deals with the personal, emotional and familial aspects . . . of the subject." As one reviewer put it: "If *Let Me Die* was the 'guide' to self-deliverance, *Final Exit* is the comprehensive shop manual." The book's subtitle, "The Practicalities of Self-Deliverance and Assisted Suicide for the Dying," explains in simple language what its contents are all about. Humphry makes it clear that his book is aimed mainly at terminally ill people who "are considering rational suicide if and when the suffering becomes unbearable."

Final Exit offers understandable, easy-to-use information about exact drug dosages, active shelf life of various drugs, their side effects, and complete information on the best routes of administering them. Humphry also devotes several chapters to the status of the law, privacy, insurance questions, and how to assist others who are in great pain. In addition, he lays to rest many long-standing suicide myths, demonstrating that a fatal bubble of injected air, cyanide, or nonprescription drugs are not only ineffective means but are also often excessively painful ways to go.

The Baptism of *Final Exit*

Humphry noted that he wrote *Final Exit* as a "workshop manual" and that it was published by the Hemlock Society with no advertising or author promotional tours, although three hundred copies were sent out to key media, TV, and other professional reviewers in February, with very few responses. He had made an optimistic gamble to print 41,000 copies of the first edition, but most of the books were stored in the warehouse of the Hemlock Society's distributor, the Carol Publishing Co. of Secaucus, New Jersey.

Within the first three months of publication, over 15,000 (or a little better than one-third of the initial printing) had been quietly bought, mainly by members of Hemlock. (Humphry had hopes of selling the remainder within two years to help provide some necessary funding for his struggling Hemlock Society.)

Then a few favorable reviews started to trickle in, but none in the major media.

The Spinoff from Dr. Quill's Action

On July 26, 1991, Dr. Timothy Quill of Rochester, New York, was freed by a local grand jury of prospective murder charges for assisting a terminally ill female leukemia patient to hasten her death. The resulting headlines, along with a front-page story in the *Wall Street Journal,* helped *Final Exit* to take off. The failure to indict Dr. Quill came in the aftermath of his heart-warming article published in the *New England Journal of Medicine* (see Appendices for complete text), detailing how he had prescribed a lethal dose of pain-killing medicine to help his patient, Diane, to commit suicide.

Although suicide is not a criminal act in the United States, physicians who assist patients to hasten their deaths can be prosecuted in *all* of the states, and be fined, incarcerated, and/or lose their licenses. But the jury in the Quill case said he was innocent of any wrongdoing and Dr. Quill, who is on the faculty of the University of Rochester Medical School, was relieved at the positive outcome of his case. (With thousands of elderly patients now lying in hospitals and nursing homes in a terminally ill or comatose state, hooked up to life-support systems, there are many doctors like Quill who are devoting more time to help their terminal patients plan to end their lives painlessly.)

After the news of the outcome of the Quill case was flashed around the country over radio, TV, and in the print media, hundreds of avid bookbuyers descended on their local bookstores seeking copies of *Final Exit,* only to discover that most of them had sold out their copies of the book, and that they would have to wait for a new shipment from the publisher.

Word of mouth and a reaction to how modern medicine was dealing with terminal illness had caused this flocking to the bookstores. They were all seeking a rational alternative to the high costs of prolonged, terminal illnesses now plaguing the country.

A Turning Point

Steve Schragis, the owner of Carol Publishing Co., who was a member of Hemlock, offered to do the trade-bookstore distribution of *Final Exit,* which until then had been handled by mail order from Hemlock's home office in Eugene, Oregon. He also worked tirelessly to get the New York media, where the heart of the publishing business is located, interested in the message of the book (Ames 1991).

In 1988, Schragis and his wife had faced a nightmare that they would never forget, when the American medical system insisted on keeping their newborn child "alive," despite a near total lack of brain function. "A decision that ought to have been ours alone was being made by others," he said sadly. That experience profoundly affected Schragis, causing him to change professions, go into book publishing, and to join Hemlock.

After writing personal letters to twenty major media outlets as well as to dozens of news, TV, and radio reporters, Schragis was about to give up when Norman Pearlstein and Meg Cox of the *Wall Street Journal* called him. That call marked a major turning point, because on August 12 the *Wall Street Journal* ran a cover story on *Final Exit,* including an interview with Humphry that told the public for the first time, coast-to-coast, what Humphry was trying to say.

Another turning point was Humphry's debate on the "Today Show" (NBC-TV) with a representative of the American Medical Association. The doctor stated that his profession was dedicated to always providing "one more sunrise for a patient if at all possible."

"Virtually anyone who has spent time with a terminally ill patient," commented Schragis, "for whom every day for the last few weeks of life is filled with pain and misery, knows just how wrong the doctor was."

This publicity break started a flurry of national media coverage on the controversial topic. The good review of the work that had appeared weeks earlier in the *New York Times* on August 9, was followed a short week later in the same paper by another favorable review by one of its regular Op/Ed-page columnists, Anna Quindlen, and a cover story was devoted to the book on August 26. These reviews, as well as a feature story in the September 30 issue of *U.S. News and World Report,* helped bring the book to the public's attention and conscience.

Why We Are Becoming Afraid to Die

In the August 14 issue of the *New York Times,* Anna Quindlen wrote a searing piece titled "Death: The Best Seller," which was based on *Final Exit.* In that column, she noted that "the questions surrounding the right to die have become central ones in American society for this very reason: *because advances in medical technology have left some of us more afraid of dying than of death.*" She went on to say:

Perhaps they [the buyers of *Final Exit*] are also people who have gone to doctors and who know that when you become a patient, often you cease to be an actor and become an acted upon. They are people who know from experience that certain illnesses leave the sick stripped of everything they think makes life worth living, prisoners of pain and indignity.

Perhaps they are men and women approaching old age who have visited nursing homes and seen people who are husks, tied upright in wheelchairs, staring at the ceiling from hospital beds, saved from death by any means possible, saved for something that is as much like life as a stone is like an egg, a twig like a finger.

That is a horrid future to contemplate for those who value their strength and competence.

2

The Impact of *Final Exit*
on America and the World

Tonight, I quit these walls,
The thought my soul appalls,
But when stern duty calls,
I must obey.
        —Gilbert and Sullivan, *The Pirates of Penzance*

The Far Right Responds

After the tremendous sales and publicity of *Final Exit,* the opposition
mounted an intense campaign to undermine its authenticity. Rita Marker,
the director of the International Anti-Euthanasia Task Force, labeled
Humphry as a "charlatan" who wrote his book in a "cold, calculating
manner" (Ames 1991).

In Canada, the Calvinist-oriented critics, strongly influenced by strict
Protestant ethical attitudes, condemned the book, but sales continued
to climb there, one book dealer alone ordering ten thousand copies and
guaranteeing Hemlock, "I will not return any of them." The National
Right to Life movement entered the fray by calling for the banning of
Final Exit both in the United States and Canada, but this led to an

avalanche of orders, which inundated the tiny central Hemlock Society office staff in Oregon. Many of the detractors made accusations that the book would increase the rate of suicide at all levels in the country.

Dissenters from the Medical Profession Speak Out

Dr. Arthur Caplan, a bioethicist at the University of Minnesota, rated *Final Exit* as "the loudest statement of protest of how medicine is dealing with terminal illness and dying." But Caplan had a warning for those who buy the book with the intent of committing suicide:

> That presumption should never be made on this subject. There has to be some room for a change of mind and people should be challenged right up to the last minute that their wish to die is authentic. I am nervous about the information getting into the hands of despondent and mentally ill people without the opportunity for counselling and discussion. This is not an argument against censorship, but I wish it had more to say about who such people could talk to and that it included hot-line numbers. (Altman 1991)

Another dissenter, Dr. Donnie Bristow, an internist in San Pablo, California, who is on the Board of the American Medical Association, called the book's message "repugnant" and declared that it goes against the medical profession's ethics.

"It strikes at the very foundation of what makes the profession noble," he said, noting that "there is no reason in this day and age for a patient to have unbearable suffering."

Bristow claimed that the philosophy behind *Final Exit* would destroy the mutual trust between doctors and patients, "if there is reason to believe that doctors are equally adept at killing as well as saving lives" (Angelo 1991).

A Warning to the Mentally Ill

In the wake of the publicity surrounding *Final Exit,* a growing number of mental health experts expressed additional worries about the impact

of Humphry's book on troubled people in our society, particularly elderly men—who have the nation's highest suicide rate. Their concern was
that such "how-to" books could push the suicide rate even higher among
the depressed elements of our population who are suffering transient
illnesses that can be treated with medication and/or psychotherapy.

That is the thesis of David Clarke, the president of the American
Society of Suicideology, an organization dedicated to preventing suicide.
"Most people who want to die are suffering transient illness, usually
depression, that is treatable with medication or psychotherapy. Most
are extraordinarily glad when they recover that someone didn't help
them die," he observed (Clarke 1991).

At the opposite extreme, Humphry insists that his book was meant
only for the "terminally-ill and not for unhappy, depressed people. I
touch on the subject in order to be responsible. . . . And I say to depressed
people, 'Seek Help.' I also say: 'Get a second opinion. Make sure you
are terminally-ill.' "

But Humphry has been criticized by such experts as Sanford Finkel,
M.D., the director of Gero-psychiatric Services at Northwestern Memorial Hospital in Chicago. "There is only one paragraph," Finkel notes,
"but he makes no attempt to explain what it is. It just says if you
are depressed, then you should get professional help. However, that
doesn't help a lot of people who are depressed, such as those who don't
have much insight into what depression really is, and who are confused
as to whether they have an illness that is indeed treatable."

Humphry has pointed out that while 2 million Americans die each
year of terminal illness, about thirty thousand commit suicide for various reasons. "I'm entitled to address my book to the 2,000,000, or those
of that group who want to read it," he says. "I don't think the 2,000,000
should be deprived of my book just because of the unhappy suicides
of 30,000" (ibid).

He received some support from several authorities in the field about
the exaggerated concerns of those objecting to the book getting into
the wrong hands. Virginia Crespo, director of Geriatric Programs at
the Neurological Institute of Columbia Presbyterian Hospital in New
York, questioned whether "how to" suicide books triggered more suicides.
"If someone wants to commit suicide," she says, "they will find a way
to do it, whether they read the book or not."

But Alan Berman, the Director of the National Center for the Study and Prevention of Suicide in Washington, stated that he was "concerned about giving an easy approach to people who would otherwise not commit suicide. Why is there a need for this book?" Humphry retorted that if the "non-terminally ill people kill themselves with this book—that's an abuse. Anything—guns, a rope, or a gas oven—can be abused. This same cry went up when we published *Let Me Die Before I Wake*. But the suicide rate did not alter. It'll be interesting to see if the rate in America alters now [in the wake of *Final Exit*], but I doubt it" (ibid.).

Is *Final Exit* a Haven for the Mentally Ill?: The Adelman Case

Humphry and other Hemlock members are aware that *Final Exit* has been utilized by some mentally sick individuals. Several news reporters called the national office to inform the author that his book had been found next to the body of a man who had killed himself by inhaling the exhaust of his car's engine. Humphry's answer to the reporters was: "One doesn't need a book to tell him when and how to commit suicide. Furthermore, using monoxide from an auto's tailpipe has been going on since the early 1900s when the auto replaced the horse as a means of travel."

The first major case in which both *Final Exit* and Humphry were accused of leading a mentally ill person to a premature death surfaced in mid-November. The mother and older brother of twenty-nine-year-old Adrian Adelman, who killed himself in September after reading the book, blamed Humphry for the tragedy that befell the deeply depressed young man. In a three-page interview printed in the November 18, 1991 issue of *Time,* Mrs. Ethel Adelman and her surviving son, Alan, both believed that Adrian would still be alive if he had not read the book. "The book took his life away. . . . We consider the book very dangerous," commented Alan, who admitted that he had confiscated the first copy of *Final Exit* when it came into their home by mail-order, addressed to Adrian, who was a new member of the Hemlock Society.

In denouncing the "suicide cookbook," the caustic Alan conceded that when his late brother went out and bought another copy of the book, he followed the instructions inside, wrote a living will, a power of attorney, and left specific written instructions, which were included with this suicide note: "If I am discovered before I have stopped breathing, I forbid anyone, including the doctors and the paramedics to attempt to revive me. If I am revived, I shall sue."

Alan was upset that the book contained instructions on "how to trick the doctor to get drugs strong enough for suicide," which his brother did when he went to three different doctors to obtain enough multiple prescriptions to take his own life. When asked by the *Time* reporter whether either he or his mother had communicated their concerns to Humphry, Alan answered, "No, I have not. I honestly don't think he cares. He is indifferent to who might read it." Alan went on to say that the "dangerous thing about the book is that it falls into the hands of teenagers and clinically depressed people" like his brother.

Even though Humphry had written that "suicide for reasons of depression has never been a part of the credo of the Hemlock Society," Alan retorted: "The only warning I found was on page 123, listed under the heading of 'Advice,' not warning. It says that: 'This information is meant for consideration only by a mature adult who is dying.' " Adelman accused Humphry of waiting until "too late in the book" to "warn" his readers, "after outlining dozens of methods of suicide." Alan told his interviewer that his mother believed that once he got the book, "we lost him. It gave him confidence. He became obsessed with the book. It showed him the way," said Alan. "The book was clearly the answer to his dilemma of how to commit suicide without feeling any pain. He said he would never shoot himself, or do anything like that."

Alan felt extremely bitter about his brother's death and asked, "Why did he [Humphry] put the book where minors could get their hands on it? . . . He knew it would fall into the hands of depressed people. Why didn't he regulate the distribution? That's why I strongly believe he's not concerned at all with the hands that the book falls into. While I don't object to euthanasia, his way of expressing his beliefs and disseminating the information is reckless."

But one thing Adelman forgot, in his plea for Humphry to exercise self-censorship and more restraint, was that the distributor and bookstores—in a free-market economy—control the placement of any book in their racks and distribution system. There is no way an author can control this aspect of his product in a free society once a book is published.

When confronted with the biting criticism of his book's indirect role in bringing about the death of Adrian Adelman, Humphry retorted: "His family made a false accusation. Why did he need *Final Exit* as a motivation to take his own life? He could have done it without the book. That young man chose a peaceful death as a way out." Humphry wrote a letter to the editor of *Time* expressing his condolences, but also noting that "suicide happens. It is part of our society."

Derek Hits the Campaign Trail to Promote His Book

Following the book's breakthrough, Humphry was inundated with dozens of radio, TV, and newspaper interviews, including a personal appearance on the top-rated Donahue TV show, in which he summarized the book's main appeal in these general terms:

> Its unusual honesty and frankness in dealing with suicide, assisted suicide, and physician-assisted suicide; being compared to a "workshop manual" with its simple language with large type; answering the need that people have to keep control of their lives when dying; and the understandable wish that many people have for a "release mechanism" should their terminal illness happen to come in an unbearable form. (Donahue 1991)

He also felt that his book marked a "significant social statement of protest about the way institutional medicine, the law and the legislatures are dealing with the dying process today."

Help from the Humor Industry

Humphry was also fascinated with the side-door assistance provided by the nation's comic and pictorial humorists, including the social and political satire offered by such celebrity network TV comics as Bob Hope, David Letterman, Arsenio Hall, and Jay Leno, as well as a featured skit presented on NBC-TV's popular "Saturday Night Live." In the latter segment, a copy of *Final Exit* jumped off a top shelf of a local bookstore allegedly committing suicide (Humphry, November 15, 1991).

Cartoons flooded the country on the topic. One of them showed a patient on a psychiatrist's couch, asking his therapist: "Tell me Doc, why don't I want to read *Final Exit*?" Another showed a library customer complaining to the librarian about being unable to find the book on the shelves. The exasperated librarian says: "Every copy of *Final Exit* is overdue and I'm overdue. I wonder why our copies of these books are never returned."

Some Light at the End of the Tunnel

By late November, with book sales averaging five thousand copies a week, plans were made to issue a paperback version and contracts were signed to translate the work into Chinese, Japanese, Turkish, French, Danish, Dutch, German, and other languages. Unfortunately, *Final Exit* could not be published in his native England, according to Humphry, since "British law labeled assisted suicide a crime," which made British publishers afraid to print the book. But copies of the American edition were shipped over to English bookstores. An audiocassette version, read by Humphry, was made available there and elsewhere to avid book buyers. The Library of Congress requested and received permission to translate *Final Exit* into Braille for the blind in both the United States and Canada.

Humphry was astonished by the phenomenal success of *Final Exit;* six printings followed the initial run and sales topped 530,000 in the hard-cover edition by December 1991. (The nonprofit Hemlock Society benefited by over $2,000,000 from these sales and a portion of Humphry's royalties went into his pension fund.) One of the intangibles that helped increase sales of the book was buyers' curiosity, according to many bookstore owners and managers. Most buyers had no intention of killing themselves.

The Legacy of *Final Exit*

Humphry believes that his book signified the recognition of the right-to-die concept as the will of the people. The book smashed the old taboo against putting such works in the bookstores, many of which prominently displayed multiple copies of *Final Exit* in front windows.

It also spurred the Harvard Medical School to host a conference on suicide in Boston during January 1992, and a national conference on suicide was scheduled elsewhere in April 1992.

There are deeper, hidden reasons, however, for the sudden popularity of *Final Exit* on the American scene. Some of these are: the fear of being kept alive by I.V. feeding tubes in a nursing home, or of being injected with life-prolonging drugs that can turn you into a vegetative "zombie," the legal court battles of family members over prolonging the life of an incurably ill patient, the dread of losing control over your quality of life and of being treated by poorly trained physicians, and the fear of having your health insurance (most of which does not cover nursing homes) cancelled by the supplier at any time.

These are only some of the major concerns expressed by correspondents who have written about their fears to Humphry and his staff at Hemlock. They seem to be saying that *Final Exit* has provided them with a handy reference book for them to use in choosing their own future alternatives in life and death. Even the medical profession, according to Humphry, has made a quiet, subtle shift from saying "no" to euthanasia to a new attitude of "perhaps" and "when."

Ronald P. Hamel, a Senior Associate for Theology, Ethics and Clinical Practice at Chicago's Park Ridge Center for the Study of Health, Faith and Ethics, noted that the popularity of *Final Exit* could "be viewed as an indictment of the medical establishment for failing to come to grips with reality." He further criticized the medical professionals by suggesting that "they need to recognize that a cure-oriented model of care is inappropriate for a dying patient, and accept the necessity of allowing people to die when their time has come." He went on to say, "Most obviously the health care profession needs to confront the overuse of medical technology that merely prolongs the dying process while producing no real benefit for the patient" (Hamel 1991)

But Hamel did not just hurl his barbs at the doctors, he also found fault with the technological "quick-fix" solution of the Hemlock Society and other advocates of suicide and active euthanasia, who are "short-circuiting the process that should instead attack the underlying causes of the problem."

Several months after *Final Exit* caused a major stir in American society, Derek Humphry assessed one of its hidden messages, when he said: "The popularity of the book represents a revolt of the people who seemed to be offering the most American of a self-examining dialogue, to wit: '*If you won't help me, I will help myself*' " (Humphry, November 15, 1991).

On page 97 of *Final Exit* Humphry notes that when reforms in medical procedures of treating terminally ill patients occur in America, then books like *Final Exit* will *not* be needed in the marketplace. So, in a sense, Humphry's tome has already served a similar purpose as Tom Paine's *Common Sense* did 215 years earlier, when he penned a battle cry for the colonists to use in resisting the British overlords.

Humphry's book of recipes provided a clarion call in response to the public's thirst for knowledge in a sensitive area of their own lives, where they could get none from their own physicians.

Final Exit Banned in Two Countries Down Under

By early spring of 1992, Derek Humphry's latest euthanasia book had been translated into a dozen foreign languages and was selling well around the world. But several right-to-life groups in Australia and New Zealand sought its banning, and government censors in both those countries finally issued an official ban and ordered all unsold copies to be seized from bookstores and forfeited. (By midyear, it was also banned in France.) The Office of Film and Literature Classification issued the ruling in Australia, and within three days the Indecent Publications Tribunal in New Zealand followed suit. The reason given for the double banning was that the book was "unacceptable" because assisted suicide is a "crime" in both countries and is punishable by twelve months imprisonment. The New South Wales state branch of the Australian Medical Association advised the government censoring agencies to ban the book because of its "potent recipes." (Humphry 1992)

The Australian book publishers Association condemned the banning of *Final Exit* as a "retrograde step" and made an appeal to the two national tribunals to lift the ban. Derek Humphry was quoted as saying: "I am shocked to find that they have censorship in those two countries. Freedom to publish and read is a basic human right." By August 1992 the Euthanasia Society in Australia made a plea to government officials in Canberra, and less than a year later the Chief Censor was forced to lift the ban in both New Zealand and Australia. Humphry was relieved by this reversal and also by the fact that customs officers in his homeland, Great Britain, allowed over five thousand copies of the book to be imported from the United States, even though not one book publisher in England dared to print the book.

Despite censorship problems, other publishers tried to cash in on the great public interest in this new topic, and soon new books with similar titles began popping up in bookstores: *Final Rites, Final Passages,* and even *Final Exit for Cats.*

Humphry's book was a pioneering work, a first "baby step" for health care professionals to use with their patients in the field of euthanasia where no similar work had existed before. *Final Exit* has helped to build bridges between terminally ill patients and health care professionals, and has furthered the growing movement to educate the public at large.

3

The Birth of the Hemlock Society

I will not relish old age unless it leaves my mind intact . . . but if
I know when I will suffer forever, I will depart. . . . Just as I choose
a ship to sail in or a house to live in, so I choose a death for my
passage from life.
                    —Seneca (8 B.C.–65 A.D.), who eventually committed suicide

In 1980, Derek Humphry, his second wife, Ann Wickett, and Gerald
Larue (who was later to become president of the infant organization)
stood on the sidewalk of Humphry's Santa Monica home and formed
the Hemlock Society. It had no identifying name until Ann suggested
"Hemlock," which was the poison used by Socrates in what has been
deemed to be his honorable death by suicide. The other two agreed,
and the name stuck, even though it has been criticized as having negative
connotations that do not reflect the true mission of the society. But
the motto of the society—Good Life, Good Death—has helped to
accentuate the positive aspects of the society.

Ann and Derek then got to work remodelling the garage in the
back of their home and converting it into the first office and workroom
of the Hemlock Society. The three pioneers, along with Richard Scott,
sat for hours in that small Hemlock "nursery" room, stuffing and sealing
envelopes to solicit memberships and funding to help the infant mature
into a national nonprofit active-euthanasia organization.

44

It has indeed grown to a national membership of over 40,000, marking Hemlock as the bellwether of one of the most visible social and human rights movements in America in the last years of the twentieth century.

Who Is Derek Humphry?

Humphry, the main founder of the Hemlock Society, was born in Bath, Somerset, southwest of London, on April 29, 1930, to an Irish model and a travelling salesman. He was the younger of two sons, his older brother being named Garth. The future founder and "Pied Piper" of the Hemlock Society went through several family turmoils as a youth. First, his parents split and his father got custody of both boys. Then his mother mysteriously left him when he was still small during the World War II years, married an Australian, and didn't reappear until he was twenty-three. He thought they would have an endless time ahead of them so that he could get to know her and make up for the lost years while he was being brought up by relatives in Somerset. But then, suddenly, she announced: "I am going back to Australia. You come and visit me" (McCrystal 1992).

Humphry never heard from his mother again, though he put ads in magazines trying to track her and even traveled to Australia in an attempt to find her. He thought she would surely show up when *Jean's Way*—his first book on euthanasia—was published, since she would recognize that it was authored by her son, when it made world headlines. "I didn't think that I would lose her again," he said wistfully, "since I am someone who likes to tie up loose ends." But he never found her.

He also suffered pangs when he lived with an aunt in Bristol as a young boy and was forced to write letters to his father who was "away at work somewhere." Years later, he discovered that the letters were put into another envelope and sent to a prison where his father was incarcerated—serving time for fraud. His father ultimately repented his youthful mistakes, straightened out his married life, and Derek was with him when he died at age seventy-nine. Today, when he talks about his late father, there is still a feeling of something lost in his family roots that he can never recover.

Derek is often nostalgic for his early years growing up on a farm in Somerset near Bath, educating himself by copious reading, walking, and listening to the BBC radio news during the World War II years. He also remembers pedalling furiously on his bike to see where British and Nazi bombers had crashed nearby. He was too young to serve in the military. Since there was no money for college, he was largely self-educated beyond his early secondary school years.

HIS FIRST JOBS: CLIMBING A CAREER LADDER

He left school at fifteen and entered the profession of journalism at the bottom of the career ladder, as a messenger boy with the *Yorkshire Post* in London from 1945 to 1946. Within one year, he became a junior (cub) reporter for the *Bristol Evening World,* and quickly progressed to a full-fledged journalist's post, first at the *Manchester Evening News* and then at the more prestigious *London Daily Mail.* He never got to go to college but perfected his craft on the job.

By thirty-three he became editor of the *Havering Recorder,* a suburban London newspaper, and held that post for five years until he moved to the London *Sunday Times,* where he wrote about race relations in Britain and established himself as a rising star in the field. In 1971, he published his first book, *Because They're Black,* a book explaining the lives of black people to white people. It won the coveted Martin Luther King, Jr. Memorial Prize for its contribution to racial harmony in Great Britain. He soon followed this with other books on race and civil liberties, including a biography of Malcolm X., the American civil rights and Muslim leader.

HIS FIRST MARRIAGE

While pursuing his career as a reporter, Humphry courted and married Jean Crane and fathered two sons by her; the couple adopted a third son. Unfortunately, Jean contracted an incurable breast and bone cancer while she was still in her forties. Her affliction would ultimately lead Derek to a new career—one which he would never have foreseen and which would consume his energies for the rest of his life.

Today Is the Day

"It was a clear, spring Saturday morning 16 years ago, and his dying wife, Jean, awoke, worn out from the pain from the cancer that started in her breast and now made her bones so brittle they snapped like breadsticks, and asked for tea and toast, then picked up the morning paper and put it down. And then she asked him, as they agreed she would when she was ready, 'Derek, is this the day?' and he replied, 'Yes, darling, it is.' "

This is the way Derek Humphry begins the description of his first wife's passing in 1975 at their home in the Cotswolds in his tender 1978 volume, *Jean's Way.* He also recounts how he assisted her to die and end her increasing pain with drugs prescribed by a sympathetic doctor. Before she drank her cup of coffee, laced with secobarbital and codeine, Humphry and Jean talked, laughed, and reminisced about their twenty years of marriage and their three children; they played her favorite music and sorted out their infrequent quarrels; and then he showed her how he would dedicate his next book to her. (He was so upset at this point that he couldn't speak and had to write the words down.) He hugged her and sat by the bed as she gulped down the lethal potion. Soon she faded into unconsciousness and died peacefully fifty minutes later. "It was the most vivid morning of my life," he recollected later.

After her death, Scotland Yard sent representatives to interview Humphry and tried to force him to give them his physician's name. They wanted to prosecute the doctor for prescribing a lethal dose of secobarbital. Humphry refused to compromise the doctor-patient right to privacy by divulging the doctor's name (Humphry 1990).

After Jean's death, Humphry got angry and asked himself several questions: "Why did I risk having to smother her if the pills did not work? How much better would it have been if a doctor administered the drugs legally?"

A Fatal Attraction

A few months after Jean's death, Humphry met a young lady from Boston named Ann Wickett, who was doing some post-Masters-degree research into the Bard of Avon at the Shakespeare Institute in Birmingham. They were married in the next year, and together wrote the story of his wife's death, during a protracted honeymoon. It was called *Jean's Way*.

After ten years at the *Sunday Times,* Derek and Ann emigrated to America, settling in a small house in Los Angeles where he obtained a position at the *Los Angeles Times* in 1978. He was exuberant at the prospects of a new life on the other side of the Atlantic. He no longer had to worry about the threat of future prosecution for assisting in Jean's death. "I could have got up to fourteen years in prison," he mused. "But I was very careful in preparing *Jean's Way*. I spent a lot of time in the library with law books. And once I was finished writing it, I destroyed all of my notes." (Humphry 1990)

In one respect, his first euthanasia book explained his own torment at the circumstances of his first wife's passing; it was his attempt to rationalize his own actions in helping his wife end the pain of her cancer-wracked body. After publication, Humphry made the rounds of book signings, press interviews, and TV talk shows, to promote the printed eulogy to his late wife. His new career was beginning to blossom.

A Career Change

Within a few years, Humphry discovered that the international acceptance of *Jean's Way* had launched him into a new career as an author-promoter of the right-to-die concept. When asked later whether he found his preoccupation with dying depressing, Humphry retorted: "No, because it involves *all* of life, good and bad." Overnight, thanks to the reception of *Jean's Way,* his life changed. He assumed a new role on the world stage as a messenger of what was right and wrong about the sensitive issue of helping terminally ill patients to die a pain-free death.

The topic of euthanasia soon overwhelmed Humphry's career as a journalist. He was invited to address medical schools and other professional groups throughout the United States, Canada, and Australia, where there were many individuals who were deeply troubled over the Catch-22 ethical dilemma created by the advances in high-tech medical technology. The size and enthusiasm of the crowds in his audiences astonished him, and he knew he had tapped into profound, widely shared concerns that had been dormant for too long. "My journalistic antennae told me that this was going to be a big subject," he told a *New York Times'* writer. He received scores of letters following the publication of *Jean's Way,* in which distraught patients and family members pleaded with him to disclose what drugs were used to ease the pain of his wife's dying and how he'd acquired them. He was at first reluctant to disclose the information.

A Second Book Makes Its Debut

But he later changed his mind on this point, when he authored *Let Me Die Before I Wake* in 1981. The subtitle of his soon to be popular new book was *How Dying People End Their Suffering.* Its anecdotal accounts of assisted suicides contained specific drug information buried in the text. His information on drug dosages (which was later expanded in the prescription tables embedded in the middle of *Final Exit*) was gleaned from twelve years of research by Humphry and in conversations that he had had with dozens of pharmacists, physicians, and "many hundreds of informants" who assisted their loved ones to die. Humphry broke new ground with *Let Me Die Before I Wake,* because it was the first book published in English that was designed to be a guide to self-deliverance for the terminally ill. The book presented detailed accounts of people with incurable illnesses who hastened their own deaths in a humane and dignified manner.

With these two books Hemlock had suddenly become a successful small publishing company. Over 150,000 copies of this volume had been sold by late 1991, a phenomenal record in the publishing business for a book that had not been promoted. The book sells regularly over 15,000 copies a year and its success led, in turn, to the writing and publication of *Final Exit.*

No other euthanasia society or publishing company in the world offers such a variety of helpful literature in choosing alternative ways to die. As a small publishing company, the Hemlock Society channels the profits from its books, newsletters, and pamphlets to support its work in the field, helping regional and local branches to get on their feet.

These two books helped, indirectly, to publicize the mission of the Hemlock Society and to attract new members to the organization.

Meanwhile, Humphry and Hemlock moved their national headquarters from Los Angeles to Eugene, Oregon, since Derek wished to move from the city to the country and had purchased a farm there.

4

The Flowering of Hemlock

Norman, I have been a surgeon for almost 50 years. In that time,
I have seen physicians torture dying patients in vain attempts to prolong life. I have taken care of you most of your life. Now I must
ask for your help. Don't let them abuse me. No surgery. No chemotherapy. . . . They are treating me like an animal. Please get me out
of here!

> —Father, age seventy-five, dying of pancreatic cancer,
> speaking to his son, Dr. Norman Paradis, Director of
> Emergency Medicine Research, New York University,
> Bellevue Hospital, New York (*New York Times,* April 25, 1992)

Turmoil Behind the Scenes

Behind the facade of his success, Humphry's second marriage was beginning to unravel under the strain of multiple tragedies. First, his wife
Ann was diagnosed with breast cancer and became severely depressed.
Compounding the anxieties aroused by her own health problems was
the double suicide of her parents, which occurred around the time of
her cancer diagnosis. Both Derek and Ann were present at their suicide
and funeral in Maine.

During this same period, Derek was also experiencing great emo-

51

tional pain from tragedies on his side of the family in England. One of his sons was jailed on drug charges. Then his brother Garth suffered irreparable brain damage as a result of a medical accident during minor surgery, and he soon died (McCrystal 1992).

The pressure on both sides precipitated the deterioration of Derek and Ann's marriage, and Derek finally asked for a divorce. Their private dispute quickly escalated into public attacks and counterattacks aired by the media, none of which had a good effect on the Hemlock Society. But most of Hemlock's officials supported Derek and accepted his explanation that his wife's mental illness had caused their marriage to break up.

After his divorce from Ann, Humphry was married again, this time to Gretchen Crocker, an Oregon farm neighbor. But the rancor of his recent divorce continued to plague him and the Hemlock Society. Ann brought a 6 million dollar lawsuit against him and the society. The suit was eventually dropped, but on the very next day, during a period of despondence on October 2, Ann drove to a remote location and took an overdose of drugs.

In her farewell message written just before her suicide, Ann accused Humphry of becoming an "agent of death and dying," and she seemed intent on pulling the plug on the right-to-die movement that they had helped to nurture, both together and apart. Her friend, Julie Horvath, who videotaped Ann's final message made just before her death, commented later: "Ann took her life because Derek had emotionally raped her." Derek's response, made on ABC-TV's "Prime Time Live" network program (aired on March 26, 1992), was an angry: "That's an outrageously stupid statement!" And he repeated his defense of his actions during the unravelling of his second marriage. "My marital breakup was an awful, awful period of my life. My wife was emotionally unstable and she was doing her best to destroy me."

Damage Control

In a three-quarter-page "damage control" ad, which he and the Hemlock Society placed in the *New York Times* (October 14 and October 26, 1991), Humphry issued a tender statement concerning the suicide of his second wife Ann. He described her as being "dogged by emotional problems" (which were well known to the inner circle of the Society's members). His eulogy attempted to clarify the circumstances about her death and to erase any lingering suspicions about his "moral culpability" in her death.

Her civil suit had charged him with libel, inflicting "grievous mental harm," turning Hemlock Society members against her, and trying to "induce her to despair and suicide," all of which allegations he categorically denied. He did note, however, that Hemlock does not "endorse suicide for reasons of depression." And he paid a sincere tribute to her for her "pioneering work . . . for the right of the terminally ill to choose to die. That she chose another path takes nothing away from that."

Significantly, there has been no upsurge in membership defections in the Society in the months following Ann's suicide.

The Growth of Hemlock

Despite these potentially devastating disruptions, Hemlock continued to flourish. In less than a decade, the Society has grown to over forty thousand members with more than seventy chapters (in the United States). Over ten thousand members reside in California alone (or one quarter of the national membership), making this state the largest contingent in the nation. Florida and New York follow far behind the Golden State, each with just under three thousand members.

Humphry presided over a full-time staff of eleven. In addition, one field liaison and four field directors were assigned to supervise present and new field offices around the country, which the Society hoped to open in the near future. The Society is kept alive by $500,000 from the annual membership dues of more than forty thousand members, plus profits from the book sales.

Although the law in most places currently prohibits the practice of euthanasia in the United States, the publication of how-to manuals like *Final Exit* and the Hemlock Society's numerous case studies of "auto-euthanasia" (or the mercy killing of oneself) is protected by the First Amendment to the Constitution. While one Hemlock publication claims that 80 percent of Americans support the concept of passive euthanasia (commonly known as the doctor "pulling the plug") and that 60 percent support "auto-euthanasia," the Society points out that its credo on the latter method is that it be "nonviolent, bloodless and painless." Hemlock feels that the process should be carried out preferably in the presence of loved ones to give them a chance to say goodbye, rather than dying alone. It also cautions to avoid such violent methods as ingesting cyanide, which has been likened to "your blood boiling."

Hemlock Goes Global

Hemlock is also a founding member of the World Federation of Right to Die Societies (WFRDS), an umbrella group of thirty-one societies in nineteen nations, which was formed in the late 1980s. The WFRDS had its eighth international conference in Amsterdam in July 1990, and the success of that meeting foreshadowed continued global growth in the future as the problems of dignified death take on worldwide implications. The ninth biennial conference of the World Federation of Right to Die Societies was held on October 23–26, 1992 in Kyoto, Japan, where the first world conference was held back in 1976. English was the primary language at the affair with simultaneous translations.

Derek: the Prophet of a Good Death

Humphry does not appear to be overly concerned with the critics who have labelled him too cavalier toward the subject of dying. Like David taking on Goliath, he is also not afraid of challenging the conservative American Medical Association for its arrogance about dying and its narrow focus on relieving physical pain while ignoring the loss of dignity and control that is the primary concern of patients. He does not like the epithets hurled by those who call him "a second Hitler" with the "Nazi solution," or the evangelists who accuse him of "doing the Devil's work" and of being a "murderer." But he does not lie awake at night worrying about his detractors. When some new crisis erupts in the Hemlock Society, he invariably exudes a reassuring calmness (Gabriel 1991).

Derek Humphry is a warm man, with a friendly smile, high-pitched giggle, long sideburns, and receding hairline. He is that rare breed of writer who can also speak effectively to an audience. As a long time journalist, he has perfected his craft, so that as a messenger of a new socio-political movement, he is able to communicate his point in simple, straightforward language to explain a complex medical subject, which is fraught with land mines. Having suffered the loss of two wives and two in-laws to suicide, he has suffered many times over through the pangs of family tragedy, which gives him a close personal insight into the problem.

Part II: Nancy's Legacy

I would rather be ashes than dust.
I would rather my spark should burn out in a brilliant blaze
Than it should be stifled in dry-rot.
I would rather be a superb meteor,
Every atom of me in magnificent glow,
Than a sleepy and permanent planet.
Man's chief purpose is to live, not exist.
I shall not waste my days trying to prolong them.
I shall use my time.

—Jack London

5

The Origins of the Modern
Right-to-Die Movement

Death is not the enemy. It is a sacrament, part of the normal life process.
—Norman Cousins, late editor of *The Saturday Review*

Origins of the Modern Euthanasia Movement

In 1935, a group of English intellectual mavericks, headed by George
Bernard Shaw, Harold Laski, Bertrand Russell, and H. G. Wells, founded
the British Euthanasia Society. The organization garnered only a few
thousand members into its fold, yet it marked a start in a global movement that wasn't to flower until half a century later—not in Britain
but rather in the Netherlands and the United States, where the idea
has finally caught on in modern times. Since the birth of the euthanasia
movement in England, there have been five attempts to change the law
in Parliament to make the concept acceptable to the medical community there, but they have all been unsuccessful. Then, in 1981, the Voluntary Euthanasia Society published a little booklet in Britain called *A
Guide to Self-Deliverance.* But for some unexplained reason, publication was stopped even though it contained no information that was
not currently available in other literature on the subject of euthanasia.

A Merger Occurs in the United States

In America, the first euthanasia group was founded in 1938 by a Unitarian Minister, Rev. Charles Potter. It was first called the Euthanasia Society (later changed to the Society for the Right-to-Die) and was a passive-euthanasia organization stressing living wills and powers of attorney. By 1990 another group, Concern for Dying, had been formed.

Then on April 12, 1990, the two right-to-die groups (with a combined membership of 120,000) announced that they were moving toward a merger. The newly merged group, called the "National Council on Death and Dying" (NCDD), is continuing the activities of the two former groups, which were more conservative in their approach than the more activist Hemlock Society. They stressed legal and medical education seminars, winning court cases, and passing legislation to assist in passive death as their chief methods of attacking the problem. Fenella Rouse, the founder of the Society for the Right-to-Die, became the first executive director of the new combined association.

It was significant that the NCDD did not extend an offer to the Hemlock Society to include it in their merger plans. The NCDD is not interested in going beyond the removal of tubes and respirators for the terminally ill, but hopes that its membership, plus some 380,000 nonmember supporters, will help to lobby legislatures to legalize living wills and powers of attorney. At the time of the merger, nine states— Massachusetts, Michigan, Pennsylvania, Rhode Island, Nebraska, New Jersey, New York, South Dakota, and Ohio—did not recognize living wills. By early 1993, all the states but Nebraska had approved them. But the NCDD is not yet ready to take the next step to push for doctor-assisted-suicide legislation in the states.

Ms. Rouse recognizes the colossal change that has taken place in public attitudes in recent years on the subject. "Our goal," she said, "is to make more people in this country accept death as an inevitable part of their living, and if they want to have any say in their future, to take responsibility for planning for that inevitability, as we do for taxes, college, children and retirement" (Mero 1991).

Our Changing Views on Suicide

To understand the modern euthanasia debate properly, we need to pause and examine briefly the various perspectives on suicide at different points in civilized history.

George Howe Colt, a staff writer for *Life* and the author of *The Enigma of Suicide* (1991), postulates that in classical times most suicides were considered rational, and the right to end one's life was taken for granted; it is only in more recent times that suicide has been looked upon as irrational. The word "suicide" (taken from the Latin and meaning literally "to kill one's self") was first used in English documents in 1651. David Hume, in England, and Voltaire, in France, both tried to establish the philosophic principle that suicide is a moral, rational act and should not be judged a crime.

It was not until the nineteenth century that discussion and controversy over the rationality or irrationality of suicide took root, so that today suicide is no longer viewed as a philosophical or moral problem, but as a reaction to mental instability. Although many current observers believe that suicide can be rational, and that everyone has the right to take one's life, there are exceptions, especially involving those who have suffered from periodic depression. In the late twentieth century, most people feel that the majority of contemporary suicides are committed by mentally ill persons. A recent Harvard research study confirmed this assessment, finding that 90 percent of suicides were committed by mentally ill people.

According to recent National Institute of Mental Health figures, in the 1960s, 10 percent of Americans were predicted to become mentally ill; in 1980, the figures jumped to 15 percent; and in 1984, they went up to 19 percent (due largely to an increased consumption of alcohol and drugs). The easy access to these products adds to this equation. Witnesss the landmark case of Karen Ann Quinlan: alcohol plus drugs equal coma and death (see chapter 6).

Thus, if one believes the results of the Harvard study, then it is understandable why the suicide rates among elderly Americans today are double those of Europeans. In fact, suicide among this aged mentally ill group far outnumbers those suffering from cancer. (See Colt, *The Enigma of Suicide*, 1991).

The Growth of English Common Law on Suicide

The United States adopted its laws on suicide from the English, where suicide was considered not only immoral, but unlawful. The penalties in this country included a forfeiture of property to the government and ignominious or dishonored burial. Property forfeiture was gradually abolished as a punishment beginning in 1701 and finally discontinued in the mid-nineteenth century. The rationale behind this switch was a desire not to punish the surviving family members any further. The majority of the original thirteen American colonies also had case law which made assisted suicide a crime.

In 1961, England decriminalized suicide and attempted suicide, but left assisted suicide a crime punishable by fourteen years imprisonment. Three attempts in the past thirty years to modify this law in Parliament have failed.

In the United States, New York became the first state to pass a law making assisted suicide a crime in 1978. Ten more states or territories soon followed suit.

The United States has taken a cue from the mother country by not enacting any pro-assisted suicide laws in the fifty states through 1991. Furthermore, no state or territory in the United States currently has a statute on the books that makes suicide or attempted suicide criminal and unlawful. However, a majority of states do have provisions for involuntary commitment of individuals who are in danger to themselves. Some of these laws specifically mention suicidal behavior as a justification. But these are public health and not criminal laws.

Criminal Law in the United States

Despite the fact that suicide is no longer illegal in the United States, many jurisdictions still make assisting suicide a unique criminal defense. Those twenty-six states and three territories that do make such actions an offense, generally characterize such acts as either a unique offense or a class of murder or manslaughter.

An example of the "unique offense" is Florida's law, which states: "Every person assisting another in the commission of self-murder shall be guilty of manslaughter." In contrast, the Oregon statute states, "Criminal homicide constitutes manslaughter in the second degree when . . . a person intentionally causes or aids another person to commit suicide."

In the rest of the states that do not have specific criminal prohibitions against assisting suicide, the act may generally be prosecuted as a homicide (either as murder or manslaughter). The one exception is the state of Michigan, which found itself in several headline-making hassles with Dr. Kevorkian and his "suicide machine" in 1990–91 (see chapters 8 and 9).

The Dilemma of the Living Dead

According to Dr. Ronald Cranford, the chairman of the Ethics Committee of the American Academy of Neurology, there are an estimated five to ten thousand "human vegetables" lying in irreversible comas in the U.S. and Canadian hospitals, and doctors do not know what to do with them. "They are the living dead and how we treat them is clearly one of the major ethical debates in the United States right now." He made this analysis before an international gathering in Ottawa on August 22, 1989, as he estimated the staggering medical costs involved in keeping alive comatose patients who have only a small part of their brain stem functioning. But as long as there is a flicker of life left in the brain stem, a doctor cannot give the order to remove the tubes that provide nutrition to the dying patient. He figured that it costs between $120 million and $1.2 billion a year to cover their hospital bills in the United States. In Canada, $200 million a year is spent annually to keep some eight hundred vegetative patients alive. That figure was provided by Dr. Leslie Ivan, a professor of surgery at the University of Ottawa, who stressed the point that there was no hope that any of them could be revived (Cranford 1992).

Just a few decades ago, most comatose accident or heart attack patients would have died in a matter of minutes or hours, but now with the development of sophisticated machines like the defibrillator, doctors and medics can jump-start an unconscious victim with an electric shock to the heart. This machine has saved thousands of patients, many of whom have completely recovered, but there are other patients who, though revived, remain unfortunately in a vegetative state.

Dr. Ivan believes that "it can be considered an act of human kindness to permit a vegetative patient to die. It is the most degrading existence for a human being."

"Negotiated Death"

People no longer die at home as they did in the eighteenth, nineteenth, and twentieth centuries. Now they die mainly in hospitals and nursing homes, in which a reputed half of the "guest" patients die of a "negotiated death"; i.e., the nurses and doctors are given a "message" by loved ones to "turn off" the life-sustaining support monitors. The American Hospital Association estimated in late 1990 that 70 percent of the six thousand deaths that occur in the United States on an average day are already somehow negotiated, all concerned parties privately concurring on the time of withdrawal of some death-delaying technology or whether to start it in the first place. This subterranean understanding reached between loved ones of comatose patients and medical officials has been one of the unwritten new practices of our health care delivery system because of the dark shadow of new technologies that hover over the emergency rooms of our medical facilities.

Despite the de facto practice of assisting death in one way or another, by 1990, there were ten men serving jail terms for helping their loved ones to die, illegally. Two of them, Roswell Gilbert and Charles Griffith, were each serving twenty-five years for assisting in a suicide, "the secret crime of the bedroom," as Derek Humphry describes it. (Gilbert has recently been released but has been forbidden to speak publicly about his case.) How many more Americans will be imprisoned before this controversial issue of assisted-suicide will be resolved legally?

The Man Who Feared the Dawn

There have been several little-publicized cases of passive euthanasia in recent years, in which the courts, doctors, or both have performed humane acts to hasten and assist terminally ill patients to their deaths.

One of them involved a thirty-three-year-old quadriplegic named Larry James McAfee, who was paralyzed from the neck down in a 1985 motorcycle accident in Georgia. Four years later, McAfee filed an affidavit in an Atlanta Court stating: "I understand turning off the ventilator will result in my death." The affidavit was written with a pencil clenched between his teeth. When Georgia Supreme Court Judge Edward Johnson came to hold a hearing by his hospital bed, McAfee told him that he woke up every morning fearful of each new day (Associated Press 1991).

In a later court hearing before the judge, his mother, father, and three sisters testified that their paralyzed family member, who had been an avid outdoorsman prior to the accident, found that his ventilator-dependent existence deprived him of the things that had made his life worth living. His insurance had run out and he was surviving on Medicaid, confined to his apartment with round-the-clock nursing care. "He said he did not want to live like this," his sister Patsy McAfee Perry told the judge. Although most right-to-die cases have involved comatose patients, McAfee was still lucid, had made his own decision about the removal of the medical systems that were keeping him alive, and had informed his immediate family of his wishes.

The judge recognized Larry's desire and, with his family's concurrence, ruled on that same day (September 6, 1989) that the patient, who no longer got any enjoyment out of life, had the right to turn off the ventilator. The judge also apologized from the bench for forcing the family to endure such a private tragedy in a public forum. Several representatives of handicapped organizations deplored the decision and the court hearing as an ominous portent of state-sanctioned participation in ending the life of a severely handicapped person who was not in a comatose vegetative state.

McAfee was then sent to an Alabama nursing home still in pain. A former civil engineer, he helped a friend design a timing device, which would allow him to shut off his ventilator valve with his mouth, so that he could end his life when he was ready with this self-designed suicide device. He then planned to return home to his apartment near Atlanta, where he desired to be when he would remove his own life-support system. McAfee did go home to die as he wished.

This case, along with many others, highlighted the growing complexities that forced the U.S. Supreme Court, at the end of its spring term in 1989, to agree to hear its first right-to-die case involving the comatose Nancy Cruzan, another vehicle-accident victim who had been lying in a vegetative coma in Missouri for six years (see the next chapter).

Thomas Russell, an Associate Dean of the National Judicial College, a school for judges located on the University of Nevada's campus in Reno, said: "Many of the cases that now come regularly before the courts [like McAfee's] have no precedent in human experience, much less legal." But they crop up every day in America and will do so increasingly in the future.

How the Dutch Do It

The Netherlands is the only Western country outside of the United States where active euthanasia has made much headway. In the Netherlands, only residents of that country can take advantage of a Dutch Supreme Court decision passed in 1984, which protects Dutch physicians from being prosecuted for helping their own patients to die in certain defined circumstances. Many Americans have been turned away when they flew to Holland for help in dying. Both a group of Dutch physicians and the Netherlands voluntary euthanasia society have warned Americans not to come to their country expecting aid which cannot be given to outsiders (Clines 1986).

In the seventies and eighties, many Dutch physicians were hauled into Netherlands' courts for assisting patients to their deaths, but none have ever been sued for malpractice or lost their licenses. A Royal Dutch poll in the late eighties reported that a majority of the citizens were in favor of euthanasia, which most probably influenced the Dutch Supreme Court in 1984 to acquit a physician in helping a ninety-five-year-old woman to die. In 1989, the Dutch Parliament had a death-with-dignity bill on the docket for over a year but was reluctant to tackle it.

The Dutch Waffle Over the Right-to-Die

On January 17, 1990, the Ministry of Justice issued a Report of a special Remelink Commission Inquiry into "Medical Practices with Regard to Euthanasia," in which it was determined that twenty-three hundred deaths (about 1.8 percent of the one hundred thirty thousand a year that occur in the Netherlands) were the result of euthanasia. The commission determined that only a small number, about four hundred, were assisted

suicide cases, and that this does "not warrant the assumption that euthanasia in the Netherlands occurs on an excessive scale" or that it "is
used increasingly as an alternative to good palliative or terminal care."

The 1990 report also stated that there are about nine thousand
requests each year to doctors for the termination of a patient's life,
but less than a fifth of these receive some sort of assistance. The commission concluded that the doctors' "prime responsibility was to keep
their patients alive" and recommended these additional considerations
(Ministry of Justice, the Netherlands 1991):

- that doctors report any "active interference on their part" in treating
  a dying patient, whose vital functions had begun to fail, without
  an "explicit request from the patient" to continue the system that
  had been in effect since November 1990.
- that the general practitioner who is considering the administration
  of euthanasia on his patient "get an independent judgment . . .
  from a specialist, preferably one who is already in attendance
  . . . for the sake of the quality of the decision process."
- that each doctor "must strictly observe the requirements for scrupu-
  lous care . . . especially the requirement of a written report."
- that "in the future doctors will be increasingly faced with important medical decisions with regard to the end of life" . . . and
  that those decisions "be of high quality."

The commission, chaired by Prof. J. Remelink, the Procurator
Generalo of the Supreme Court of the Netherlands, made it clear that
it was up to the members of the "government in question to decide
what value that they want to attach to each of the above additional
considerations." The commission appeared to leave many loopholes,
however, in its recommendations, which recognized that euthanasia was
a growing issue in that country and was no longer an affair that could
be ignored.

1991 Dutch Survey on Patients Who Choose to Die

Physician aid-in-dying is still technically a crime in the Netherlands.
Yet requests from terminally ill patients for their doctors to hasten their

deaths have been honored more openly and tolerated more widely than in any other place in the world. The physicians abide by seven guidelines issued by a committee of the Royal Dutch Medical Association. The guidelines are as follows:

1. The patient must repeatedly and explicitly express the desire to die.
2. The patient's decision must be well informed, free, and enduring.
3. The patient must be suffering from severe physical and mental pain with no prospect for relief.
4. All other options for care must have been exhausted or refused by the patient.
5. Euthanasia must be carried out by a qualified physician.
6. The physician must consult at least one other physician.
7. The physician must inform the local coroner that euthanasia has occurred.

However, after almost two decades of acceptance of the patient's right to choose death-with-dignity, the Dutch knew little about who was choosing to die, why they sought death, and who was helping them to obtain it. Now a study, recently published in the *Netherlands Journal of Medicine,* and reported in the *New York Times* on September 11, 1991, reveals the results of anonymous questionnaires sent to general practitioners in Holland. Of the 1,042 surveyed, 676 general practitioners replied, 388 with extensive details of cases in which they had cooperated to end a patient's life. Many doctors reported having helped two or more patients.

Most deaths had come about via the injection of a large dose of barbiturates to bring on coma, followed by an injection of curare to stop the breathing and the heart. In other cases of physician aid-in-dying, the physician had prescribed a large dose of barbiturates for the patient to take in the presence of the doctor.

Of all the patients, 85 percent suffered from cancer and were in the final weeks of life. The average age of those requesting physician aid-in-dying was sixty-three for men and sixty-six for women. Men and women requested physician aid-in-dying about equally, the most frequent reasons for men being lung or bronchial cancer, and for women breast cancer. Close to 3 percent of the men had AIDS.

Researchers estimated that doctors in the Netherlands help about 3,000 patients to die each year, less than half of the previously publicized estimates. About two-thirds of the deaths occur at home, with only about 25 percent happening in nursing homes. All told, Dutch doctors comply with only about two out of every five requests for physician aid-in-dying.

Roadblocks in the Netherlands to Legalization of Euthanasia

Dr. Pieter Admiraal, a leading Dutch pro-euthanasia doctor, has noted that according to recent opinion polls over 60 percent of Dutch citizens are in favor of euthanasia, including more than half of the lay members of the Roman Catholic Church, whose hierarchy is opposed to legalization. Nonetheless, Article 293 of the Dutch criminal code provides for twelve years imprisonment for anyone who "takes the life of another at his or her explicit and serious request." This stricture has made many Dutch doctors fearful of openly challenging this article.

The minority opposition to the proposed euthanasia legislation in the Dutch Parliament consists mainly of Christian Democrats. Their spokesman, Jan Schinkalshoak, gives the following reason for their opposition: "In a case of life and death, we must be very careful. The core of the argument is that people are the creation of God, and do not have the right to determine about their own living, or about ending it." Reservations based on religious beliefs constitute one reason why so many Dutch politicians have been wary of this explosive issue, despite so much popular support. The supporters of the proposition in parliament have been hoping that the Supreme Court would settle the issue by deciding on several cases that are lying before it. But it hasn't considered them yet.

Mr. Schinkalshoak further explained his position: "We are the first country in the world moving this way [toward more and more euthanasia requests from citizens]. And maybe we don't know what we are doing." Yet, one has to ask the question of the Christian Democratic Party: "Would God approve of all the tubes and hoses now used to keep patients alive indefinitely?"

Although legislation approving aid-in-dying has been rejected again and again by the Dutch parliament and its penal code, no physicians who have engaged in it have been indicted, which gives an observer the impression that Netherlands officials are "looking the other way" on this hot issue. The Netherlands grants physicians immunity from prosecution, and any doctor who terminates life at the request of a patient will not be punished if the doctor invokes a defense of *force majeur,* and satisfies the strict judicial guidelines concerning euthanasia that have been published there.

The Netherlands served as a bellwether for what would soon be occurring in the United States on the euthanasia frontier. America was just embarking on her first painful steps to come to terms with this difficult issue.

6

Breakthrough on the Euthanasia Frontier

The invasion of armies can be resisted, but not an idea whose time
has come.

—Victor Hugo

It was not until the late eighties and early nineties that the problem of
euthanasia received national attention. The headline-making cases involved
five patients, all of whom were women. Lead stories on the controversial
deaths of these terminally ill women became more and more frequent in
the media. In Missouri, the landmark Cruzan case finally came to an end
with Cruzan's death in 1990, following a U.S. Supreme Court case and
a Missouri judge's decision that her feeding tubes should be removed. In
Michigan, three doctor-assisted deaths in 1990 and 1991 by Dr. Jack Kevorkian resulted in a series of court cases and widespread media coverage.

But setting the stage for these later controversies was the pioneer
1976 case in New Jersey centering on the comatose Karen Ann Quinlan,
who subsequently remained alive until 1986.

The Legacy of Karen Ann Quinlan

The turning point of America's concern about euthanasia was the Quinlan
case. Having consumed a near fatal potion of alcohol and sleeping pills

71

in 1971, Karen Ann Quinlan lived on in a brain-dead, vegetative state for nine more years, even though her respirator had been removed by court order in 1976. She survived with the help of feeding tubes containing liquid nutrition until 1985, when the tubes were removed. Death by this means is a classic form of passive euthanasia. Her case became the catalyst for the rebirth of the long-dormant euthanasia movement, because the whole world watched her prolonged ordeal.

When the New Jersey Court ordered the removal of the respirator from Quinlan's inert body in 1976, it gave the impetus to many of the advanced directive laws which states enacted in the last decade and which led indirectly to congressional action on the same matter in 1990. In that case, the New Jersey court held that an individual's right to privacy grows as the "degree of bodily invasion increases and the prognosis dims. Ultimately, there comes a point at which the individual's right overcomes the state's interest," the court said.

This formula stood the test of time for twelve years, until 1988, when the ombudsman for the Institutionalized Elderly in New Jersey caused a public furor when he issued some strict directives to nursing-home administrators, which effectively reversed the court's formula. So intense was the negative reaction of health care providers and the general public in the Garden State to his directives, that the ombudsman was forced to withdraw his directives, and he eventually resigned in disgrace a year later in April 1989.

This approach by the New Jersey Court mirrors the one that the U.S. Supreme Court took in the 1973 landmark *Roe* v. *Wade* case, which delineated the shifting balance between the state's interest in potential life and a pregnant woman's interest in terminating an unwanted pregnancy. Before the point of fetal viability, the high court said, a woman's interest, protected by the constitutional right to privacy, outweighs the state's interest. But once the fetus is able to live outside the womb, the balance shifts and the state may ban abortions that are not necessary to preserve the woman's life or health.

A Dissenter's Voice is Heard

In the mid-1970s, Dr. C. Everett Koop, who was then the chief surgeon at Children's Hospital in Philadelphia, wrote an article entitled: "The Slide to Auschwitz," in which he propounded the "slippery slope" thesis of what might happen if passive euthanasia techniques became the order of the day. In his piece, Koop (who later became the nation's most celebrated Surgeon General during the decade of the eighties) wrote that he opposed the New Jersey Supreme Court decision allowing Karen Ann Quinlan to be taken off the respirator. He feared that the withdrawal of care from the hopelessly ill would lead to active euthanasia, which he despised then and still did as late as the fall of 1991, when he openly opposed Initiative #119 in the state of Washington. (See chapter 13.)

When the New Jersey Supreme Court ruled that Karen Ann Quinlan had a right to privacy, it did more than just allow her parents the right to remove their comatose daughter from the respirator; since then, in various spinoffs, there have been more than fifty court decisions in sixteen states supporting the right to refuse medical treatment. The Quinlan ruling, however, still did not settle the issue nationally, even though many people thought that it had been resolved. "Initially, we thought in the aftermath of the Quinlan case, it would be dealt with and quickly fade away," said Daniel Callahan, the director of the Hastings Medical Research Center (which studies medical ethics) in New York in December 1989. "But here it is twenty years later, and we still haven't solved the problem" (Greenhouse, July 25, 1989).

The year after Karen Ann Quinlan's death, the New Jersey Supreme Court ruled *In the Matter of Jobes* (1987) that a thirty-one-year-old woman in a persistent vegetative state was entitled to the removal of her feeding tubes based on the substituted judgment of family and friends, since the patient had left no living will. This case received no publicity, even though it came four years after the beginning of the most famous euthanasia case to date. There was no controversy over the court's decision in this case.

The Ordeal of Nancy Cruzan

On the dark, snowy night of January 11, 1983, Nancy Cruzan, then twenty-five, was driving home in her 1963 Nash Rambler, when it overturned several times on Elm Road just outside of Carthage, Missouri. Miss Cruzan's brain was deprived of oxygen for fifteen or twenty minutes after she was thrown from the car and knocked unconscious.

She lay face down in a water-filled ditch until paramedics arrived and restarted her heart. But it was too late to hope that Nancy would ever come out of her unconscious state. She was brain dead, suffering from an irreversible coma.

She soon fell into a persistent vegetative state for the next seven years and her doctors speculated that she could live another thirty years. Despite the protests of her parents to let her die peacefully, the state and the hospital kept her on tubes for the next seven years.

Beginning in 1986, her parents, Lester and Joyce Cruzan, pleaded with the authorities to have the plastic feeding tubes that surgeons had connected to her stomach disconnected, since they believed that their vivacious, active daughter would not want to spend up to thirty years in a hopeless coma. But their pleadings went unheeded.

No Living Will

Unfortunately, Nancy had not left a living will or any oral statement of her wishes in the event she should be left unable to communicate by a life-threatening accident. She was like the estimated 90 percent of Americans who have not left instructions with loved ones in similar situations. Because of this absence, Missouri's attorney general, William Webster, challenged the family's plan to disconnect the feeding tube. The state then took custody of their daughter for the next four years and every day nurses flushed water and other nutrients through the tube, a sad sight witnessed by millions of TV viewers who saw several documentaries focused on Nancy's plight.

The Missouri Court Acts

In 1988, the Missouri Supreme Court rendered a split 4-3 decision that Nancy's tubes could not be removed at her parents' request because "life is precious and worthy of preservation." In the aftermath of the Missouri decision, many clerics argued that the state should stay out of the way of death. The "Missouri court decision which severs family ties," said the Evangelical Lutheran Church of America, in a brief on the ruling against the Cruzans, "substitutes moral and religious judgment on the state of that person."

There is some irony in the fact that the Evangelical Lutherans argued for a family's right to privacy, while the state of Missouri promoted the "sanctity of life." Yet the notion that life is sacred and worthy of the state's protection is embedded throughout the American legal tradition, along with the protection of individual liberty. When these two rights clash and are at odds, the ensuing debate grows fierce. The state permits the taking of life in war, self-defense, or as punishment for a heinous crime. The Cruzan case, however, raised the question of whether personal choice and great suffering, by either patients or their families, should join that set of circumstances!

It was obvious that an appeal of the close Missouri decision would ultimately wend its way to the highest court in the land. (Two years later, the Supreme Court rendered the *first* right-to-die decision in the nation's history, based on an appeal from this Missouri court's close finding in the case of Nancy Cruzan.)

The Supreme Court Hears Arguments

On December 6, 1989, the U.S. Supreme Court heard opening arguments in the Cruzan appeal, the first ever held on this type of case. Missouri Attorney General William Webster, who had also been involved in a landmark Supreme Court case involving abortion in federally financed clinics, was slated to testify in defense of the Missouri Supreme Court decision to deny the Cruzan's their request on behalf of their daughter, Nancy. He had said a few months earlier: "The slipperiest slope is to start moving toward placing a value on a particular quality of life, because then you can move into people who are handicapped or people who are retarded." This was still his position before the Supreme Court (Greenhouse, December 17, 1989).

The American Academy of Neurology argued that a doctor's duty is to continue treating unconscious patients as long as there is some chance of improvement, which the brain-dead Nancy Cruzan did not have. When all hope is gone, the doctor's duty ends. But the Association of American Physicians and Surgeons argued precisely the opposite: "The obligation of the physician to the comatose, vegetative, or developmentally disabled patient does not depend on the prospect for recovery," it wrote in its brief. "The physician must always act on behalf of the patient's well being" (Greenhouse, July 25, 1989).

During the initial hour-long argument on the Cruzan case, there was much skepticism voiced by several judges, hinting at a resistance to a sweeping ruling on the status of the comatose Nancy. Knowing this was the first time that the court had confronted this supersensitive issue, there was the expected intense questioning as the justices probed the lawyers on both sides with penetrating questions and then appeared to be unpersuaded by the answers. There were no hints of any middle ground between the two poles.

Justice Antonin Scalia, one of the most intellectually astute judges, asked Mr. William Colby, the Cruzan family lawyer, "What if a person says, 'I am of sound mind but it is my desire to die. I'm in pain and my quality of life is nil'? Must a state allow that person to refuse food and water?" (Greenhouse, December 17, 1989)

Colby replied that the Fourteenth Amendment's guarantee of liberty "protects that person's right to be free from state intrusion." But he also said a refusal to accept medical treatment need not be honored if it is "irrational," as in the case of a Jehovah's Witness who wanted to prevent life-saving treatment for a child. Such refusals were motivated, he said, not by the child's best interest but by the parent's religion.

Mr. Colby then made the following point: "The question is: Who decides? This court has always deferred to the special competency of families to know what values are important to family members." Justice Scalia sarcastically replied: "But that's not what you said about the Jehovah's Witness. You said that was a religious belief. Decisions about whether life is worth living are based on 'philosophical beliefs.' It's a philosophical debate. I can read the ancient philosophers and find it there. Why can't the state say: 'We don't deal with philosophy, we deal with physics, and life must be preserved.' "

Robert L. Presson, an assistant attorney general for Missouri, said there was no constitutional role for the family in deciding whether an unconscious person should be permitted to die. In any event, he said, a state can never be required to participate in "state-assisted suicide." Justice John Paul Stevens chimed in: "Does that mean that even 'a competent person' would be unable to refuse food and water?" And Justice Anthony M. Kennedy observed, "If that's true, there is no need to inquire about whether an unconscious person has such a right."

The liberal Justice Harry Blackmun, the author of the controversial *Roe* v. *Wade* abortion-rights decision in 1973, who had been largely silent through the argument, then became exasperated with the Missouri lawyer. "Have you ever seen a person in a persistent vegetative state?" he asked. Presson replied: "I have seen Nancy Cruzan herself." But that was not the answer that Justice Blackmun expected. "You have seen Nancy. Have you seen others?" Blackmun asked pointedly. Mr. Presson said that he had seen other similar patients in the state rehabilitation hospital.

Presson was supported by the U.S. Solicitor General, Kenneth Starr, who had sought and been granted the court's permission to argue on behalf of Missouri, even though the federal government had not been involved in the Cruzan case heretofore. He told the court that the Fourteenth Amendment "should not be interpreted to force the states or the federal government to embrace a particular procedure or approach" to the care of incompetent patients. Starr asked that the court rule that any policy is acceptable as long as it is "reasonably designed to serve a legitimate state interest."

Justice Byron White asked Mr. Starr whether a state could decide that it would never permit the withdrawal of a feeding tube, no matter how clear the evidence of the patient's wishes. Starr retorted: "That raises a very difficult question that I'm not prepared to answer authoritatively." Then Justice Stevens asked Starr whether, in the case of a patient suffering "continuous pain," the Constitution would permit a state to insist that life-support measures continue. "I think not," Starr answered, adding that such a policy would amount to oppression by the state.

"So you do agree that the Federal Constitution is implicated," Stevens said. Starr replied: "If there is a condition of suffering." Justice Stevens pressed him further: "What if a patient felt no pain, but had given unequivocal evidence of intent not to remain alive?" Mr. Starr replied that the Constitution would be "clearly implicated" in that case. He then described the constitutional right at issue as a "significant liberty interest in being free of unwanted intrusions." In the legal jargon, this phrase—"liberty interest"—means the "lowest-level of constitutional protection."

Significantly, neither the justices nor the lawyers mentioned the constitutional right of privacy during the argument, a specific right to which the court gives a higher level of protection. This omission was curious because the case had been originally brought to the court by the Cruzan family as a right-to-privacy case, in which their daughter had a right to be free of unwanted treatment. But the justices' silence on the privacy issue seemed to signal either that the court had concluded that the right to privacy was not implicated or that there was no need for a decision based on broad constitutional grounds. They seemed to be searching for a narrow solution to a profound issue.

High Court observers also noted that the results of the case would be an indicator of the justices' inclinations about the right to privacy inferred from the Bill of Rights and how they might rule in the future on follow-up cases, like abortion, which often turn on privacy questions. "They never said before that there was a general right to privacy in the receipt of medical care," said Larry Gostin, the executive director of the American Society of Law and Medicine. But he noted that the court was narrowing the right to privacy in other areas outside of health. "If they were to decide there was no right to privacy in the Cruzan case, it would be a nail in the coffin," he predicted. "But if they rule the other way, it offers a ray of hope that the court is not so doctrinaire."

Which way would the court decide?

A Minnesota Octogenarian Speaks Out

In mid-1991, Helga Wanglie, eighty-seven, had lain in a Minneapolis Hospital for eight months with severe brain damage. Her physician, Dr. Michael Belzer, wanted to remove the tubes keeping her alive: "We now have the technology to keep fifty Helga Wanglie's alive for indefinite periods, because we can do it. *But do we have to?*" (my italics) he asked. Helga's last wish, before she went into a life-ending coma, was: "Only God can take me." Her husband concurred with her desire, so she remained alive for a while longer, against the doctor's recommendations. Helga Wanglie's case represents the opposite pole of the ethical dilemma. Between her case and Nancy Cruzan's there exists an unexplored gulf of complex ethical, legal, and medical issues that still await a sane resolution.

7

The Right to Die Becomes the Law of the Land

We would all draw a different line at which we wouldn't want to live any longer. We have a strong recognition in this country that you are the master of your body. If we begin to deny the freedom of an individual to choose to participate or not in medical care, we could become a medical police state.

—Nancy Dickey, M.D., former chairwoman of the Council on Ethical & Judicial Affairs, AMA, 1988

The Supreme Court Decides Its First Modern Euthanasia Case

In June 1990, six months after beginning its hearing on Nancy Cruzan's case, the court acted. The official title of the "right-to-die case" before the high court was *Cruzan* v. *Director, Missouri Dept. of Health.* In the 5-4 decision written by Chief Justice Rehnquist (see Appendix 3 for excerpts), the court, for the first time, endorsed the view that the Fourteenth Amendment guarantees the right to avoid unwanted medical treatment.* The court specifically applied that principle to all patients,

---

*In 1914, Justice Benjamin Cardozo said: "Every human of adult years and sound mind has a right to make medical decisions regarding their own bodies."

conscious and comatose, who have made their wishes known. But it also found that states like Missouri could require that "clear and convincing evidence, like a living will, be offered in evidence" to state the patient's wishes.

Justice William Brennan, Jr., in his dissenting opinion, wrote: "The state's general interest in life must accede to Nancy Cruzan's particularized and intense interest in self-determination in her choice of medical treatment. There is simply nothing legitimately within the state's purview to be gained by superseding her decision." In other words, Brennan was issuing a strong recommendation to the states to recognize the rights of the individual in such cases, and it sent a clear message to other states to do the same thing if future Cruzan cases cropped up within their borders (Greenhouse 1990).

Brennan was joined by Justices Thurgood Marshall and Harry Blackmun in agreeing that "Nancy Cruzan is entitled to choose to die with dignity. . . . Yet Missouri and this court . . . have discarded evidence of her will, ignored her values, and deprived her of the right to a decision as closely approximating her own choice as humanly possible."

The fourth dissenting Justice, John Paul Stevens, in a separate opinion added: "The meaning and completion of her life should be controlled by persons who have her best interests at heart—not by a state legislature concerned only with the preservation of human life." These dissents practically guaranteed that more cases on similarly sensitive human-rights issues would continue to be decided on a case-by-case basis. The foggy high court decision cried out for clarification and guidelines to help the states in their tortuous series of decisions.

What the Court Did for Nancy

Although the court rejected specifically her parents' plea to have her tubes disconnected, it left an opening for the comatose Nancy Cruzan and her parents to seek redress by passing the buck back to the states, so that she could die with dignity. The nebulous decision motivated the public to think about the cruelty of continuing to force such an indignity on her inert body. On the plus side, the court did not turn away from the overall problem of the right to die. Eight justices (all except Antonin Scalia) said the problem *does* engage the Constitution, opening up the possibility that in the near future this sensitive question could be explored further in constitutional law. Thus, the Cruzan case marked a hidden breakthrough. As Justice Brennan wrote in his important dissent, the case affects the million Americans who die each year (out of two million) after some form of life-sustaining treatment is ended. He noted that all these cases involve a decision on a "medical procedure that could prolong the process of dying."

Where the Constitution comes into play is the Fourteenth Amendment, which provides that no state may deprive any person of "liberty without the due process of the law." In the past seventy years (since World War I), the Supreme Court has read that general, open-ended language to forbid state intrusions into certain vital areas of the individual's privacy and autonomy. One constant theme of these decisions has been the integrity of the human body. For instance, the court condemned the forcible pumping of a prisoner's body to look for criminal evidence.

It has also said that the injection of antipsychotic drugs interferes with the person's liberty under the Fourteenth Amendment. Even the conservative, strict-constructionist Chief Justice Rehnquist, writing for the narrow 5-4 majority in the Cruzan case, noted that past court decisions pointed toward a constitutional liberty of patients to refuse life-sustaining medical treatment, or water and food. Yet, he waffled on this admission by stating that a state was "still entitled to guard against potential abuses in such situations."

But was pulling the tube on Cruzan an abuse? The court inferred that it was. Because the Missouri courts had found that Nancy had never clearly expressed her wish, the high court majority noted that Missouri law required that there "be clear and convincing evidence" of an incompetent patient's prior expressed wish not to be kept artificially alive. On this delicate point, the court sided with the state against Nancy and her family.

On the other hand, the four dissenters said that Missouri's high standard of evidence unconstitutionally burdened Nancy Cruzan's desire to avoid artificial mechanisms, which they felt she had sufficiently expressed orally before her accident. (These four votes, along with Justice O'Connor's, would be enough to establish a constitutional right to die in a future case where the patient's wish is clear and convincing.)

But for this first case, the court tiptoed with a tentative step around what Chief Justice Rehnquist termed a "perplexing question with unusual strong moral and ethical overtones." Nevertheless, the court did enter the thicket and at the same time confounded conservative legal arguments and expectations; former judge Robert Bork, for example, had argued before the Senate in his failed nomination to the high court in 1987, that the guarantee of "liberty" in the Fourteenth Amendment was "too vague for the courts to enforce." The high court's mixed bag of decisions on the Cruzan case had the immediate effect of defeating the Cruzan family, but in the long-run it gave persons whose wishes on death and dying are clearly known a constitutional right to the discontinuance of life-sustaining treatment.

A Glimmer of Hope for the Future

In an opinion concurring with the majority, Justice Sandra Day O'Connor noted that the decision did not bar other states from following paths different from Missouri's, nor did it prevent the high court from backing a family's wish to remove life-sustaining treatment in a future case. Justice O'Connor, who was part of the majority of five, went further in a separate opinion (see Cruzan Case in Appendix 3), when she noted that if, before becoming disabled, a person designates parents or someone else to make life-and-death decisions for her, then the Constitution might well require the state to carry out those decisions. O'Connor opened the door for future litigation before the Supreme Court, when she wrote: "Today we decide only that one state's practice does not violate the Constitution. The more challenging task of crafting appropriate procedures for safe-guarding incompetents' liberty interests is entrusted to the laboratory of the states" (Greenhouse 1990).

Thus, the other four states would each have to face up to their own problems and enact meaningful right-to-die laws and legislation to approve doctor-assisted suicide. The case put a premium on foresight by alerting citizens to register some written statement of intent to guide a family through future crises. As the *New York Times* editorialized on June 27 in the wake of the Cruzan case: "It's no consolation to the Cruzans, but this Supreme Court offers a monumental example of law adjusting to life."

Paul Armstrong, the New Jersey attorney who represented Karen

Ann Quinlan, was amazed at the change in right-to-die attitudes since 1976. "Fourteen years ago," he said in a 1990 interview, "we were arguing successfully that Karen Ann's family could remove her respirator. Now in Cruzan, the Supreme Court has already found a Constitutional right in refusing any artificial life support." He predicted that a "quiet consensus" would form among Americans on the issue, and this was soon reflected in the half million requests for living-will forms that flooded the offices of the Society for the Right to Die in New York, as a result of the great publicity surrounding the Cruzan case. When one considers that only one-third of Americans have a traditional signed will when they die, the rush to obtain living wills signified a significant change and a continued, passionate debate between the right-to-life and the right-to-die proponents. Armstrong called the decision "an elegant accretion of common law, case by case, adding to the national consensus" (Lewis 1990).

The Supreme Court ruling in the Cruzan case set no national guidelines, however, on the right to die, but left it to the states to set their own standards. The court further argued that the patient had a "liberty interest" under the Due Process clause of the Fifth Amendment in refusing unwanted medical treatment. But the liberty interest does not stand alone. Questions regarding whether a constitutional right has been violated must be answered by balancing the liberty interest against the relevant state interests.

A Kickback to the States

While upholding the individual's right to die, the U.S. Supreme Court also held that the State of Missouri had a right to stop the Cruzans from withdrawing treatment in the absence of "clear and convincing" evidence that their daughter would have wanted to die. So, Nancy's parents went back to the state court with additional witnesses who provided the necessary evidence. At the November 1990 hearing, Miss Cruzan's coworkers testified that they recalled her saying she would never want to live "like a vegetable."

Before Judge Charles S. Teel, Jr., made his decision, Dr. John Bagby, the director of the Missouri Department of Health, testified that state officials had signed an affidavit pledging to "carry out the court's order, whichever way it goes." He said that he had already talked with the hospital officials and that "they understand our approach clearly." He and others noted that her intensive care was costing the state $112,000 a year at the rehabilitation center, and that if she continued to receive nourishment through a tube, she "could remain in that condition for another forty years."

A Doctor Reverses Himself

Nancy's physician, Dr. James Davis, who had originally opposed removing the tubes and respirators from his patient's body, finally reversed himself late in 1990. He knew that Nancy's colon upsets, increasing obesity, incontinence, bleeding gums, eye problems, body seizures, and increasing stomach upsets made her case hopeless. Asked by Nancy's court-appointed guardian if it was in her best interests to continue in a vegetative state, Dr. Davis paused and then asserted strongly: "No sir," he said. "I think it would be personally a living hell!"

In his brief court order, Judge Teel, of Jasper County, overruled the 1988 decision of the state court, which had withdrawn from the case in the fall following the June 1990 U.S. Supreme Court decision. With both the doctor, the state-appointed guardians, and her parents—all in agreement that she be allowed to die—the judge ruled simply that there was clear evidence on three points regarding Nancy, a ward of the court:

- "That the intent of our ward, if, mentally able, would be to terminate her nutrition and hydration."
- "That there is no evidence of substance to cause belief that our ward would continue her present existence, hopeless as it is, and slowly progressively worsening."
- "That the co-guardians, Lester and Joyce Cruzan, are authorized to cause the removal of nutrition and hydration from our ward, Nancy Beth Cruzan." (Nachtigal 1990)

There being no person or organization with any legal standing for further challenges, this move represented the final legal resolution in the long tortured fight of her parents to let Nancy die a dignified death.

Controversy Erupts at Nancy's Death Watch

When her case and death watch became the staple of TV talk shows and news commentaries, a loose collection of anti-euthanasia and anti-abortion groups, calling themselves "right to life" advocates, quickly took up what they considered to be Nancy's cause. They argued that every life has a meaning, even life in a vegetative state, and that removing the feeding tube and starving Ms. Cruzan to death devalues life. These opponents had gone to court seven times to try to force the state of Missouri to resume feeding Ms. Cruzan, but they found no legal standing to intervene. Nineteen demonstrators were arrested on December 18, when they entered the hospital in an effort to reattach Nancy's feeding tube. They failed.

Nancy's last days evolved into the centerpiece of a controversial national debate over what direction the country would be taking in the years ahead as similar cases cropped up. On one side, David O'Steen, of the anti-abortion National Right to Life Committee, said her death "diminishes hope for thousands of medically dependent people nationwide." Others, in the same vein, expressed troubled fears that the nation was moving toward both passive and ultimately active euthanasia. The Rev. Joseph Foreman of Atlanta, a founder of the anti-abortion group, Operation Rescue, called Cruzan's death "a tragedy with dangerous implications." He was one of ten who participated in a prayer vigil outside the hospital where Cruzan was housed. He predicted:

> I think the next few years will see an entire industry spring up around putting people to death whom family and friends have deemed to be no longer of use to anybody. There will be wings in hospitals devoted to putting people [like Nancy] to death like this. . . .
>
> I sympathize with the hardships of caring for a helpless woman, but I have no sympathy for a family who solves their problems by starving their daughter to death when there were hundreds of bona-fide offers to care for her regardless of her condition. Even a dog in Missouri cannot be legally starved to death. (Belkin 1991)

Yet on the other side of the fence, there were comments like that of John McCabe, the legal counsel for the National Conference of Commissioners for Uniform State Laws, who credited the Cruzan case with "sensitizing people, especially young people, to the need for planning in advance how to deal with such catastrophies." (At the time of her death, all but nine states had specific statutes spelling out right-to-die rights, but in several of those nine, court rulings and common law provided some limited rights of individual determination. Cruzan's legacy helped to spur action in these remaining states to recognize patients' rights.)

And Doron Weber, a spokesperson for the National Right-to-Die organization in New York, said "The ramifications of this case will be far reaching. The Supreme Court found there is a constitutional basis for the right to refuse treatment. . . . We feel that Nancy Cruzan has made legal history. But her dying is entirely a private matter."

When her father and mother, Lester and Joyce Cruzan, heard the news about the local court's granting their wish, they issued a statement implying that their daughter—"our bright flaming star who flew through the heavens of our lives"—had already "gone" seven years ago. "Because of Nancy," her father said, "I suspect thousands of people can rest free, knowing that when death beckons, they can meet it face to face, with dignity, free from the fear of unwanted and useless medical treatment. I think this is quite an accomplishment for a twenty-year-old kid and I'm damned proud of her."

The family's lawyer, William Colby, said that the surgically implanted feeding tube would be removed within twenty-four hours at the Missouri Rehabilitation Center in Mt. Vernon, where Nancy lay at the end of her seven-year struggle to stay alive in a vegetative state. The result would mean the now thirty-two-year-old Nancy would die of natural causes within a week. After the tube was removed on December 14, Nancy lingered for twelve more days and finally expired on the day after Christmas, December 26, 1990.*

---

*On November 30, two weeks prior to Judge Teel's order to remove Nancy's feeding tube from her stomach, the Court of Common Pleas in Lackawanna County (Scranton), Pennsylvania, held that a sixty-four-year-old incompetent woman in a persistent vegetative state was entitled to have a naso-gastric feeding tube withdrawn. The hospital removed the tube and the woman died peacefully and quietly, in sharp contrast to the front-page publicity that enveloped Cruzan's death a few weeks later.

The Aftermath of Nancy Cruzan's Death

Nancy's death intensified the intensive and bitter national debate between those who believe that people should be allowed to die with dignity and others who have argued that even life in a vegetative state has a meaning. While the debate raged, her case generated a new interest in living wills and other directives to allow people to specify, in advance, what kind of care they desire if they become incapacitated and who should make medical decisions for them if they become terminally ill.

Reaction around the country to the judge's decision was mostly one of relief, like that of Fenella Rouse, the executive director of the Society for the Right to Die, who said: "By their courage in making public a personal tragedy, Lester and Joyce Cruzan have helped us all deal with issues that we would sometimes rather not think about. It is now up to each of us to make sure that our wishes are known so they can be honored."

But the Anti-Euthanasia Task Force (headed by Rita Marker) at the University of Steubenville in Ohio denounced the Missouri decision as "a frenzy to kill Nancy Beth Cruzan that has set in place the cornerstone for a full-scale anti-euthanasia program." And James Bopp, Jr., the general counsel for the National Right to Life Committee, called the ruling "very distressing. It is clear that the evidence does not support denying her food and water."

Because the Cruzan case was an example of passive euthanasia, Arthur Caplan, the director of the Center for Biomedical Research at the University of Minnesota, called Judge Teel's decision "good, tragic and overdue." Ellen Goodman, the columnist, has written:

> The Cruzan case, like that of Karen Ann Quinlan, left a legacy that touches everyone and became a story that made America talk publicly and at length about death in the technological age. . . . Our gratitude to science, our own passionate pursuit of medical salvation, now comes with increasing unease about this same technology. We fear that there may be too much of a good thing. That we can't stop it.
>
> This is what Nancy Cruzan came to represent as she lay twisted, bloated, unconscious in her hospital bed. . . . She came to represent the unintended consequences of technology, the side-effects of our best intentions, the cruelty of our modern medical mercy. She came to

represent something worse than death. . . . Every hospital that has been forced to think about aggressive treatment, every medical school that has been prodded to teach young doctors about dying, has a piece of Nancy Cruzan's legacy. (Goodman 1991)

On the first anniversary of Nancy's death (December 26, 1991), her family announced that they were establishing the Cruzan Foundation in her honor, to help other families who face similar circumstances and have no recourse to legal relief. They felt that this foundation would be the best way to commemorate their daughter's long struggle to die, which has become a symbol of the continuing campaign to establish the right to die as a national right for all Americans.

The First Post-Cruzan Legal Spin-Off

Just over a year after the precedent-setting Nancy Cruzan decision in the Missouri court, Massachusetts' highest court rendered a similar ruling when it ordered that feeding tubes be removed from a thirty-three-year-old, mentally retarded woman who was in a persistent vegetative state. On January 6, 1992, the Supreme Judicial Court, in a 4-3 ruling ordered that the woman, named "Jane Doe," who was also suffering from a degenerative disease, be allowed to die. The justices ruled, in upholding a lower court decision, that if the woman were competent, she would want treatment withheld so that she could "go in peace." But Justice Joseph Nolan, in a dissenting opinion, accused his brethren of playing God. "Death by starvation and dehydration," he wrote, "will not assist Jane Doe in her unquestionable desire to go in peace" (Associated Press, 1992).

The woman, who had been mentally retarded since infancy, was also suffering from Canavan's Disease, which causes progressive destruction of the central nervous system. Her parents, a guardian, the State Department of Mental Retardation, and her doctors all wanted her feeding tubes removed, although her lawyer was opposed to this action. She had been a patient in the Wrentham State Hospital since she was five years old. According to the ruling, written by Justice Ruth Abrams for the majority, Jane Doe displayed no awareness of her surroundings and showed no response even to intense pain. She was also blind and deaf and was completely dependent on the hospital staff for all of her care. The high court also said that the views of the woman's parents were "the best mirror" of her wishes.

The significance of the Jane Doe case was that it marked the first time since the Cruzan case that another state court had rendered a similar decision allowing tubes to be removed from an incurable patient. Others would undoubtedly follow in years to come in other states.

Part III: Doctors Finally Wade Into the Controversy

No decent human being would allow an animal to suffer without putting it out of its misery. It is only to human beings that human beings are so cruel as to allow them to live in pain, in hopelessness, in living death, without moving a muscle to help them.

—Isaac Asimov

8

"Dr. Death" Concocts a Suicide Machine

The eyes are open, but the sense is shut.

—Shakespeare, *King Lear*

The ethical and medical dilemma of doctor-assisted suicide captured the national spotlight in mid-1990, when an obscure, newly retired Michigan pathologist helped a victim of incurable Alzheimer's disease to her death. The resulting headlines placed the name of Dr. Jack Kevorkian on page one and his name became synonymous with the active euthanasia movement.

Who is Dr. Kevorkian?

Jack Kevorkian, sixty-four, graduated from the University of Michigan Medical School in Ann Arbor in 1952, and then took further postgraduate training in pathology. He was an outstanding student, according to his professors, and also an accomplished painter and musician. He spent his career working in hospitals in California and Michigan, taking a special interest in the death process.

While in medical school at the University of Michigan, he was warned by his superiors that he would have to leave the institution if he did not back away from a proposal that death-row prisoners be made permanently unconscious and their bodies then be used for medical experiments. Years later, he also proposed that blood be transferred from dead soldiers lying on the battlefield to wounded soldiers nearby. These controversial proposals were pooh-poohed by his colleagues as being bizarre.

Dr. K. Becomes "Dr. Death"

Dr. Kevorkian, a lifelong bachelor, lives on a small $514-a-month pension in a one-room, second-floor apartment located over a flower shop in downtown Royal Oak, Michigan. According to observers, he never married because he never wanted to be tied down with a family, thus making him able to "say what he wanted to say, and do what he wanted to do." Over the years, his controversial views made it difficult for him to get a steady hospital appointment and he became ostracized by the medical profession.

Kevorkian ceased to practice medicine in 1988, but still retained his license. His business card reads: "Jack Kevorkian, M.D., Bioethics and Obiatry. Special Death Counseling." (He defines the term "obiatry" as "going to one's death with the aid of a doctor.")

Kevorkian is a committed atheist and possesses a hot temper when challenged. He is basically a reclusive person, who nonetheless relishes the publicity whenever he feels he has garnered wide public support for his solo medical actions. He gets a psychological uplift every time he walks down the street in Royal Oak, and neighbors offer him thumbs-up gestures of support. He likes to hear them call out: "Hi, Doc. Keep it up."

Kevorkian and Hemlock

Dr. Kevorkian approached Hemlock in 1988 with the idea of opening a suicide clinic in southern California to which Hemlock would refer terminally ill people who wanted to die. His rationale was that such a clinic would become a necessity and that if he was ever prosecuted for assisting in suicides, the resulting publicity would benefit the cause of euthanasia and Hemlock.

During that same year, a quasi-competitive sister group to Hemlock was battling to qualify the Death With Dignity Act for inclusion on the ballot in California. The campaign failed through poor organization and lack of sufficient signatures. Since the euthanasia movement was attempting to legitimize doctor-assisted suicide for the terminally ill through that act, Humphry suggested to Kevorkian that such law-breaking as he suggested would result in a backlash and bad publicity for the infant movement. He agreed and did not approach Hemlock again.

The First "Suicide Machine" Is Born

Kevorkian invented his "self-execution" apparatus—a kind of "Rube Goldberg" device consisting of forty-five dollars worth of local hardware-store items—after visiting a quadriplegic named David Rivlin, who had asked to have the state of Michigan turn his ventilator off. His request for a passive suicide was granted and he died later in 1989. "Anyone who saw him," Kevorkian told an interviewer, "would say, 'My God, that's not a life.' But a couple of religious nuts were keeping him alive against his will. That's when I knew I needed a device" (Belkin 1990).

The resulting suicide machine was completed in the late summer of 1989, but the Oakland County Medical Society's seven-person board unanimously turned down the physician's request to advertise his product in their medical journal in September. He did receive publicity, however, in newspapers and news services throughout the country. He was also invited to show his machine to the nation for the first time on the Phil Donahue TV show.

Near the end of 1989, Dr. Kevorkian publicly presented to a national television audience his invention of a homemade "suicide machine." It consisted of three bottles inverted in a rack, from which tubes descended to be inserted into a willing patient's veins. For several weeks the media latched onto this gadget, and hundreds of TV viewers became spellbound by its potential. Some, who were really sick, saw Dr.

Kevorkian as "the new messiah" and scores contacted him.

Now all he needed was a willing, credible patient, and one such person soon gave him the opportunity to conduct his lethal experiment.

The Specter of Alzheimer's Descends on Janet Adkins

In 1989, Janet Adkins, a fifty-four-year-old, happily married school-teacher and mother of three grown sons, was diagnosed by her doctor as suffering from the first stages of Alzheimer's Disease—a degenerative disease of the brain that is still incurable. As a member of the Hemlock Society prior to her traumatic discovery, Janet Adkins became horrified as the progressive illness began to affect her faculties, including her speech and memory. Janet was both a physically and intellectually active woman who loved hang-gliding in the mountains nearby, where she also became an avid mountain climber. In addition, she enjoyed playing the flute and beating her thirty-two-year-old son in tennis.

With her husband Ronald's consent, they resolved together that she somehow would end her life before the creeping symptoms became more serious. She had received all of the then known standard and experimental medical treatments for her deteriorating condition, but to no avail. She knew of other similar cases, like that of the late film actress Rita Hayworth, who died of the disease, and Janet didn't want to linger as the movie actress had until her heart stopped.

She approached three doctors in the vicinity of her home town, Portland, Oregon, and asked them to help her to die. Two of the doctors were members of Hemlock. The Adkins also sought counselling from a skilled family therapist, Miriam Coppens, who helped her make her final decision to die. Unfortunately, despite their obvious sympathy with her plight, none of the three doctors whom she consulted would help her directly. She told her Unitarian-Universalist minister about her plans to die soon, and he sympathized with her decision but offered no further advice.

She desired that one of the three doctors administer the lethal drugs in her possession, because she feared that she might make a mistake if she did it to herself, which could prolong her agony. Their rationale for refusing to help her boiled down to the fact that none of them was her physician. They all feared the risk of prosecution for their act, even though one of them confessed to Derek Humphry that he had helped six people to die with drugs. (See page 132 of *Final Exit*.)

Janet Adkins had heard about Dr. Jack Kevorkian in late 1989 through stories in the media and watching his demonstration of the suicide machine on the "Phil Donahue" show. Since she hoped for a gentle death with dignity, she made contact with him and he suggested that she come to him in his home state of Michigan when she was ready to die. Her three sons urged her first to try some experimental treatments for Alzheimer's. But when that approach failed and her memory faded, along with her ability to play her beloved flute, she vowed to go through with her decision to end her life—somehow.

She then sent Dr. Kevorkian her medical records to examine. Since the state of Michigan had murky laws regarding the legality of suicide, Mrs. Adkins decided to go there if he would accept her, since the doctors in her hospital said that they would never recommend suicide as an option in her case.

So, Janet and her husband Ronald, an investment broker, flew the two thousand air miles to Michigan in early June, vowing to go through with her desire to die. He hoped she would change her mind at the last minute and bought her a round-trip air ticket, just in case she did. Upon the Adkins' arrival and without the aid of any lab equipment, Kevorkian soon confirmed the Alzheimer's diagnosis of his new patient and judged Janet to be lucid.

D-Day for the Medical Profession

Kevorkian had previously searched for a suitable place where the procedure could be carried out. The local funeral home, offices, churches, and motels all refused his request to use their premises, as did members of the local Hemlock Society when he asked if he could use one of their homes. He did not wish to use his own apartment—"My landlord would have thrown me out," he said—so, he fell back on his rusty 1968 Volkswagen van as the site for his operation. "There was no other place that I could do it," he explained (Gibbs 1990).

Two days later, on June 4, 1990, Dr. Kevorkian drove his van to a public campground called Grovelands, outside of Royal Oak. As Janet Adkins settled down on a small cot in the back of the curtained van,

Kevorkian hooked her up to a heart monitor, slid an intravenous needle into her arm, and started a harmless saline solution flowing through the tube in one of the three bottles of his machine.

Kevorkian then sat back and watched her push a big red button at the base of the machine, which replaced the saline solution with a sodium pentathol pain killer. One minute later came the poison—potassium chloride mixed with succinylcholine—from the third bottle. Just before she became unconscious, Janet looked up at the doctor and said, "Thank you, thank you, thank you." (She refused to allow her husband of thirty-four years to be with her so he stayed at a nearby motel.) Within five minutes Janet Adkins was dead of heart stoppage.

When her EKG flattened out on the electrocardiograph, he then called the police to tell them what he had done. Kevorkian's only regret was that Mrs. Adkins' organs could not be donated because her body remained in the van for several hours before it was taken to a nearby hospital. "The medical examiner wouldn't let me touch the body," Kevorkian said later. "They were there for four hours walking around and scratching their heads. Had it not been for the delay", he lamented, "you could have sliced her liver in half and saved two babies, and her bone marrow could have been taken, her heart, two kidneys, two lungs and the pancreas. Think of the people that could have been saved. If you were waiting for a new heart, you'd be all for what I'm doing. She had a good, strong heart. I know, I watched it on the screen until it gave out" (ibid.).

Criticisms from the Medical Community

Kevorkian saw himself as a medical missionary. The day after Adkins' death, in a front-page interview in the *New York Times,* he admitted that he took the action "to force the medical and legal professions to consider this idea" (ibid.).

As a result of the *Times'* story, Kevorkian immediately became a controversial figure in the medical profession. Although some right-to-die advocates called him a "brave pioneer," most doctors and ethicists challenged him on both moral and procedural grounds. The majority of right-to-die groups stress that safeguards must be placed on a patient's request via a living will and having at least two independent doctors confirm in writing that the patient desires to die and that his or her condition is both unbearable and irreversible.

Kevorkian went beyond these strictures, however. As ethicist Susan Wolfe of the Hastings Center in New York put it: "Even the staunchest proponents of physician assisted suicide should be horrified at this case because there were no procedural protections." Other doctors commented that Alzheimer's is a very difficult disease to diagnose because of the conflicting symptoms, one of which is the deteriorating mental ability to make decisions. Much of the medical community rejected Kevorkian's solution, voicing fears that damage would be done to their profession if doctors routinely acted as executioners. "With the doctor-patient relationship being based on mutual trust," said Dr. Nancy Dickey, a trustee of the AMA, "our patients should not have to be concerned that we are going to make a value judgment that their lives are no longer worth living" (*Associated Press,* June 8, 1990).

Some physicians considered Kevorkian's use of a machine to pass control to the patient an "ethical copout," one doctor saying: "Even if he gets off the hook legally, there is a moral accountability that cannot be ignored." Several months later, the Michigan State Medical Association took a similar stance when it declared: "We don't think an individual physician can arbitrarily decide that euthanasia is legally and morally correct. But giving someone a medicine or allowing them to take medicine is not necessarily different than stopping chemotherapy or stopping antibiotics." The medical society declined to condemn the "suicide machine," however, and made no recommendation to remove Kevorkian's medical license.

The Politicians and the Pulpit Lash Out at Kevorkian

An irate Republican state senator, Fred Dillingham, was quoted as saying after the Adkins affair: "My feelings are that we need to punch Kevorkian's light out right now. He's proven himself to be a danger." Dillingham said he was going to introduce a bill in the legislature to stop this "bizarre" form of death, and to make assisted suicide a felony:

> Here in this state he is referred to as "Dr. Death." We are looking at somebody who wants to be Dr. God. It's a very scary concept.

He violated a court order, violated medical ethics, then turns around and broadens it to the chronically ill. It makes me wonder what's next if we don't get him checked in this state.

Several prominent religious leaders also condemned Kevorkian. A spokesman for the archdiocese of Detroit stated unequivocally that "God alone is the author of life, from beginning to end." But Adkins' own church, the Unitarian Universalist, defended her right to act according to her conscience. Other critics labeled him "Dr. Death" and some even called him a "serial mercy killer."

Dr. K. Fights Back

He later claimed that he never wanted any publicity, but Dr. Kevorkian took center stage a week later when he appeared on successive TV shows, including "Crossfire," "Good Morning America," and "Geraldo." Before a national television audience, he described his device as "humane, dignified and painless," and he claimed that his critics were "brainwashed ethicists" or "religious nuts," and that he only wanted to help patients in deep distress. "My biggest enemies," he said, "are the medical organizations because independent doctors tell me that they are behind me, but they can't speak out" (ABC-TV, June 12, 1990).

For the next two months the media courted him and both the medical and the psychiatric professions were thrown into turmoil about the ethics of mercy killing. Adkins became a symbol of all those thousands of patients who are suffering the pangs of an incurable, debilitating disease and who seek a pain-free death with dignity. As Kevorkian carried his crusade for legal mercy killing via the TV networks, he too became a standardbearer for a distinct minority of doctors who failed to see a moral difference between unplugging a respirator—known as passive euthanasia—and plugging in a poison machine for an active-euthanasia operation.

Dr. K. fought back against his critics, announcing that he would help more people to die as soon as he cleared up his legal problems. Yet he soon expressed doubts about how best to conduct physician-assisted suicide. Three months after the medical association waffled on his Adkins' action, he told the *Detroit News* about his new plan. "If a terminally-ill person wanted to die, I would go to their home and consult with them; their family, their minister and all the relevant doctors would then determine if the case qualifies for what the person wants. A decision could then be made by a specially appointed panel."

The Hemlock Society opposed Kevorkian on this approach, arguing that suicide centers were unnecessary, because with a simple change of the law, through the proposed Death with Dignity Act, help with death could take place quietly at home, hospital, or in a hospice, as a privately negotiated arrangement between the doctor and patient. Secondly, there could never be enough such "suicide centers" across the country to be within easy distance of sick patients who were unable to travel far from their homes. And thirdly, such centers could encourage massive abuse unless heavily regulated (Smith 1990).

The Hemlock Society approved Kevorkian's helping Janet Adkins since it knew that she had been contemplating her action for six months and had been going through psychological counselling. But the society felt "it is hardly death with dignity to travel 2000 miles and die in the back of a van on a campside lot. We need to change the law so that this sort of compassionate help by a doctor can happen at home or in the hospital" (Humphry 1991).

Turning over the fate of a patient to a panel of doctors would also remove the patient's right to make a decision about quality of life and the right to determine when that life should be ended. Dr. Kevorkian did provide a public service, however, by forcing the conservative medical profession to rethink its head-in-the-sand attitude on euthanasia and the rights of patients.

9

The Double Deaths in Cabin 2

We're looking at somebody [Dr. Kevorkian] who wants to be God!
—Michigan Republican State Senator Fred Dillingham

Did Kevorkian Go Too Far?

Kevorkian knew that his home state of Michigan had the most ambiguous set of laws on assisted suicide in the United States. In previous cases, some of the defendants had been exonerated and others had received punitive sentences. The first known prosecution in America for euthanasia assistance took place in Michigan in 1920 when Frank Roberts assisted his wife to take her own life. She had multiple sclerosis and had unsuccessfully previously attempted suicide on earlier occasions. At her urging, her husband mixed Paris Green (containing arsenic) with water and placed it within her reach. She drank it and died, after which he was convicted of first-degree murder and received life imprisonment at hard labor. His case, *People* v. *Roberts,* became a classic in the legal history books. He presumably died in prison since he was never released on parole.

Over sixty years later, the pendulum swung in the other direction in Michigan, when Steven Paul Campbell was convicted of leaving a gun and ammunition with a friend, who used it to take his own life. He later walked free, however. The deceased victim had been severely depressed and had been drinking heavily, but the Michigan Court of Appeals said: "The legislature has not defined aiding a suicide as a crime. Aiding suicide does not fall within any definitions of suicide." (The law was changed in 1992.)

But after Kevorkian's headline-making act in 1990, the Michigan law enforcement authorities moved swiftly to prevent him from doing it again by issuing a temporary restraining order to impound his battered Volkswagen, his suicide machine, and the drugs, and to forbid him to help anyone else. Part of the official legal complaint against him was that "it is likely other candidates for his 'machine' will be turning up." That prediction came true when Kevorkian was swamped with inquiries and entreaties, but he decided not to build another machine like the one used to aid Janet Adkins. For the moment, he decided to go underground.

Was It Murder?

On December 3, 1990, six months after Janet Adkins' death,* Dr. Kevorkian was charged with murder. This indictment was handed down one day before he was to go on trial in connection with the temporary restraining order, which prohibited him from using the so-called "suicide machine" again. The Hemlock Society offered to help him in the courts, but he rebuffed the offer. One of his attorneys stated that the reason for his rejection was the fact that "he doesn't support the Hemlock Society standards" (Associated Press, 1990).

Just ten days later, on December 13, after a day and a half of the preliminary examination, the criminal charges were suddenly dropped. District Judge Gerald McNally of Clarkson, Michigan, dismissed the first-degree murder charge against Dr. Kevorkian after hearing a tape on which Janet Adkins discussed her fight against Alzheimer's. "I've had enough," she said, near the end of the tape. "I want to get out,"

---

*Many legal experts felt that in any other state Kevorkian would have been charged with murder the day after Adkins' death. It is unclear why Michigan waited a half year to bring charges against him.

she complained on the tape, and when asked by Kevorkian whether he had solicited her business, she answered: "No, no, no, no." Because Michigan law did not outlaw assisting suicide, the prosecutors had no case against the retired pathologist.

There was scattered applause in the courtroom as Kevorkian shook the hand of his lawyer. "I feel like I'm walking on a cloud," he said. Despite his dismissal Kevorkian—who received no fee from the Adkins for his assistance—was told by the court that he was not free to use his death machine again, and that his old one would remain in police custody. The issue of whether to make the temporary restraining order a permanent one to prevent the doctor from any future use of new suicide machines was still pending (Irwain 1990).

The effect of Judge McNally's decision was to maintain the status quo that assisted suicide was not a crime in Michigan—for the time being. But in announcing his decision, the judge called on the Michigan legislature to address the issues raised by Kevorkian. State Senator Fred Dillingham had recently introduced a bill making assisting in a suicide a felony punishable by four years in prison and a two-thousand-dollar fine, but no action had been taken on it by the end of 1990. And the prosecutor said he would not appeal the decision.

On January 4, 1991, the prosecutors asked Judge Alice Gilbert of the Oakland County Circuit Court for a permanent order banning Dr. Kevorkian from regaining possession of his suicide machine. In a civil hearing, the state brought in expert witnesses, including psychiatrists, who testified that Janet Adkins was not competent to make her decision to die. In stressing the need for clear laws regarding the right to die, Cheryl Smith, a Hemlock Society lawyer, commented: "This type of ad-hoc assistance in suicide for the dying is wide open to abuse because there are no ground rules and no criteria." (The judge did not issue the order.)

If he did nothing else, Kevorkian put Michigan at the center of the moral and ethical debate over assisted suicide. Richard Thompson, the Oakland County prosecutor who had failed to get first-degree-murder charges to stick against Kevorkian, offered this commentary: "Dr. Kevorkian is a free man, garnering the publicity he normally seeks. We don't know what part he played, if any. It would be purely speculative on our part to characterize him in any way other than being at a cabin when the police arrived, as a witness who has refused thus far to cooperate, as have other witnesses."

Thompson's statement, however, presaged further legal action against Kevorkian after it was stated by the sheriff that it would take at least two weeks to determine whether charges should be made against the doctor. (But they were not made because Michigan had no law against assisted suicide at the time.)

Where to Draw the Line?

How do many doctors get around the dilemma of prescribing a lethal dose of medicine to their cancer patients and yet avoid the risk of being accused of malpractice? Judith Ross, a professor of medical ethics at UCLA, was reported to have said: "It's not uncommon for physicians of cancer patients to say: 'Here's some medication and make sure you don't take more than 22 pills, because 22 pills will kill you.' " If a patient wants to commit suicide, he or she can ignore the doctor's warning, and the doctor is off the hook. But Professor Ross believes that Dr. Kevorkian's suicide machine goes way beyond the ethical line illustrated by her example. "Killing patients is not a good activity for doctors to be engaged in," she said. "Even if society wants something like this done—and it not clear that they do—it sends a really problematic message to patients: 'Do you know what your doctor's up to?' "

Kevorkian agrees that doctors should *not* use his machine; rather, he envisions the establishment of suicide clinics, administered by nonmedical workers. "They should be salaried and not fee-for-service, so there's no profit motive at all," he said. But who would prevent the abuses in such a set-up, Kevorkian did not say.

Dr. Kevorkian Publishes a Book on Euthanasia

In the early fall of 1991, Dr. Kevorkian published his second book, titled *Prescription: Medicide: The Goodness of Planned Death* (Prometheus Books). This book marked a detour from the crusade that brought him to the forefront of the right-to-die movement, namely assisting Janet Adkins to her death and his public campaign for legalized active euthanasia. The major ethical and philosophical issue addressed in this new work is how the state can get something positive out of the execution of convicted felons. Kevorkian devotes most of *Medicide* to expounding his thesis on the usefulness of allowing death-row inmates to willingly donate their organs after execution or to agree to human experimentation before death. He notes how many patients' lives could be saved if the organs of prisoners on death row could be donated to those who needed them. He spends very little time explaining the circumstances surrounding Janet Adkins' death and stops short of discussing any legal action that was brought against him or is likely to be brought in the future.

Nonetheless, Kevorkian shows a profound understanding of the misguided nature of the medical profession, noting that the real dilemma facing doctors is the issue of the proper care of patients rather than curing diseases. In taking on the medical establishment, theologians, and politicians, the maverick physician challenges them to stop resisting a "rational and comprehensive program of dignified, humane and beneficial planned death." He defends the ethical basis of his proposal, which he says has often been thwarted by "the vestiges of medieval thinking that continue to grip the law makers, the medical community and the society at large."

The author of the previously published *Stone Age Ethics and Space Age Medicine* claims he has conducted a thirty-three-year campaign to get both "medicide" and his lethal-injection device approved. He calls his machine the "Mercitron," a name he prefers to "suicide machine."

But he still prefers to go it alone rather than to ally himself with any right-to-die groups like the Hemlock Society. In response to a question posed to him at a televised National Press Club luncheon in Washington in October 1992, Dr. Kevorkian answered: "I do not believe the nation's doctors will follow the leadership of a lay-led organization like Hemlock on doctor-assisted suicide" (C-SPAN TV, October 12, 1992).

The Trek to Cabin #2

On October 23, 1991, two women rented a rustic cabin for thirty-five in the Bald Mountain Recreation Area, forty-five miles north of Detroit. Cabin #2, which had no electricity or indoor plumbing, overlooked the picturesque Tamarack Lake. But the lack of modern conveniences didn't matter to the two women—Sherry Miller, forty-three, of Roseville, Michigan, who was suffering from multiple sclerosis, and Marjorie Wantz, fifty-eight, a former elementary-school teacher of Sodus, Michigan, who was afflicted with a very painful but not terminal pelvic disease. Wantz's genital-pelvic disorder had become so painful that her neighbors in the Meadow Streams Trailer Park could hear her screaming in agony at night. Even heavy doses of painkilling Demorol and ten operations to remove inflamed tissues could not relieve her distress. Both women were haunted by the thought that they would face years of incapacitation; and so they had come to Cabin #2 to end their suffering with the help of Dr. Kevorkian, who was prepared to assist them with a newly constructed suicide machine, similar to the one that had been used on Janet Adkins sixteen months earlier.

Kevorkian made the solo decision to assist both women to commit suicide at the same time because, according to his lawyer Geoffrey Fieger: "He was afraid he would betray one, if he left the other. Kevorkian was fearful of being stopped and leaving one to suffer."

Kevorkian's second experiment with the suicide machine did not have a propitious start. First, he and his sister, Margo Janus, got lost in the woods on the winding dirt roads leading to the death cabin. But they managed to find the cabin before the two women, who arrived soon afterward in another vehicle, accompanied by three supporters. Then Kevorkian discovered that he had forgotten some medical equipment that he needed, so he had to make his patients and their families and friends wait several hours there while he returned to his home in Royal Oak, a Detroit suburb, to retrieve the medical equipment.

Hemlock's Concerns

Meanwhile word had filtered back to Hemlock's national headquarters in Oregon that Dr. Kevorkian was going to help someone just before the vote was taken on Washington State Initiative #119 (see chapter 13) to legalize doctor-assisted suicide in that state. "We had heard rumors about it," Humphry told this writer in a post-election interview, "and one of our staff (the Rev. Ralph Mero) communicated with him [via phone calls and a letter] and begged him not to do it. But he ignored our request."

Besides this political consideration, Hemlock differed with Kevorkian's philosophy, which envisions "suicide clinics," having the power to experiment for medical reasons on terminally ill patients both before and after death occurs.

Kevorkian Videotapes the Last Statements of Miller and Wantz

On the hour-long videotape made the night before the event (which Kevorkian released after the deaths of the two women), Miller said in a faltering voice, "I thought about it for a long time, a long time. I have no qualms about my decision. I want to die, and I know there's no turning back." On the same tape Wantz said that she had unsuccessfully attempted suicide on her own three times by inhaling carbon monoxide from a hose connected to a car exhaust pipe, and that she had twice tried overdosing herself on Halcion, the sleeping medication. "I tried loading a gun, but I didn't know how," she told Kevorkian on the tape. "If you do it yourself, you don't know what you are doing. I wish I could have done it a year ago, or two years ago." Miller lamented, "I went from a cane to a walker to a wheelchair. I can't walk, I can't write. It's hard for me to talk. I can't function as a human being." Looking down and weeping, Miller added: "What can anybody do? Nothing! I want the right to die" (Kole 1991).

(The tape had been made at the Roseville home of Miller's parents. At times both women were able to chat amiably about their forthcoming suicides despite their complaints; they even joked about the choice of accommodations at the cabin, when Kevorkian said it had twenty bunks. Kevorkian also spent twenty minutes describing in detail the device that he planned to use to administer the lethal drugs the next day.)

Wantz was the first to go. Kevorkian attached strings to her index and middle fingers, while Bill Wantz, sixty-five, her husband of five years, told her: "I'm going to miss you." Then she pulled the string on her index finger, and Brevital, a fast-acting anesthetic, began flowing through a tube into her arm. She soon fell asleep, and when her hand fell by her side, it automatically pulled the second string, releasing a fatal intravenous dose of potassium chloride and anextine. Within three minutes she was dead (Svoboda 1991).

Watching this doctor-assisted suicide was Sherry Miller, a former housewife who had been suffering from multiple sclerosis for thirteen years since 1978. Five years after the onset of her deteriorating affliction, she and her husband, Wayne Polachiwski, were divorced, and their two children, Jennifer, now twenty, and Kevin, seventeen, moved in with their father. Miller, left alone, was so incapacitated that she was forced to live with her parents. Once a vigorous swimmer and roller skater, she had lost the use of her arm, leg, and neck muscles and was confined to a wheelchair. Despite this imprisonment in a wheelchair, she confessed in 1990: "I am not in any pain, I just can't do anything anymore. I'm just existing, and I no longer care just to exist."

Kevorkian had originally planned to use the same machine for both patients, but when he found Miller's veins to be too weak, he had to use an alternative back-up method. This consisted of a face mask, normally used for administering oxygen to a patient, attached to a canister of deadly carbon monoxide (which is spewed out of the tailpipes of autos, trucks, and buses).

"Are you sure that this is what you want?" he asked her.

"Absolutely, positively," she replied firmly.

Two close friends each told her: "I love you," after which she pulled a string that opened a valve. Her death took about half an hour, quite a bit longer than Wantz's.

Then Kevorkian called the Oakland County Sheriff's Office to report a "double doctor-assisted suicide." He was not arrested when the authorities came to the cabin to claim the bodies, but his latest action touched off another escalation in the national debate on the issue. Even the National Hemlock Society, which supported him in the Adkins' death (but not officially), expressed qualms over this latest twin-death episode. The Society was concerned that Kevorkian was no longer restricting himself to the terminally ill. (The Michigan chapter of Hemlock did support him, however.)

After their deaths, Geoffrey Fieger, Kevorkian's attorney, stated that his client felt "compelled as a human being to render compassionate treatment to patients who have no alternative." Fieger also released a last letter written by Wantz before her passing that read in part: "I have begged him to help me for two years. After 3½ years, I cannot go on with this pain and agony. No doctor can help me anymore. If God won't come to me, I'm going to find God."

Dr. Susan Block, a Harvard University psychiatrist, who has interviewed seventeen physicians who participated in euthanasia cases and who believes in it under limited circumstances, made this comment when apprised of the latest two deaths in the cabin: "I am stunned. Kevorkian is an irresponsible, unprofessional madman, who is capitalizing on this issue" (Treen, November 11, 1991).

Michigan Acts Against Dr. Kevorkian

The Michigan Board of Medicine made a critical decision on November 20, 1991, when its eight-member panel voted unanimously to suspend indefinitely Dr. Kevorkian's license to practice medicine. Their decision came in response to a request by State Attorney General Frank Kelley, after the local prosecutor had failed to pursue criminal charges against him. Several board members said they wanted to send a message that the doctor's methods were unacceptable, even though they expected him to appeal the ruling almost immediately, which set off a long hearing process before the Michigan Board of Medicine. Dr. Philip Margolis, a board member who abstained from the vote, said that the medical, ethical, and legal issues were too complex to address with a summary suspension of Dr. Kevorkian's license. "I think at least from my point of view," the dissenting physician said, "there is no immediate menace to his activities. This is a very complex issue, which will take a lot of thought on everybody's part, whether it be the legislature or us or whomever" (Associated Press, November 21, 1991).

Kevorkian had made few public appearances since his latest two assisted deaths in late October and did not answer his telephone. The board hoped that their suspension would have two positive effects, even though Kevorkian had not practiced medicine in recent years. First, he would become vulnerable to a criminal charge if he continued to practice medicine without a license, and, second, they hoped it would make it impossible for him either to prescribe or to gain access to drugs. But they quietly acknowledged that there was no way of knowing how many lethal drugs he had stockpiled before he lost his license.

Kevorkian had earlier hurled down the gauntlet at the state board when he stated that he would help more ill people to commit suicide, even if he lost his license. "He's clearly intentionally prepared to violate the public health code," board member Dr. Rachel Keth commented. One of Kevorkian's lawyers, Michael Schwartz, told a Detroit TV audience in an interview on WDIV that "no license was required to help people to kill themselves. Dr. Kevorkian can do anything that any unlicensed human being can do if asked for advice."

So the issue was joined, even though the legal status of Kevorkian's ability to help future incurable patients to die had been put temporarily into limbo.

10

Was It Really Murder?

Michigan leads the country and the world [in euthanasia cases], outside
of the Netherlands, where euthanasia is legal.
> —Dr. Jack Kevorkian, July 21, 1992 (after being freed of two
> first-degree murder charges for the October 1991 deaths)

The Next Step for Dr. Kevorkian and the Law

On December 18, two months after the twin suicides of Wantz and
Miller, the Michigan prosecutor, Richard Thompson, issued a homicide
ruling against Dr. Kevorkian for his assistance in the deaths of the
two women. If convicted, Kevorkian could be given a long prison term.
But the question remained: would these charges stand up in court? One
of his lawyers, Allan Adler, said: "There is no way that the prosecutor
could make such an indictment stick since Michigan has no law against
assisted suicide."

On December 19, the day after the Oakland County Medical Examiner, Dr. Ljubisa Dragovic, issued homicide rulings in the deaths
of Wantz and Miller—declaring that the deaths were *not* suicides because
"suicide is reserved for self-inflicted death"—the county prosecutor asked
a grand jury whether to bring murder charges against Dr. Kevorkian.

Prosecutor Thompson also said he would seek to have Kevorkian held in contempt of court for violating a judge's order imposed after the 1990 suicide of Janet Adkins, which demanded that he refrain from helping people kill themselves again. Thompson was playing hardball now in his attempt to put Kevorkian behind bars.

The suicide doctor sat quietly in the courtroom as his lawyer called Mr. Thompson a "buffoon living two thousand years behind the times," and then accused the prosecutor of being an "arch-Machiavellian manipulator" who was waging a personal campaign against his client. "The prosecutor of Oakland County is sworn to uphold the law, not take on a personal vendetta because of his own peculiar political or religious beliefs," Mr. Geoffrey Fieger said.

Thompson responded to this name calling by saying: "Kevorkian, through his attorney, is attempting to turn these serious proceedings into a media circus. There seems to be no limit to the extent Dr. Kevorkian and his sidekicks will go to promote their views and distract public attention from the profound issues involved here." Thompson then announced that the secret grand jury would meet on January 6, 1992, to begin hearing witnesses, including relatives of the two dead women, who had been subpoenaed to testify under oath (Hoogterp 1992).

The new career of the retired pathologist had now taken on an ominous twist in his conflict with the law enforcement agencies in his home state. The nation had not yet heard the last of Dr. Kevorkian and his suicide machines.

The Grand Jury Brings Forth an Indictment

On February 4, after a month of deliberations, the grand jury brought forth a murder indictment against Dr. Kevorkian, based on the assertion that, while Janet Adkins had been terminally ill when he assisted her suicide in 1990, the two women whom he helped to their deaths in 1991 were not. The grand jury also noted that he defied the judge's order after the 1990 episode not to do it again (editorial, *Oakland Press,* February 16, 1992).

Three and a half weeks later, District Judge James Sheehy ordered the smiling doctor to stand trial for first-degree murder in helping Wantz and Miller to die before their time. The judge dismissed a drug-trafficking charge against the retired physician, and scheduled a March 12 arraignment for Kevorkian on the two murder counts. He did agree to let him go free on a $10,000 personal bond. His attorney, Geoffrey Fieger, stated that he and Kevorkian were not surprised at the ruling and anticipated a victory at the coming show trial, even though they both knew a conviction would mean a mandatory life prison term without parole.

One of the prosecutors, however, noted that the Michigan legislature, which had several bills in the hopper, needed to give the courts some guidance in handling physician-assisted-suicide cases, since the state had no law on that point. Judge Sheehy acknowledged the lack of a law to guide him, but said that some serious questions had arisen since the October 23, 1991, deaths of the two women in the cabin in the woods.

"Causation of the deaths has become a question of fact," the Judge said, "and questions of fact are decided by jury trial."

But on the day after the judge's announcement, February 28, defense attorney Fieger announced that he would file a motion to head off the trial after his client's forthcoming arraignment. He stated that his motion would focus on an apparent oversight in the judge's opinion. Sheehy had noted that Kevorkian must be tried because there was a lack of testimony from observer witnesses as to who activated the machines that caused the two women's deaths. The judge had said, "Only Kevorkian and his sister were present in the cabin to witness the deaths, and no testimony was presented as to who activated the two death devices." Unfortunately, Sheehy's opinion did not mention that Sharon Welsh, a friend of Sherry Miller, had testified before Sheehy at a preliminary hearing, that she personally saw the two women trigger the death machines. "I saw Sherry pull the screwdriver that started the [fatal dose of carbon monoxide] gas and I testified to that. I can't explain how it was omitted after Sheehy's decision was released," Welsh said (Hoogterp 1992).

After this embarrassment on the part of the court, the judge could not be reached for comment and the arraignment date was quietly postponed. A confident Kevorkian and Fieger both felt that they had trumped the judge's ace and were hoping for a dismissal of the charges.

A Welcome Respite

Realizing his oversight, the judge made a decision on March 14, 1992 that Mr. Fieger would be given thirty days to submit a new brief outlining his arguments why Dr. Kevorkian should not be tried for murder because of the presence of the third party at the double suicide. He then added on an extra two weeks grace period (with no announced reason) bringing the due date for submission to the court May 1. So, the case of *Michigan* v. *Kevorkian* was put on an extended hold pending the court's reaction to Fieger's brief to dismiss all charges against his client ("Kevorkian," *Hemlock News,* April 1992).

Experts in legal circles opined that any state other than Michigan could in all likelihood successfully charge Dr. Kevorkian with a crime of assisted suicide because neither of the two women were terminally ill. But that state's present law is such a mess, due to conflicting prior court decisions rendered over the past seventy years, that it has become practically unworkable. (See chapter 14 for the proposed new Michigan law that is aimed at rectifying the present one.)

Even if Kevorkian was ultimately tried, a conviction was unlikely. A growing phenomena called "jury nullification" had been a factor in other recent euthanasia trials around the country. In these cases, the juries considered the defendant guilty, but threw the case out because the law was found to be wrong. Similarly, many grand juries refused to issue indictments.

These cases, like Kevorkian's, are forcing reluctant state legislatures to face up to the issue of legalizing doctor-assisted suicide. Unfortunately, Kevorkian's actions in the two most recent "suicide machine" cases do not appear to have aided law reform. Most doctors, with families and children of their own, have more to lose than Kevorkian and would not risk losing their licenses by imitating his actions. Public opinion is now being tested at the polls, as various states consider euthanasia bills (see chapter 15).

Dr. Kevorkian Helps a Fourth Woman to Die

While still facing a resolution of the two October 23, 1991, first-degree-murder charges, Dr. Kevorkian helped another woman to commit suicide on May 15, 1992 in Clawson, Michigan. Fifty-two-year-old Susan Williams took her own life by inhaling carbon monoxide through a mask she placed over her face in the bedroom of her suburban Detroit home. Williams, who was legally blind and had been confined to a wheelchair for more than a decade because of degenerative multiple sclerosis, had been counselled for some time by the "suicide doctor" before she agreed to take her own life. She made her choice in the presence of her two sisters, her twenty-nine-year-old son, and Kevorkian's own sister (who was also present at the October 23 twin suicides).

When the authorities came to confirm the death of the terminally ill woman, who wrote a short letter just before she died absolving the pathologist of any responsibility in her death, no arrest was made, although the Oakland County prosecutor announced that an investigation would be made. (Because Kevorkian was restrained from writing prescriptions, he felt this lethal alternative method to high powered drugs provided him with a legal escape hatch to help those who came to him to end their lives.) In her note, Williams wrote (*Associated Press,* May 16, 1992):

> I don't want to live any longer and feel that I have the right to end my life. . . . The quality of my life is just existing, not living. . . . Dr. Kevorkian has counselled me not to do this until I am absolutely sure this is what I want. I pray Dr. Kevorkian will be exonerated of any wrongdoing in this case. I am so thankful he was able to help me.

After the county authorities came to view the body and found the sixty-three-year-old pathologist standing at Mrs. Williams' side, Kevorkian's attorney, Geoffrey Fieger, told a news conference that his client would refuse to eat if he were imprisoned for this latest headline-making "obiatric" treatment of a patient, as he termed it.

Unlike the previous two women, who were painfully but not terminally ill, Mrs. Williams was "terminal" in the opinion of her relatives and the doctor. Although Kevorkian still faced an appeals court regarding the 1991 case of Wantz and Miller, which could result in imprisonment for life, Kevorkian and his defense counsel felt that he was within the law of Michigan in aiding Susan Williams to end her life.

To critics, he was still a "loose cannon" who was harming the profession of medicine, but since Michigan had no law barring his "compassionate act," he went ahead anyway. One of his staunchest critics has been Ellen Goodman, a prominent syndicated columnist for years, based at the *Boston Globe*. On May 24, she published a column that blasted the actions of the man who she claimed was "on the loose again."

> The State of Michigan has a serial killer on its hands. Or a serial mercy killer. Or a serial aide and abettor to suicide. Choose one of the above. But the distinctions are becoming more blurred all the time.
>
> Kevorkian, trained pathologist and self-proclaimed "obiatrist," thinks of himself as a maverick and martyr in the spirit of Mahatma Gandhi. "Dr. Death," the man with the motive—"My motto is a rational policy of planned death"—believes he's a crusader like the Rev. Dr. Martin Luther King, Jr. But as the count of the dead grows he looks a lot more like Jack the Ripper, M.D.

Even though she conceded that each of the four women wanted to die, had prepared living wills, and had said how grateful they were to the maverick physician for providing them with the means to die, she attacked Kevorkian's character: "But that doesn't diminish the fact that Kevorkian has become an ethical outlaw, a free-lance death dealer providing paraphernalia and know-how to the users," she wrote. But Goodman conceded that Kevorkian's escapades "ratcheted up the national discussion on [right to die] covering everything from disconnecting life support to aiding suicide."

She quoted Dr. George Annas, a medical ethicist of Boston University, who said sharply:

> He [Kevorkian] doesn't have a doctor-patient relationship with these people. He's not there for treatment or diagnosis. He doesn't give them alternatives or reasons to live. He's there to help you die. . . . The only question is whether he should be in a mental institution or a prison.

Goodman also conceded:

> As long as Janet, Sherry, Marjorie, and Susan [the four women who came to him for help in dying] pushed the button, he may not be guilty of first-degree murder. But he has provided the means and

recklessly endangered lives. If nothing else, that's respectable grounds
for a manslaughter charge, or in this case, womanslaughter.

She concluded her acerbic column by quoting Kevorkian's 1990
challenge to the system: "If it's legal, let me do it. If it's illegal, stop
me." She adds: "Now this renegade—have carbon monoxide, will travel—
has issued a new challenge: 'Stop me before I kill again.' That's exactly
what Michigan must do."

And in due time, it looked like the Michigan legislature would finally act to do just that.

The Coroner Calls It Homicide

A new twist in the Kevorkian-assisted death of Susan Williams occurred
on June 5, 1992, when Dr. Kanu Virani, the Oakland County Deputy
Chief Medical Examiner, declared that the doctor's help to the patient
constituted homicide on his part. The key to the homicide finding, the
coroner said, "is that somebody actively participated in the process of
when she died." While he conceded that Williams could have triggered
a valve to release the carbon monoxide poison, he maintained that
someone else must have operated the valves to control its flow. But
Kevorkian's attorney, Geoffrey Fieger, countered that there was no need
for anyone to operate the valves after the patient started the flow of
gas, since Kevorkian had put the valve and mask within her reach.
"If she had not chosen to start the flow of gas, she wouldn't have died,"
he said. "She took the action that killed herself," implying that just
providing the lethal materials, which Kevorkian made available, did not
violate the court order prohibiting Kevorkian from assisting in suicides
(Drummond 1992).

Meanwhile, Oakland County Circuit Judge David Breck heard four
hours of Fieger's motion to dismiss the case against his client, despite
this latest bombshell by the coroner. Breck declared that he would not
"rule for quite a while" on the charges and set a tentative date for
a trial in early September if he ruled that one was warranted in this
latest case involving the doctor.

Whatever the outcome, Kevorkian's "incidents" involving terminally
ill patients had brought the issue front and center nationwide and would

force legislative and court decisions regarding the resolution of the medical and moral dilemma.

Dual Murder Charges Dismissed Against Kevorkian

On July 21, 1992, for the first time in the growing national controversy over the morality of assisting terminally ill patients to their deaths, an obscure county judge took a firm stand and sent a clear message to the country: Oakland County Circuit Judge David Breck dismissed the first-degree-murder counts against Kevorkian for the deaths of Sherry Miller and Marjorie Wantz.

In dropping the charges, he admonished the county prosecutor, Richard Thompson, for wasting more than a million dollars of taxpayers' money in trying to show that Kevorkian had actually tripped the lethal devices of his suicide machines. Judge Breck wrote that "for those patients, whether terminal or not, who have unmanageable pain, physician-assisted suicide remains an alternative."

"This is the way it always should have been," a relieved and elated Kevorkian told a news conference. "This is a medical service. It always was. . . . Michigan leads the country and civilized world outside of the Netherlands, where euthanasia is legal. Are you going to watch people suffering in agony when we have the power to do something about it?" he asked.

But Thompson was not ready to give up. He declared that he would appeal the decision, because, he claimed, it was "legislating from the bench. This law, if left unchallenged, would make Michigan the only state in our nation that legalized active euthanasia. I feel I would be shirking my duties if I did not appeal the decision." He has worked to get the legislature to pass a law to prevent any more assisted suicides.

Another negative reaction came from Rita Marker, a charismatic self-proclaimed opponent of active euthanasia and the director of the International Anti-Euthanasia Task Force of Steubenville, Ohio. She expressed her disappointment that Breck did not allow the case to go to trial with bitter words: "We've already seen that Dr. Kevorkian is prone to placing himself in the headlines standing on the dead bodies of disabled women" (*Associated Press,* July 22, 1992).

Kevorkian retorted that his state was "blazing a path in people's rights to decide to die if they are chronically ill."

The ongoing struggle would have to await the decision of California voters in November 1992 on Initiative #161. California would have the opportunity to send a message to the nation on the issue.

Dr. K. Strikes Again

In September 1992, Dr. Kevorkian attempted to sway the Michigan Medical Board to establish a new policy to favor his assisted suicide position. He gave them a week to decide and if they didn't make up their minds to come around to his point of view (and he hoped give him back his license to practice medicine), he would then consider himself free to engage in further assisted suicides.

Since he did not receive a positive reply from the board, he took it upon himself to help a fifth patient seeking self-deliverance from her terminal lung cancer. Lois Hawkes, fifty-two, who was suffering great pain from her illness, pushed a button on Dr. Kevorkian's carbon-monoxide-dispensing machine on September 26, 1992, and she soon expired, as family members and a videotape recorder acted as witnesses.

The Hemlock Society, then in session at its sixth annual conference in Long Beach, California, issued a press release written by its president, Sidney Rosoff, which extended its "compassion to the family of Lois Hawkes." But the Society differed with Kevorkian's methodology, opting instead for the passage of Initiative #161, which the National Hemlock Society had endorsed on the Nov. 3, 1992, ballot in that state, because it would provide "an orderly, structured system with proper legal safeguards to help others . . . who become terminally ill and request physician aid-in-dying."

Number Six for Dr. K.

On November 23, 1992, just two months after he assisted Lois Hawkes to her death, Dr. Kevorkian attended the suicide by carbon-monoxide poisoning of his sixth female patient in the home of one of his supporters in Waterford Township, Michigan. Catherine Andreyev, forty-five, who had been suffering from cancer since 1986, pressed the button to release the deadly gas and died while Kevorkian and four friends, including Kevorkian's sister and the homeowner, were witnesses. (Andreyev had no immediate family.)

Oakland County Prosecutor Richard Thompson, who had charged Kevorkian in three previous cases and had failed to obtain an indictment, announced that he would not file charges in this latest case. "I have tried three times," he said, "and I feel any further efforts would be useless and counterproductive. The ball is now in the court of the House of Representatives. It's time for them to do their job, which is to make public policy."

Michigan Moves Against Dr. K.

A day later, on November 24, the House did act when it voted seventy-two to twenty-nine to make assisted suicide a felony punishable by four years in prison. The state senate had previously approved a similar prohibition months before, and after it approved the House version, Republican Governor John Engler signed it, although his criticism of the bill was that it did not insure a "permanent ban."

Thus, Dr. Kevorkian's one-man crusade had brought down the wrath of the legislature, making assisted suicide a crime in Michigan. Mr. Thompson observed that the "legislature has finally made a statement after Dr. Kevorkian had been playing the Pied Piper of Death here in Michigan." But while viewing the bill's passage as a "triumph for his office," Thompson was not convinced that the law, which would take effect in March 1993 (ninety days after the 1992 legislative session ended), would stop Dr. Kevorkian. "This doesn't mean that Dr. Kevorkian will follow the law," he said. "So far, he has thumbed his nose at us." Thompson knew that even though the sixty-four-year-old pathologist had lost his license to practice in Michigan, he still retained his license in California. Also to be considered were the deliberations of a state commission, which had been appointed to study the matter and report back to the governor. That study was expected to take fifteen months and would have an impact on the next act of the running battle between Kevorkian and the state.

One of Kevorkian's more vocal opponents, Republican State Senator Fred Dillingham (who was cosponsor of the ban adopted in March

1992 in the Senate), declared, "We have been in a two-year struggle here in Michigan. It took us not only two years, but six deaths. Dr. Kevorkian's actions yesterday added to the necessity to deal with the issue. It has continued to build. Now Dr. Kevorkian will be out of business in Michigan."

But no voices in opposition have yet arisen in Michigan in support of propositions similar to those in Washington and California to make doctor-assisted suicide legal (see chapters 14, 15, and 16). Kevorkian's taunting actions have wrought a conservative political backlash, which is holding up progress in that state to enact legislation to move forward on the issue of death with dignity.

Meanwhile, in early 1993, Kevorkian continued his crusade, helping the first two male patients and several more women to end their lives via his carbon-monoxide machine. Many observers wondered whether he would become a martyr to his cause by assisting a terminally ill patient to his or her death after April 1, 1993, which would lead to his incarceration and a fine.

11

Other Doctors Speak Out: Their Trials and Tribulations

Rational suicide is like a decision of a firm's Board of Directors to declare bankruptcy.
—Richard Brant, contemporary American philosopher

In the 1930s, some doctors prescribed such powerful drugs as opium and bella donna for terminally ill patients. Using these narcotics, a patient could easily take an overdose and die. But in those days there was no prosecution for malpractice. Today, however, writing such a prescription, if discovered, could lead to the arrest of the prescriber. A half a century ago, the medical establishment had not yet developed the tubes, respirators, pumps, and liquid nutrition used today to artificially prolong the life of a terminally ill, bedridden patient. When someone at home could no longer eat through the mouth, they died a natural death shortly thereafter. But in this age, with all the modern facilities to keep comatose patients alive indefinitely, as in the case of the late Karen Ann Quinlan and Nancy Cruzan, doctors, families, and society as a whole must decide when the lives of brain-dead patients in a vegetative state should no longer be sustained.

Dr. Kevorkian is not the only doctor to grapple with this difficult issue, although he has made the most spectacular headlines with his suicide machine. There have been several other cases that have not received as much publicity, but they merit retelling here to show that Dr. Kevorkian was not alone.

One of them involved Dr. Peter Rosier, a Florida pathologist, and his cancer-ridden wife.

The Patti Rosier Case

DR. ROSIER'S ACQUITTAL: A VICTORY AND A WARNING

Patricia Rosier, forty-three, a resident of Fort Myers, Florida, and the wife of a prominent local physician, Dr. Peter Rosier, was suffering from cancer of the lung, brain, and adrenal glands. Her physicians were in agreement that she had just a few days or, at most, a couple of weeks to live. Her pain was under reasonable control, but she suffered from continuous vomiting. Knowing that her death could be gruesome, Patti wanted personal control over her dying, not only to preserve her own dignity but also because she could see how her terminal illness was affecting her husband's mental state. He was depressed to the extent that he had already given up his medical practice at the young age of forty-five. His insurance company had granted Dr. Rosier disability.

Patti told Peter that she wanted to commit suicide by taking an overdose of drugs. In his depression, he responded that he wished to die with her, but later, at the request of their two children, agreed not to do it. So, Patti fixed the day of her death on a January night in 1986, and arranged a "last supper" for her family and closest friends. Everybody dressed for dinner and they consumed lobster and champagne brought in by local caterers.

There were toasts all around with the most poignant one being to "the lady." After dinner, Patti gave away her lifelong possessions to her family and friends, and then she suggested to her husband that he call a local TV station and ask them to come over to the house for a final interview. She had earlier appeared on the same station to talk about the personal problems of dealing with cancer, and she had even agreed to be filmed shaving off her hair because of the deleterious effects of chemotherapy. At that point, Patti did not reveal her intended suicide, only that she would be dead soon.

Her family and friends all sensed that suicide was the chosen avenue for the woman whose personality, intelligence, and concern for others were universally admired. After that evening together with their two children (in their late teens), her stepfather, two stepbrothers, and an aunt, Patti and Peter announced that they were leaving to make love for the last time. Around midnight they returned to the family room and Patti kissed everyone goodbye.

As she prepared for bed, Patti vomited up her lobster and alcohol, so she probably had an empty stomach. In the presence of her husband and one of her brothers, she took twenty Seconal tablets and washed them down with a glass of water. Up to that point, no possible crime had been committed. Unfortunately, however, her pathologist-husband had not planned the event carefully enough. He had previously asked a medical colleague how much Seconal would be a lethal dose, and was told that two grams (or twenty tablets) would do it. Because Patti was robust and had a strong heart, she was able to withstand this nonlethal, minimum dosage, although she did fall asleep immediately.

In the morning she was still alive, but in a deep coma. Her husband now realized that he had failed and was desperate to make amends. He could not bear the thought of her awakening after being so well prepared for death. He knew, sadly, that the extra Seconal and morphine tablets stashed in his house could not be consumed by a comatose person.

Rosier then called one of Patti's doctors, who rushed over to the house and confirmed that Patti was still alive but breathing shallowly. Peter asked him to provide sufficient liquid morphine to end Patti's life, but he refused to give him more than 8 mg, a trifling amount. There was a row between the two doctors and the visiting doctor left in a hurry.

Rosier then injected the morphine into Patti's buttocks. He made no secret of this act, since her brothers saw him do it. But a few hours later, she was still just barely breathing, so Rosier contacted another treating doctor and asked for his assistance. This doctor wrote a prescription for four morphine suppositories, which Peter inserted into his comatose wife.

Still she did not die, as the combined drugs did not prove to be lethal, as hoped for. Everybody in the household was distraught. Around noon the next day, some twelve hours after the drugs had been taken, while sitting around the pool outside the house, one of Patti's brothers remarked that if he had the courage, he'd go into the bedroom and smother his sister to end her ordeal.

Shortly afterward, Patti's father, Vincent Delman said, "Enough is enough," and went into the bedroom, followed by his sons, and put his hand over his daughter's mouth, thereby suffocating her. She was too far gone to resist and soon expired from a lack of oxygen. When the three Delmans emerged from the bedroom, Peter said: "Don't tell me what happened in there." (The father and sons then made a pact not to tell anyone.)

Patti was mourned by her family, cremated, and then the family grieving started, according to their religious custom. This process was very difficult for Peter and, for a catharsis, he began to write a book about her life as a monument to her. He entitled it "The Lady." He also tried to arrange a TV play to be done about her life, but twenty publishers rejected his hastily written book, and his TV project foundered. Unfortunately, in the manuscript of "The Lady," Rosier openly admitted that he helped his wife to end her life. This would soon lead him into trouble with the state attorney. Assisting a suicide is illegal in Florida and admitting it publicly was viewed as a challenge to the system. (See *Murder of Mercy* by Stanley Rosenblatt for the complete story of the Rosier case.)

DR. ROSIER'S MURDER TRIAL

During the postmortem investigation into the circumstances surrounding her death, Patti's father and brothers were interviewed. They showed more legal savy than Peter Rosier and agreed to the interview only after they had secured immunity from prosecution. With that court safeguard, they confessed to the suffocation, but no charges were pressed against them. Instead, Dr. Rosier was charged with murder.

The trial, which opened on October 31, 1988, was held in St. Petersburg, Florida. It was moved from Ft. Myers at the request of the defense, which demonstrated to the court that Dr. Rosier could not get a fair trial in his home town because of the negative publicity about the case and malicious gossip.

During the trial the state attorney pounced on Rosier's blatant act of appearing on local TV to promote his book and admitting on camera that he had given his wife something to end her life. (This had been

Rosier's major mistake and the prosecution used it to initiate the criminal investigation that led to the charges and the trial.) The prosecutor was armed chiefly with the book manuscript, which told every detail of her lingering death except the suffocation (which Dr. Rosier did not know about) and the televised confession. Three charges were offered to the jury and to the court: murder one, conspiracy to murder, and attempted murder.

THE JURY MAKES UP ITS MIND

Most juries would have probably convicted Rosier based on the evidence presented. But with the help of a brilliant defense offered by Susan and Stanley Rosenblatt of Miami, who poured scorn on the prosecution, Dr. Rosier felt that he might be vindicated. The jury deliberated on December 1, 1988, for only three hours and returned with an acquittal for Dr. Rosier—on all counts. They even declined to consider five lesser counts, which were offered by Judge Thompson, who seemed to be leaning towards a conviction. The *Tampa Tribune* reported the next day that the foreman of the jury of seven women and five men had told them: "No one at any time during the jury pollings said 'guilty' to any one of the charges." They all admitted, however, that the five-week trial had been both emotionally and physically draining.

THE LESSONS OF THE ROSIER TRIAL

The Rosier case was the first case in the United States in almost seventy years (since the Roberts trial in 1920) where the matter of assisted suicide had brought about a charge of murder. Some observers wondered whether this trial marked a dangerous portent of things to come in similar cases in the future. In *The Hemlock Quarterly* (Spring 1989) Derek Humphry's assessment of the postmortems of the Rosier trial led to the following conclusions:

- Juries are increasingly reluctant to send people guilty of any form of euthanasia to prison.
- Until the law is changed, people must be discreet about helping a loved one to die.

- Don't trust a doctor to tell you how to end your life. Most American doctors do not know, although in the Netherlands it is part of every future doctor's medical training.
- Meticulous planning is required for self-deliverance from a terminal illness. (The Rosiers were too casual and overconfident in their plans.)
- It is time to amend the law to permit doctors to accede to requests from terminally ill patients for euthanasia.
- Finally, don't invite the whole family to the deliverance.

The Quill-"Diane" Case: A Physician Breaks Through the Doctor-Patient Confidentiality Barrier

Dr. Timothy Quill, a forty-one-year-old internist at the University of Rochester School of Medicine, has focused much of his clinical work on efforts to increase patient autonomy in medical treatment. One of his long-time patients, "Diane," whom he had been treating for progressive leukemia deterioration for eight years, consulted with him, her family, and a psychologist about her decision to refuse chemotherapy in her case. She knew that she had only about a one-in-four chance of surviving chemotherapy, a bone marrow transplant, and the long-term painful side-effects when she became very ill. She said no to this alternative. When her time to die came, she wanted to go quickly.

So, after long talks Dr. Quill wrote her a prescription for sleeping pills at her request and told her how many she needed to kill herself. A short while later she did just that, but her date and place of death remained a mystery, since the name "Diane" was a pseudonym.

AN ECHO FROM THE "SOUNDING BOARD"

On March 7, 1991, Dr. Quill published a significant three-page article in the prestigious and widely read *New England Journal of Medicine*—in the back-of-the-book section known as "The Sounding Board." (See appendix 5 for the reprint of the complete article.) This space is usually devoted to letters to the editor and brief summaries of medical events of interest to the journal's physician readers. Quill's article—a first in the profession—detailed in specific steps how he helped his leukemia-wracked patient (identified only by the name of "Diane") to die. He knew he was taking a bold chance and that someone opposed to physician-assisted death would object to his courageous confession.

He was heartened to discover, however, that many doctors recognized his article as a "milestone," particularly because he described *how* and *why* he took various medical steps over the eight years that he had treated his patient. He answered the ethical questions left hanging in the wake of the Kevorkian-Adkins case, which would help him if he were taken to court for his admissions.

Quill wrote that he acceded to Diane's wishes because "she was convinced she would die during the period of treatment and would suffer unspeakably in the process." He also made sure that she understood her decision, although he disagreed at first. He gradually adjusted to her wish not to undergo further treatment and finally to end her life.

"It was extraordinarily important to Diane to maintain control of herself and her own dignity during the time remaining to her," Quill wrote. "When this was no longer possible, she clearly wanted to die." She wanted no part of the drugged netherworld of terminal care, and when she was ready, she wanted to take her own life as painlessly as possible.

But Dr. Quill made a damaging admission when he wrote that he told the medical examiner Diane had died of "acute leukemia," even though that was not the whole story. Under New York law, "offering a false statement for filing," as in a death certificate, is a misdemeanor punishable by up to a week in jail. Quill also wrote that Diane visited him to say goodbye two days before committing suicide. He described a discussion he had had with her the day she asked for the prescription. He knew she wanted enough barbiturates to be able to commit suicide, so she could live fully and concentrate on the present until she entered the final stage of her disease:

> I wrote the prescription with an uneasy feeling about the boundaries I was exploring—*spiritual, legal, professional,* and *personal* [emphasis added]. Yet I also felt strongly that I was setting her free to get the most out of the time she had left, and to maintain dignity and control on her own terms until her death.

Quill, who spends half of his time in practice and the other half in research, had already published a series of academic articles on how best to increase patient autonomy during all phases of treatment, including the last stage of terminal illnesses. He was upset that the desires of many patients were often ignored.

POST-PUBLICATION REACTION

Dr. Anthony L. Suchman, a close friend of Quill and a fellow internist who also teaches medicine and psychiatry at the University of Rochester School of Medicine, stated that Quill's article about Diane was "just one piece of a large body of work at giving patients more control over their medical care. . . . Stopping the medical steamroller has been something that has mattered to him for a long time."

Arthur Caplan, a bioethicist at the University of Minnesota, commented on the article: "This story comes as close as I can imagine to a morally defensible role of a physician in the suicide of a patient." But Dr. Nancy Dickey of Richmond, Texas, a trustee of the American Medical Association, said: "I would be more than a little uncomfortable writing a prescription [knowing it would be used in this way]. By the letter of the law, this doctor comes about as close as he can get but didn't actually cross the gray line" [of assisting a patient during suicide]. Some other doctors praised Quill for describing a compassionate way to assist patients facing death and for exposing what many said was a "common, but hidden practice in modern medicine."

In interviews after he published his now famous article, Dr. Quill said he decided to go public partly to present an alternative to Dr. Kevorkian's suicide-machine approach. Legal experts in Michigan stated, after a local judge had dismissed homicide charges against Kevorkian in December 1990, that a clear test of the legal boundaries governing doctors who help in suicides would have to be decided at a later date in a state such as New York, which has a law on assisted suicide. In New York the law says that any person "commits a crime" when "he intentionally causes or aids another person to commit suicide." (Punishment for such an act is five to fifteen years in prison.)

After Dr. Quill published his article in March, Howard Relin, the district attorney, declined at first to prosecute, explaining that the victim, Diane, was not clearly identified in the article, and that prosecutors could not prove that there had been a crime without a body. Then, an anonymous tip to the D.A.'s office identified Quill's deceased patient as Patricia Diane Trumbull, forty-five, of Pittsford, N.Y. The tip led the local authorities to a cadaver at Monroe Community College, where the body had been stored for dissection. Now Relin had a body.

In June, the Monroe County Medical Examiner did an autopsy and concluded that there was a fatal dose of barbiturates in the body. At this point, Relin stated that he would indeed now take the case to the grand jury. The circumstances and intensity of emotions on the issue left Mr. Relin with little choice. "He's in a box," said Michael DiPrima, a local defense lawyer who was a close observer of the case. "In all fairness to Dr. Quill, he put himself and Relin in that box."

In another post-publication interview, Quill said that his hidden agenda for writing the article was to force the issue out into the open. "We can't do things like that [referring to his prescription for Diane] without talking about real examples," he noted. "I hope this will cause doctors who take care of severely ill patients to think about what they did and how they handle these situations." In a statement made in June, Dr. Quill said that he hoped to get some time to explore the legal boundary further if and when he got to testify before a grand jury. "I hope a deeper appreciation of the suffering of dying people is achieved as a result of this process," he said.

A GRAND JURY DELIBERATES A NEW FRONTIER OF LAW

While twenty-three states have laws that make assisting a suicide a crime, none of them has a law that makes such an act noncriminal, as the people of Washington tried to accomplish at the polls in November 1991. However, despite these laws, prosecutions of doctors have been virtually unknown, with the exceptions of Drs. Rosier and Kevorkian. That was the challenge facing a grand jury panel of twenty-three men and women on Monday, July 22, 1991 in Rochester, New York, when they met to determine whether Dr. Quill had committed a crime when he helped Diane commit suicide with an overdose of barbiturates.

The grand jury's examination of the facts in the case and their decision whether to recommend the indictment of Dr. Quill would mark the clearest test to date of what constitutes assisting a suicide and whether a doctor could legally help end the life of a patient under any circumstances.

Jay E. Kantor, a medical ethicist at the New York University Medical Center and the Bellevue Hospital in Manhattan, prophesied: "He is a test of what the public sentiment is going to be on assisted suicide."

The alternatives for the grand jury in this case were possible indictments for manslaughter, misdemeanor charges, or an acquittal for Dr. Quill. If the jury chose the last option, it would be saying that Dr. Quill had committed no crime, which would effectively ratify his decision to tell his patient how to end her life by taking the drugs that he had prescribed. Quill stated that he would waive his immunity and would testify, since his lawyer, Douglas Rowe, believed that he had committed no crime.

MEDICINE VS. THE LAW

Several medical and legal experts, who praised Quill for shedding light on this subterranean practice, openly criticized Rochester District Attorney Howard R. Relin for shutting off open discussion of the issues by the threat of prosecution of other doctors. Free speech and First Amendment rights were now at stake as well as the right to privacy, the right to choose how to end one's life, and the dignity of the medical profession. "If Dr. Quill is indicted, it's not going to stop the practice," said Irwin Birnbaum, a lawyer who advises hospitals in New York City. "What it's going to do is to stop the debate."

On the other side of the debate, Relin was championed by euthanasia opponents who said they were horrified by Dr. Quill's action because it appeared to present a blueprint for other doctors to end the lives of their patients who were in despair. Rita Marker, the director of the International Anti-Euthanasia Task Force, said: "I think he very clearly assisted her and nudged her toward taking her own life. I believe that is a crime and should be a crime."

Some lawyers said that Dr. Quill's article placed the district attorney, who had formerly been the Monroe County prosecutor, in an untenable position, since the law on assisted suicide in New York was "murky." But the same lawyers admitted that Quill's article came so close to admitting violations that it was clearly a challenge to prosecutors. Relin could have refused to take any action against Dr. Quill, but a failure to at least present the case to a grand jury could have been interpreted as an invitation to other doctors to violate New York laws in future cases.

Feeling the pressure from the doctor's colleagues, Mr. Relin avoided taking a position on whether Dr. Quill violated any laws. He stated only that the precedent-setting legal and moral issues entwined in the Quill case warranted an "impartial presentation" to the jury. "This is not a black and white case," he said bluntly. "This is not a bank robbery. This is a case that not only has criminal law questions, but medical ethics questions. You're going to have twenty-three ordinary citizens representing the community" [for this controversial case].

During the grand jury proceedings, the prosecution would have to answer the legal questions: Did Dr. Quill have to do something more active than prescribe a drug to be guilty of "intentionally" assisting in a suicide? What is the definition of lethal dose? It varies with each individual patient.

THE JURY SPEAKS OUT

The jury in the Quill case knew that they would be sending a signal about the possible prosecution of doctors and the impact of their decision would go far beyond the borders of their county located in the northwestern part of New York. On July 26, 1991, after listening to Charles J. Siragusa, an assistant district attorney of Monroe County, present his case for an indictment, the jury declined to indict Dr. Quill on the three charges brought to them by the prosecutors. This decision ended the possibility of any further criminal prosecution against the doctor.

Dr. Quill, relieved at the outcome, said: "The debate needs to go on and be broadened, since people grasp the issue and are now willing to discuss it. The response to my article was very positive in that it had moved the debate away from the suicide machine of Dr. Kevorkian." Quill said that he had learned from many accounts that his story was "the tip of the iceberg" since several doctors had told him how they had taken similar action in secret but had been reluctant to discuss it. He also noted that "the process had taken some difficult and unpredictable turns" (referring to the unauthorized release of Diane's full name).

THE AFTERMATH

Dr. Ronald Cranford, a neurologist and medical ethicist of the Hennepin County Medical Center in Minneapolis, who opposed physician-assisted suicide, commented that "this is a very important case that will set a precedent nationwide." He was not surprised at the failure of the grand jury to return criminal indictments and admitted that Dr. Quill had acted "courageously" and that "many Americans would support what Dr. Quill did and the way he did it. I think it reflects a loss of confidence in medicine by the American public and a feeling that they will lose all control over their lives and that their lives will be unduly prolonged."

Mr. Siragusa pointed out, however, that the decision was specific only to the Quill case and that "it would be irresponsible for anyone to take the grand jury's decision on these specific facts as any type of directive involving medical or legal conclusions involving terminally-ill patients. Nevertheless, I will admit, obviously the case has attracted a lot of attention."

Although he could no longer be tried on criminal charges in the "Diane" Trumbull case, Dr. Quill could possibly have faced professional misconduct charges from the New York State Health Department. Kathleen Tanner, the head of the department's office of professional conduct, said that an investigation into Dr. Quill's activities had been postponed pending the grand jury's decision. If he had been convicted of a crime, he would have been subjected to professional discipline.

Nonetheless, a committee from that office had been looking into whether Dr. Quill had "inappropriately prescribed drugs" in Diane's case, and whether he filed a false document when he told the Monroe County medical examiner that Diane had died of "acute leukemia," but had withheld information about the barbiturates and the suicide. The State Medical Society of New York, to which Dr. Quill belongs, but which has no legal powers, has a policy which says: "The use of euthanasia is *not* in the province of the physician."

Dr. Quill performed a courageous act in his written confession regarding his patient Diane. He didn't have to tell his story to the world. He could have kept his sleeping pill prescription under wraps, but he chose to take a stand, not to bring himself notoriety but to clear the air and make it easier for other doctors and patients in the future to make similar decisions in parallel situations. Kris Larson, a spokeswoman for the Hemlock Society, applauded the decision, saying: "Juries are seeing this conduct as a compassion, a help."

DR. QUILL IN RETROSPECT

At the end of his three-page article in the Sounding Board section of the March 7, 1991, edition of the *New England Journal of Medicine,* Dr. Quill offered some poetic, philosophical, and retrospective afterthoughts, which included this final paragraph:

> I wonder how many families and physicians secretly help patients over the edge into death in the face of such severe suffering. I wonder how many severely ill or dying patients secretly take their lives, dying alone in despair. I wonder whether the image of Diane's final aloneness will persist in the minds of her family, or if they will remember the more intense, meaningful months they had together before she died. I wonder whether Diane struggled in that last hour, and whether the Hemlock Society's way of death by suicide is the most benign. I wonder why Diane, who gave so much to so many of us, had to be alone for the last hour of her life. I wonder whether I will see Diane again, on the shore of Lake Geneva at sunset, with dragons swimming on the horizon.

Dr. Bettelheim Takes His Own Life

When obituaries appeared in mid-1991 concerning the death of the renowned psychoanalyst Bruno Bettelheim at age eighty-six, after a full life of rich accomplishments, most people assumed that his death was the normal benign passing of old age. But it wasn't. His body was discovered on the floor of his apartment with sleeping pills in his system and a plastic bag over his head; it was obvious that he had committed suicide. The death of his wife, and a debilitating stroke that had limited his work, a move from one coast to another, a shift from independence to the limited freedoms of a retirement home, and his rumored estrangement from one of his children all appeared to play on his mind before his death.

But "did all these clues add up to a reason?" the columnist Ellen Goodman asked. She concluded that he "left this legacy: In his memory, in his name, we inherit a moral quandary of our era. Are there good and bad reasons for suicide?"

Recent statistics show that suicide rates have jumped over 25 percent among the elderly in the decade of the eighties, with elderly white men, like Bettelheim, heading the list. But many more die without adding to this statistic because of the shame of suicide and its effect on their loved ones, plus the worry about their beneficiaries losing the insurance benefits. The psychiatrist and ethicist Dr. William Gaylin, has postulated that more modern Americans have come to reject what he has called: "the tyranny of survival. One can simply get to a point where the pain and grief of life is in excess of the joy and pride."

Bettelheim, a survivor of a concentration camp in World War II, spent most of this century trying to understand the meaning of life and to communicate his thoughts to millions of followers, particularly on parenting. In his classic book, *Surviving,* he wrote eloquently about the challenges that a concentration camp offered to the inmates' will to live:

> So intricately, so inextricably interwoven are death and life, when life seems to have lost all meaning, suicide seems the inescapable consequence. . . . To have found meaning in life is thus the only certain antidote to the deliberate seeking of death. But at the same time in a strange dialectical way, it is death that endows life with its deeper, most unique meaning.

Dr. Gaylin summed up his assessment of Bettelheim's act this way: "He paid his dues. He tolerated suffering. He understood life and exercised his privilege to leave it." He made his choice in privacy and that's the way he wanted to go.

Part IV: The People Speak

LIVING WILL

Take me off the tubes and hose.
Stop the IV as it flows.
God forbid that I should live
punctured like a bloody sieve.

Respirator, bags and dope
chain me here where there's no hope.
Free my body from the machine.
Let the end be quick and clean.

Sense and spirit long have fled
from the body on this bed.
Send my organs to the banks.
All will be received with thanks.

What good reason can there be
for prolonging misery?
When my vital functions cease
let me go in grateful peace.

—Mary Traeger, senior citizen,
Sun City, Arizona (1990)
(*Hemlock Quarterly,* January 1992)

12

Of Living Wills
and an Act of Congress

Worldwide, the death rate is one per person.
                    —Richard Lamm, former governor of Colorado

We are always attending other people's funerals and never our own.
                    —Hans Uffelmann, professor of Philosophy,
                    University of Missouri, 1991

How the Courts Treat Women vis-à-vis Men
in Euthanasia Cases

In mid-1990, Dr. Steven Miles, a geriatrician at the Hennepin County
Hospital in Minneapolis, Minnesota, conducted a study of right-to-die
cases and found that the courts treat women differently from men.
According to his findings, published in the July 1990 issue of *Law,
Medicine and Health Care,* the courts were far less likely to give weight
to women's wishes regarding life support than to men's. Miles examined
twenty-two right-to-die decisions and found that women have been
consistently portrayed as less capable than men of rational decision-
making. The twenty-two cases studied formed the bulk of the appellate

decisions involving patients who had been found to be mentally competent but had left no written directives for their care. In such cases, judges may try to "construct" the patient's preference from evidence presented about his or her values in life. Dr. Miles noted:

> Women are referred to by their first names, and "constructed" as emotional, immature, unreflective, and vulnerable to medical neglect, while men are called by their last names, and "constructed" as rational, mature, decisive, and assaulted by medical technology. Only women are described as curled in a fetal position, while men are described as having "contractures" [the medical term].

Miles noted the contrast between the ways in which the comments of a thirty-one-year-old woman on life support and the comments of a thirty-three-year-old man were characterized. The woman's remarks were described as "offhand remarks made by a person when young," while the man's were judged to be "deeply held," and showing "solemn intelligent determination." The study further found that in cases involving women, the courts said that they could not construct the patient's preferences regarding life support in twelve of fourteen cases, while in cases involving men, the court refused to construct the patient's preferences in only two of eight cases.

Dr. Miles concluded that "living wills, particularly pertaining to women, often wind up being a cipher [being ignored by most doctors], unless you know the patient, and the patient has been directly, chronically ill."

The Insurance Factor

Many depressed men and women (with or without a living will) do not like to contemplate suicide out of ignorance and fear that their life insurance policies will become null and void. Prior to 1929, most companies paid in full on suicide claims. But after the stock-market crash of 1929, when so many financially ruined citizens committed suicide, the companies inserted a two-year noncontestability clause, which meant that claims could be processed only *after* a two-year waiting period had occurred from the time the policy was written. That two-year waiting period is still standard practice today as liability "insurance" for most life insurance companies.

The Legacy of the Cruzan Case on Right-to-Die Legislation

The Supreme Court's ruling on the Cruzan case in June 1990 stated that, although it was a constitutional right for a patient to refuse medical care, a state could require "clear and convincing evidence" that the cessation of treatment was in agreement with the patient's prior wishes. Such "evidence," known as an "advance directive," could be in the form of a health-care document called a living will. The living will should specify what kinds of treatment a patient has the right to refuse simply to be kept alive when his or her quality of life has drastically deteriorated.

By mid-1992, forty-nine states had already passed such living-will legislation or a stand-in. Three states (Michigan, Massachusetts, and New York) recognize the authority of some form of advance directive by the patients. (New York recognizes only the authority of a health-care proxy, a power of attorney, or proxy in place of a living will. Only Nebraska has failed to pass a living-will act or case law supporting its concept.)

But it was not just at the state level that Nancy Cruzan's ordeal had a positive impact. It also spurred a reluctant Congress to get into the act, instead of continuing to bury its collective head in the sand by failing to respond to the will of the people.

The Quiet Birth of the Patient Self-Determination Act

The Patient Self-Determination Act (PSDA) in Congress took shape back in 1989, a year before the Supreme Court issued its breakthrough opinion on the Cruzan case, but more than five years after the case first made headlines. U.S. Senator John Danforth (Republican, Missouri) had felt the heat from his constituents to do something constructive in the area as far back as 1985, so he quietly introduced the PSDA in 1989 and it was passed in November 1990, a month before Nancy died. The June 1990 Supreme Court decision undoubtedly helped to insure passage of the act in the Congress. It went into effect in the nation's hospitals on December 1, 1991. This process was an excellent example of the working of democracy: one branch of the federal government, the Supreme Court, helped to push another branch, the Congress, into taking action that it might not have taken otherwise (Spears 1990).

One of the main purposes of the law was to prevent future tortured dramas like the one that surrounded Miss Cruzan from being repeated throughout the land. The new law requires that all health-care centers receiving federal aid must inform patients of their rights to accept or refuse medical treatment and to provide advance medical directives like living wills and powers of attorney to make clear their desires. (See Appendix 6 for the complete text of the PSDA.) The Congressional legislation gives all patients an opportunity to place critical life-sustaining decisions in the hands of a loved one rather than leaving them up to the doctor or the courts. "It's one of the best ideas they have come up with yet," said Gloria Davis, a forty-eight-year-old kidney patient as she was enrolled in a New York City hospital on December 1 (Weber 1990). The PSDA caused a general sigh of relief among both patients and staff members in the nation's hospitals and helped to clarify the need to sign some form of advance medical directive before the patient ever arrives at the hospital.

The passage of the PSDA meant that state living-will legislation had, in a sense, been superseded by the federal act, which served as de facto national living-will legislation. So Nebraska and Pennsylvania, which had not yet joined the other forty-eight states by passing their own living-will legislation, were now bypassed and forced to go along with Washington's edict.

Before December 1, 1991, according to several news services,* it was estimated that fewer than half of the nation's doctors had ever discussed the option of living wills with their patients. Many felt that the passage of the act and its mandatory implementation caught them by surprise, but most were relieved to have this law at their disposal (Weber 1990).

---

*New York Times, December 2, 1990; Associated Press, December 2, 1990.

The Advent of Advance Directives

The new law specifically empowers the admission clerks in a hospital, or any other health-care facility that accepts Medicare or Medicaid patients, to ask you about your attitude toward a "living will" or "health-care proxy" and your wishes if you become "terminally ill or unconscious." Patients must be told that they have the right to accept or refuse treatment should they become gravely ill. These choices, when signed and entered into hospital records, amount to an "advance directive" to the doctors, nurses, and hospital officials. Thus, December 1, 1991, marked a historic date in the nation's health-care delivery system.

Prior to the passage of this act, a 1991 study conducted by the Gallup organization showed that only about 20 percent of Americans had signed living wills. But in the wake of the Supreme Court decision in the Cruzan case and the passage of the PSDA, a flood of requests descended on the offices of the right-to-die organizations for the proper living-will and power-of-attorney forms. The Durable Power of Attorney, which is the enabling document to help validate the living will as an advance directive, is a fallback insurance document to allow others to decide your ultimate fate should you become incapacitated. Dr. John La Puma, the director for Clinical Ethics at the Lutheran General Hospital in Park Ridge, Illinois, has stressed that living wills, powers of attorney, and advance directives are not "death plans" as they have been erroneously labeled in some media stories:

> Rather, advance directives are flags. They signal the need for a discussion about the potential goals of care, preferably before a critical illness, perhaps in an office or clinic visit. Patients with advance directives are not telling the doctors that they want to die. They are saying: "I want to know about my treatment. Talk with me." (Lewin 1990)

The Long-Range Impact of the PSDA on Health Care

When Congress passed the PSDA, the lawmakers could not have realized that their legislation would have the long-range effect of forcing people to deal with their own deaths while they are still in their prime, enjoying relatively good health, and fully competent to understand the consequences of such life-and-death decisions. The new federal law encourages, but does *not* require, that patients being admitted to a hospital enter into a conversation regarding the procedures to be followed in the event of a life-threatening situation.

Those patients who agree to this useful conversation with hospital personnel about the process of dying will have the rare chance to determine the manner of their own death before it's too late. Those who refuse to deal with the issue while they are still mentally competent will either have to deal with it during more trying times later or dump the burden onto loved ones and possibly high-priced legal and medical professionals who may not act as the patient would wish. As the *New York Times* editorialized on November 19, 1990, the PSDA is a "prudent and compassionate law that could greatly ease the confusion, anger and litigation that now attends many deaths."

Both the PSDA and the Supreme Court ruling on the Cruzan case have put new pressure on all citizens to face the issue of life-extending treatment for the terminally ill in terms that are far more specific and legally binding than vague bromides like: "I wouldn't want to live like a vegetable." This result may be more important in the future for the euthanasia movement than the actions of Congress or the Supreme Court. As the late sociopsychologist, Havelock Ellis, put it: "The by product is sometimes more valuable than the product."

Does the PSDA Go Far Enough?

Despite breaking through the legal thicket that has prevented more advances on the right-to-die frontier, the PSDA, according to some critics, did not go far enough. Dr. Alan D. Lieberson, a patients' rights advocate and physician in Westport, Connecticut, who is the author of *The Living Will Handbook,* has noted that the law is too limited. For instance, it requires only that the hospitals tell patients of their constitutional and common-law rights to execute a living-will proxy form and about the relevant state laws, but it does not require that the hospitals assist in the preparation of these documents or question patients about their personal desires unless the patients volunteer to do the extra paperwork. The failure of many patients to spell out their specific desires before death, has led to several postmortem court cases.

Lieberson claims that most hospitals plan to take a medical "Miranda" approach; i.e., they will inform the patients of their rights and then tell them to call a lawyer. He feels that, because of the high cost and time considerations involved in fulfilling the letter of the law, most hospitals will try to avoid advising patients. And many physicians, already overburdened with paperwork from Blue Cross, Medicare, and Medicaid, will become increasingly discouraged, since they have been trained to preserve life wherever possible, not to end it.

In a letter to the editor of the *New York Times,* Lieberson states:

> Making living wills clinically significant will require more than patient, doctor, and community education. It will require that physicians tailor medical care to the wishes of the patient. This will not be difficult once physicians accept the fact that honoring a living will does not create a legal risk.
>
> There is no reason why these advance directives should not be physician managed, just as surgical consent forms, anatomical gift forms, and "do not resuscitate" orders are. The law is much easier for a physician to learn than medicine is for a lawyer.

Dr. Bettie Jackson, the director of Professional Services at New York's Mountefiore Hospital, was acutely aware of patients' rights when she observed: "Over time, if we're to be successful, the questions need to be answered outside the hospital, before they get here. People need to make decisions like this before they get into an extreme situation." (This procedure is a fundamental part of the educational counselling of most Hemlock chapters.)

As Dr. Jackson suggests, a tremendous educational challenge confronts the nation on this issue: the proper information must be provided in the home, church, schools, and media, as well as doctors' offices and hospitals, so that future patients are prepared before they come through the hospital doors either ambulatory or on a stretcher.

The Pennsylvania Hangup over the "Incubator Amendment"

On November 19, 1991, the Pennsylvania State House of Representatives voted overwhelmingly (186–15) to allow a terminally ill person to refuse life-sustaining treatment under a living will that had been signed while the patient was still conscious and competent. This state was one of the last to act on living will legislation. (Final passage into law took until the following April.) Pennsylvania attached an important string to its bill, however, by denying the right of a living will to pregnant women. In a move similar to the controversial 1989 abortion-rights legislation passed in the Commonwealth, the anti-abortion coalition in the Pennsylvania House wrote in an "incubator clause" to the living will law. The clause would prohibit doctors from honoring the living will of a pregnant woman, whether she was alert or comatose (Motley 1991).

"There can never be a compromise with an innocent life," said State Representative Stephen Freind, the leader of the group who successfully amended the bill. His group quashed compromise amendments that would have allowed pregnant women to abort a fetus through the twenty-fourth week of a pregnancy, when a fetus becomes viable. Freind (who was also the author of the controversial Pennsylvania Abortion Control Act, the constitutionality of which was to be heard by the Supreme Court in 1992) was adamant that pregnant women had few rights from the moment of conception and would be required to remain on a life-support system until a birth resulted. The life of the fetus was paramount and could not be "killed" via an abortion at any time during the pregnancy, according to Freind and his cohorts. The mother would have to suffer through any terminal illness strapped to tubes and respirators to guarantee that the fetus had a fighting chance for survival.

His skewed logic was expressed as follows: "We know one person is going to die. The question is, is it going to be one or two," Freind said, rejecting his opponents' arguments that the compromise measure was in keeping with the time limits of the Abortion Control Act— the most restrictive in the nation. There would be no exception even for a pregnant comatose woman on crack-cocaine who is either HIV positive or has AIDS. She would have to carry her fetus to term, even if it too had been infected with the virus. The life of the fetus was judged to be more important than the life of the mother, no matter how imperfect the fetus might be and even if it had little chance of survival. Backed up by the power of the Catholic Conference in the Commonwealth, Freind wielded a powerful sword to reduce pregnant, comatose, terminally ill women to second-class citizenship (ibid.).

Pennsylvania Gets a Living Will Law—At Last

After nearly a decade of inaction, the legislature in Harrisburg, Pa., finally passed a living will law on April 7, 1992, so that the terminally ill could refuse life-sustaining medical treatment. Pennsylvania became the forty-ninth state—leaving Nebraska as the only state without a living will or a substitute. The bill passed both houses virtually unanimously and Governor Casey signed it into law a few days later.

Unfortunately, the price of passage was the retention of the so-called "incubator amendment," which would prevent an unconscious pregnant woman from making the same decision that a conscious pregnant woman could make. Such comatose mothers-in-waiting would lose their right of free choice. For this reason, it is probable that this legislation will eventually be challenged in the courts as being discriminatory and an abridgment of First Amendment rights.

Actually the hidden push given to the passage of this legislation came from the enactment of the federal Patient Self-Determination Act (PSDA), which went into effect on December 1, 1991, in all federally funded hospitals in the country. The PSDA acted as a sort of de facto living will since it forced all hospitals and nursing homes receiving federal funds for serving Medicare patients to inform those patients about state laws on the issue.

And so another bridge in the national struggle to legalize both passive and active euthanasia had been crossed in the state where the Bill of Rights was written.

New Jersey: Where It All Began

Back in 1975 Joe Quinlan walked into his lawyer's office and asked his help in getting his comatose daughter, Karen Ann, removed from the respirator which was keeping her alive in a vegetative state because of restrictive barriers in the law. Sixteen years later, on July 11, 1991, New Jersey, where the right-to-die debate began in the USA, became the forty-eighth state to legally recognize living wills. Governor James Florio signed the bill into law in the presence of the Quinlans, with the statement: "Medical technology is advancing faster and faster each day. Sometimes it gets ahead of us." Joe Quinlan remarked after the signing: "I hope that living wills will again make it a private family decision." He was referring to the implementation of a New Jersey Supreme Court decision rendered back in 1987, when the justices observed:

> Courts are not the proper place to resolve the agonizing personal problems that underlie these cases. Our legal system cannot replace the more intimate struggle that must be borne by the patient, those caring for the patient and those who care about the patient.

The columnist Ellen Goodman wrote, "A living will can help prevent a living death that we have seen in the bedside horror stores of Karen Ann Quinlan and Nancy Cruzan. And it can help families."

New Jersey got the message finally.

The First Lady Signs a Living Will

In late 1990, the First Lady, Barbara Bush, acknowledged that she had finally signed a living will: "I had a dog I loved put down, because I didn't want the dog to suffer anymore. I certainly hope that someone would do the same for me." But she never endorsed any living will legislation, which could have given a welcome push to the passage of a death-with-dignity act in Congress.

13

The Coming of Initiative #119

We need to commit ourselves less to calling 911 for relief in medical emergencies, but rather more to the principles of Proposition #119.
—Prof. Hans Uffelmann, philosopher, University of Missouri (1991)

The first major attempt in the United States to enact meaningful legislation to legalize doctor-assisted suicide for the terminally ill took place in the state of Washington in 1991.* Initiative #119, which was placed on the ballot on November 5, 1991, was an attempt to strengthen the PSDA, both to protect the rights of patients and to remove the cloud hanging over physicians who feared the loss of their licenses, a heavy fine, and even imprisonment.

In 1975, a Gallup Poll showed that 41 percent of American adults felt that people in great pain had a moral right to commit suicide to take themselves out of their misery. By 1990, in the most recent Gallup Poll, the figures had risen sharply to 66 percent. The Roper Poll reflected even more startling figures on the topic. A mid-1991 Roper Poll showed that 80 percent of all adult Americans favored passive euthanasia, while 60 percent favored active euthanasia (doctor-assisted sui-

---

*A prior attempt to change the law was undertaken in 1988 by Americans Against Human Suffering, which launched a referendum reform campaign in California. Their initiative failed because of weak organization and the inability to gather enough signatures to put a death-with-dignity act (including the right to choose) on the ballot.

cide), all of which presented to the supporters of Initiative #119 a rather optimistic forecast.

The Birth of the #119 Concept

The father of the Initiative #119 "Death With Dignity" proposal was the Rev. Ralph Mero, a Unitarian-Universalist Community Volunteer Minister in Seattle, who had also become the director of the Pacific Northwest Region of the Hemlock Society. The proposition was born in his church basement through the efforts of some of his congregants, who felt the time had come to put the next step to rational euthanasia on the ballot. Mero became the director of the nonpartisan movement in that state.

The Washington chapter of the Hemlock Society threw its weight behind the ballot item as did Derek Humphry, who lent his name and prestige to its package. During the campaign that followed, Mero noted:

> Derek took a great deal of personal abuse and an assault on his integrity, in addition to the 12 prior years of fighting for a cause. We, and the terminally-ill, all owe him a debt of deep gratitude. . . .
>
> We've reached a critical mass. There are now enough families who have been touched by the prolonged painful process of dying. It's resulted in the sense that, damn it, this is not right. (Mero, November 15, 1991)

The ethical case for doctor-assisted suicide was cogently made by the columnist Ellen Goodman, when she wrote that the concept "rests on a belief in both autonomy and mercy—that people should be allowed to make their decisions, and that we should expect mercy from others, especially doctors."

In 1990 and 1991, over 223,000 voters from all over the state of Washington signed a petition to put Initiative #119 on the ballot, the total being well above the minimum 150,000 signatures required in that state. This voter support caused the supporters of the proposition to be optimistic about its passage when it was placed on the ballot in November 1991.

What Was Initiative #119?

Initiative #119 defined persistent vegetative state as a terminal illness and nutrition and hydration machines as artificial life supports which could be withdrawn through a living will. It also allowed mentally competent terminally ill patients to voluntarily request aid-in-dying from a qualified physician. The initiative was carefully written to include nine strict safeguards for terminally ill patients:

1. The aid-in-dying provisions of #119 are totally voluntary for patients, physicians, and hospitals.

2. Only conscious, mentally competent, terminally ill patients with less than six months to live may voluntarily request aid-in-dying.

3. No one can request aid-in-dying for anyone else.

4. Two impartial people must witness the written request of the terminal patient for aid-in-dying. They cannot be family members, heirs, or employees of the physician or health-care facility.

5. A terminally ill patient may revoke his or her request at any time.

6. Two doctors must indicate in writing that the terminally ill patient has less than six months to live. One of the physicians must be the patient's primary doctor.

7. Physicians may require a psychological evaluation to insure that the patient is mentally competent, not depressed, and that the request is voluntary.

8. Aid-in-dying may only be requested at the time it is to be provided, not in advance.

9. Terminally ill patients and their physicians may seek advice from any family members or clergy they choose. (See Robinson 1991.)

It also sought to clarify portions of the 1979 Natural Death Act with the wording: "Tubes for nutrition and water are among life supports that can be withheld or removed at the written request of the patient."

As a major breakthrough in terminal-care legislation, Proposition

#119 went beyond the passive living wills and powers of attorney, which merely allowed patients to refuse artificial life support.

The Heart and Brains of Initiative #119: The Volunteers

The campaign headquarters for the Proposition #119 operation was located in an old, nearly vacant industrial building located on the Seattle waterfront. The offices were peopled mainly with volunteers who made up the bulk of the staff, and they exhibited the vitality and enthusiasm of a dedicated group who deeply believed in what they were trying to accomplish.

Without the hordes of volunteers who gave their time and in some cases took a leave of absence from their jobs, the initiative would never have gotten the recognition that it finally received. Midge Levy, a full-time social worker, quit her job in Seattle to work for its passage. One of the seven full-time central staff volunteers personally collected 22,000 signatures during the 1990 campaign. The volunteers all over the state worked seven days a week, often well into the night. Through the summer and fall of 1990, they solicited signatures from door to door, in shopping centers, and at hundreds of public events. Many voters who willingly signed the petitions described how they had watched parents and other family members die in prolonged agony.

AIDS support groups were especially helpful in getting signatures as were social workers in hospices and nurses working with cancer patients. Some of the volunteers were walking terminal cases themselves, many of whom later died from their illnesses before the issue got on the ballot. But their yeoman work was remembered by the task force that ran the operation.

Herb Robinson, the senior columnist of the *Seattle Times,* observed that "the coalition of groups and individuals backing Initiative #119 has become one of the most diverse in the state's political history" (ibid.). Among the many diverse civic organizations behind the death with dignity initiative were the following: the Seattle-King County Bar Association, the Physicians for "Yes" on Initiative #119, ACLU of Washington, Northwest AIDS Foundation, the National Organization for Women (NOW) of Washington State, the Puget Sound Council of Senior Citizens, the National Association of Social Workers, and the Washington

State Democratic Party.

The following religious organizations lined up their followers in favor of the proposal: The Interfaith Clergy for "Yes" on Initiative #119, The Northwest Annual Conference of the United Methodist Church, the National Council of Jewish Women, and the Unitarian Universalist Association of the USA. (The latter faith was the only religious denomination in the country to endorse the initiative on the national level.) (Keller 1991)

To carry this message around the state, a group of doctors, calling themselves Physicians for Death With Dignity, was formed to encourage other doctors to "come out of the closet" on the issue. Although physician-assisted dying has been occurring for years in a clandestine manner, it has not been talked about in medical conventions for fear of damaging the image of the physicians. This group attempted to shine the light of day onto the problem.

Two Heartrending Cases

Many individuals spoke out in support of #119 through public statements and letters to the editors of local papers. One bedridden absentee voter in Washington named Edna put the Catch 22 dilemma in a personal perspective, when she commented to a reporter: "If God is going to take me, then why do I need all those tubes and machines? Take them off me. God's running the show! We don't need this artificial support."

Another Washington citizen, Goldie Nickson, a terminally ill cancer patient, told the state legislature on March 20, 1991:

> I'm in favor of Initiative #119 for Death with Dignity, and I will tell you why: In January 1988 I was diagnosed with multiple myeloma, which is cancer of the bone marrow. For most of 1988, I was either in the hospital or in an adult care home, and I was in excruciating pain. The cancer is all over my body, including my skull, but mostly in my rib cage.
>
> Should my pain again become excruciating, with no hope of improvement, I would wish that I could have the aid of my doctor in dying—my doctor who knows and cares about me. Having a choice does not mean that you have to make the choice. It simply means that you have the option. I want that option.

But Goldie never got that option. On September 3, 1991, she died in great pain. Her doctors, hospice nurses, and loving family could not shut out her pain. In the end Goldie begged her friends to help her die. She also pleaded with nurses, but despite her pleas, she suffered intolerable pain during her last days—because there was no law to assist her to a pain-free death (Keller 1991).

Fund Raising for and against the Cause

On one side of the fund-raising battle in the campaign to pass #119, supporters contributed $1,700,000, of which $313,000 came from Hemlock Society members. Ralph Mero pointed out that 26,000 individuals contributed to that total, and 80 percent of the contributions were in sums of thirty dollars or less (Mero, November 16, 1991).

On the other side, the Knights of Columbus poured in $200,000 to help kill the bill, and the Archdiocese of Seattle put $100,000 on the line to defeat the initiative. These were the largest contributions out of a total of over $2,000,000, as reported to the Washington State Election Commission (Watson 1991).

Worldwide Interest in #119

The initiative attracted global attention while signatures were being collected and while the campaign to seek its passage was underway in 1991. Reporters from Japan, Britain, continental Europe, and from dozens of American journals, all visited the central offices in Seattle seeking information. Many legislators from other states, who were considering the introduction of similar proposals in their respective states, requested copies of the proposed Washington law (Egan 1990).

The Doctors' and Lawyers' Dilemmas

The campaign to pass #119 brought out the private anguish of many doctors, some of whom felt that their role as healers would be compromised if they became "agents of death." But other doctors, especially younger ones, saw the initiative as a humane and long overdue response to many of their patients who wanted as much control over their own deaths as they had over their lives. No matter which side of the issue they were on, doctors around the country said that the voters in Washington could change the nature of American medicine with the passage or rejection of the initiative.

"I am not an alarmist by nature, but I am absolutely terrified of what this could mean," said Dr. Carlos Gomez of the University of Virginia's Health Sciences Center and the author of a recent book on euthanasia, *Regulating Death.* "The proponents talk about physician-assisted suicide as a right. But I don't understand how you can have a right to be killed," he said.

James Vorenberg, a teacher of criminal law and the former dean of the Harvard Law School, commented on the Op/Ed page in the *New York Times* on November 5, 1991:

> Until recently, most of the attention given to the "right to die" has been focused on patients who are unconscious, as doctors, hospitals and the courts have struggled to decide when and on whose direction respirators and artificially administered nutrition and fluids may be turned off. The Washington initiative and Dr. Kevorkian make it clear that assisted suicide raises issues that are at least equally difficult.
>
> In effect, existing law on assisted suicide places virtually unlimited discretionary power in the hands of doctors and prosecutors, and gives patients no assurances that they can decide when to end their lives if they are terminally ill. It is not a crime to attempt or commit suicide, but in many states assisting suicide is a crime and in others someone who caused death, say by such actions as injecting poison or placing pills in a patient's mouth, could be charged with murder or man-slaughter.

Vorenberg put the controversial issue front and center, when he admitted:

> It is well known that some doctors will give a lethal dose of morphine or other medication to shorten the suffering of a terminally ill patient at the patient's request or when the patient is unable to make a request. But no doctor has ever been convicted of hastening death this way. . . .
> Assisted suicide is not the first opening wedge, or a bigger one,

than capital punishment, the authority given to the police to shoot felons and the general authorization to kill in self-defense. It is not clear that deaths arising from a merciful motive are more likely to proliferate than these other kinds of permitted deaths.

Vorenberg supported the initiative and said he would vote for it if he were a resident of Washington. The issue was decided just a few hours after Dr. Vorenberg's provocative piece appeared in the *Times*.

Breakthrough for a Cause

On June 11, 1992, support for the legalization of active euthanasia came from an unexpected front, when Washington State Attorney General Ken Eikenberry filed a lawsuit against the #119 Vote No! Committee. The suit charged that the committee had made false claims about Initiative #119 in a flyer that it had circulated throughout the state a week before the election in November 1991. The flyer claimed that Initiative #119 "would let doctors end patients' lives without benefits of safeguards." Eikenberry, a Republican gubernatorial candidate, believed that the claim violated the standards established in a statute against false political advertising, which prohibits false statements of material fact made with actual malice.

Other claims made by the opponents of Initiative #119 that Eikenberry charged were false included:

- No special qualifications are required: "Your eye doctor could kill you."
- There are no rules against coercion, i.e., nothing to prevent "selling the idea to the aged, the poor and the homeless."
- There are no reporting requirements: "No record keeping required."
- No notification is required: "Nobody even needs to tell the family members beforehand."
- There is no protection for the depressed patient: "No waiting period, no chance to change your mind."

Eikenberry's legal action focussed on the claims that #119 provided no safeguards because the language of the initiative detailed many safeguards, including some that directly contradicted the assertions in the flyer. The attorney general alleged that this claim was a false statement of material fact made with reckless disregard for its accuracy. "These claims were a flat-out contradiction of the Initiative's language and their falsity is obvious to anyone who reads it," he said. He believed that he could prove that the committee acted "with actual malice" by publishing these allegations even though they knew they were untrue. His action asked for up to $10,000 in penalties, which could be tripled if the court found circumstances merited a larger penalty, together with reasonable costs and fees.

As a gubernatorial candidate, he vowed not to let election-year politics interfere with his responsibility to the citizens of Washington State to perform his duty in a fair and impartial manner. Since the same groups who opposed the initiative in his state were marshalling their forces to kill a similar one in California on the November 1992 ballot, the significance of his lawsuit was important to warn the opponents in California to tell the truth in their flyers.

14

The Going of Initiative #119

It's not the repression by the bad people that hurts—it's the silence
of the good.

—Rev. Martin Luther King, Jr.

In early October, a national poll showed that 61 percent of the voters
in the state of Washington favored the euthanasia measure, while only
12 percent were opposed and 12 percent undecided. The supporters of
#119 were euphoric in their belief that the initiative would pass. A simi-
lar poll conducted by the *Boston Globe* and the Harvard School of
Public Health showed that 64 percent of the public favored letting doctors give lethal injections to patients asking to die.

But then came a major turnabout, wrought by the engines of two
powerful social forces who were opposed to the proposition: the Roman Catholic Church and the American Medical Association, who
both played upon the moral qualms and the practical fears of the electorate. Richard Doerflinger, a staff member of the Roman Catholic
Bishops' Conference, questioned the firmness of the poll's findings,
pointing out that the poll's question on lethal injections offered re-
spondents three choices: whether giving such injections upon request
should be "required" (only 16 percent said yes), "allowed but not required" (48 percent approved), or "prohibited" (30 percent). He claimed

158

that framing the questions in such a way invited the second or "middle of the road" response.

In the March 1988 Roper Poll, however, which showed that 58 percent of 1,982 people questioned favored active voluntary euthanasia, it was significant that 61 percent of the Roman Catholics polled supported the initiative, even though the hierarchy of the church opposed it. (This figure marked a slight increase over the previous Roper Poll taken two years earlier, when 59 percent of the nation's Catholics supported the concept.) (Associated Press 1991)

The opponents of the measure knew that they had to overcome an estimated two to one margin in favor of #119 when they started their counter-campaign in October. They hammered away at what they said was a lack of safeguards, and they pointed out that the existing Natural Death Act already allowed "death with dignity" by permitting life supports to be removed, which is a form of passive euthanasia. In their broadcast and print ads, the opposition also stressed that the initiative did not require a waiting period or family consultations to make sure that patients truly wanted to die. They used the ploy that the poor would use aid-in-dying disproportionately, so their families wouldn't be burdened with large hospital or nursing home bills. They also said that current medications effectively control pain for the terminally ill. Finally, they aroused the fear that if the initiative passed, out-of-state residents would be induced to come to Washington to be "euthanized."

The First Signs of Opposition

Letters were sent to the American Medical Association, the American Bar Association, and other professional organizations by the #119 Initiative office, asking them to review the initiative and to make any positive recommendations for improvement in the wording. None of them responded, however, although the AMA—at its 1990–91 annual meeting—took a vote opposing #119.

The National Right-to-Life Committee sent out 50,000 copies of a handbill imploring the readers to "Stop the Washington Euthanasia Bill" because it was the "moral equivalent of Nazi concentration camps" in World War II. The Washington State conference of Catholic Bishops issued a handbill aimed against the Hemlock Society entitled "Life at Risk." It also planted articles and letters to the editor in local papers. An eight-page pastoral letter was given to all the priests in the archdiocese to be read in every pulpit during mass before the election.

The Catholic Opposition Exerts its Muscle

In early October, reliable polls showed that Initiative #119 would probably pass, with a 2000-vote plurality out of 1,500,000 votes expected to be cast. However, the backers of the proposition knew that there were now some powerful minority economic and social forces arrayed against them. Chief among these were the aforementioned American Medical Association (AMA), the National Right-to-Life Committee, and the National Council of Catholic Bishops. Even though opponents to the initiative were outnumbered by its supporters, the oppositon had extraordinary power to raise money quickly to pay for expensive TV commercials, which became the backbone of the lobbying effort to sway voters before November 5 (Mero, November 16, 1991).

The Catholic Church's dogma that "only God gives life and only God can take it away" was emphasized in connection with both #119 and the abortion issue at Sunday masses and on other occasions all over the state. (Catholics received support from orthodox Jewish elements and fundamentalist Protestant sects in their joint opposition to these two controversial issues.) The Roman Catholic hierarchy in the state of Washington ordered a voter registration campaign in 1991 in all of their churches in order to bolster the vote against Proposition #119. In September, volunteers were provided with the proper forms to sign up prospective voters, and parishioners coming to daily and Sunday masses were registered and provided with arguments against abortion legislation and the right-to-die initiative.

Since Washington had traditionally been identified as a pro-choice state in regard to the issue of abortion, the right-to-life groups, including Catholics and fundamentalist Protestant denominations, announced that they "would spend two dollars against #119 for every dollar spent against the other initiative"—Proposition #120, which would legalize abortion in the state, in case *Roe* v. *Wade* was scuttled by the Supreme Court. The reasoning behind this lobbying campaign was that the movement for death with dignity could be nipped in the bud, while the anti-abortion groups conceded that the movement for abortion access was too well established in Washington to be defeated at the ballot box.

The Catholic Church was careful to say that euthanasia, per se, was not a cardinal sin; rather it argued that the intent of the initiative would be bad for patients and that doctors would be out of control, as they were in the Netherlands.

Archbishop Thomas Murphy of Seattle warned his flock that propositions similar to Initiative #119 would come up again sometime in the future. Bishop John Nevins of Venice, Florida, fearing just such an eventuality in his state, sought help from Murphy on ways to organize opposition to euthanasia proposals in the Sunshine State. Nevins was a firm believer in the "redemptive value of human suffering," a way of rationalizing physical pain, and a church strategy passed on to him by Murphy to use against euthanasia lobbying groups (Mero, November 15, 1991).

The AMA Gears Up for Action

The Washington Medical Association conducted a secret survey of two thousand of its members and found that a bare majority of 51 percent said no to #119, while 49 percent said yes. The organization poured $40,000 into an advertising campaign. They distributed a poster reading "Vote NO" and stressed that #119 had no safeguards, especially for the poor but also for society in general. Copies of their ten-point checklist of #119 negatives were found in each member's medical office.

A group of doctors organized under the banner "Washington Physicians Against 119" issued a one-page flyer that listed ten reasons why their group opposed Initiative #119 and implied that the voters should do likewise. The reasons were as follows:

1. *"We want to care for our patients and not kill them . . . "* as doctors have been doing for 2400 years.
2. *"We want to offer terminal patients compassionate care and not death."*

3. *"Initiative 119 is not in the public's interest"*—but rather offers the easy way out.
4. *"It is intentionally vague* because most people do not understand what 'aid-in-dying' and 'death with dignity' mean." (The latter involves doctors in the killing of patients by lethal injections.)
5. *"Initiative 119 could destroy patient trust in doctors."* The group fell back on a paper written by the late anthropologist Margaret Mead in 1965, in which she switched from a pro-euthanasia stance because of the abuse of its tenets by a fringe element.
6. *"119 would undermine the standard care for everyone."* The Washington physicians' group cited a 1983 study in which, they claimed, with no reliable statistical proof, that half of the doctors in the Netherlands who offered "aid in dying" admitted killing conscious patients without getting the patients' consent.
7. *"The right to refuse to be kept alive by machines in Washington is already well established* through the Natural Death Act of 1979."
8. *"It establishes the fundamental right to die,"* but it would open the door to court challenges, allowing suicide on demand for everyone—even depressed teenagers.
9. *"We don't want to be forced to participate in euthanasia"* (This was a false assumption, although the group felt that any doctor who did not agree to be an accessory could be charged with "criminal neglect, malpractice or abandonment."
10. *"Doctors are human beings"* and should not have the burden of killing other human beings.

These points caused many voters to have doubts about the intent of Initiative #119 and to misunderstand what it was trying to accomplish.

In conjunction with this flyer circulated by "Washington Physicians Against 119," the Washington AMA pressured newspapers and TV stations across the state to oppose #119 by pointing out the dangers of euthanasia. Both electronic and print reporters ran stories of how alarmed several hospitals and nursing homes had become over the prospects of the initiative's passage. "Their stories should have been relegated to a fiction features section and not [treated] as a hard news item," commented one #119 supporter.

Finally, the AMA Ethics Committee, at the national level, reaffirmed their continued opposition to doctor-assisted suicide and euthanasia by issuing statements in which Hippocrates—revered as the father of Western medicine and the author of the Hippocratic oath—was quoted. But they didn't point out that euthanasia has been a subject of constant debate since Socrates drank the cup of hemlock.

Dr. Kevorkian's Hemlock Vendetta

In March and September 1991, Ralph Mero, the author of Initiative #119, spent several hours on the phone with Dr. Kevorkian, pleading with him not to use his "suicide machine" before the November vote. He feared that the publicity surrounding Kevorkian could undermine the chances of the initiative passing. Despite two follow-up letters to the "suicide doctor" from Rev. Mero, Kevorkian remained rabidly critical of Humphry, calling the founder of Hemlock a "phony" and charging that his organization was "deceiving people."

This attitude toward Humphry and the growth of Hemlock (which extends back to a time before *Final Exit* became a best-seller) can only be explained as professional jealousy on the part of the imperious doctor toward the journalist-author who has built up a large following around the country on this sensitive issue. Kevorkian told Mero that "I believe Prop. #119 deserves to lose and I have no interest in supporting its aims." He said that Hemlock should take an interest in what he was doing to educate other doctors about building their own suicide machines and then assisting terminal patients to die. "And if they get themselves arrested," he went on, "they will be exonerated like I was" (Mero interview, November 16, 1991)

In late September, Mero again phoned Kevorkian and asked that Kevorkian call him if "a situation comes up in your medical practice before November 5th [election day] . . . since the pressure would then be on us." Kevorkian exploded with bitter anger, shouting back: "No, I won't call you first if I do anything. You will deserve whatever repercussions you get from whatever I do when I do it."

Kevorkian's antipathy toward Humphry and Hemlock is so great that he refused even to appear with Humphry on the Donahue TV show, an event that would have greatly promoted the sale of Kevorkian's 1991 book, *Prescription Medicide.*

Mero believes that Kevorkian envisioned Initiative #119 as a "creation of the Hemlock Society and that Hemlock, in turn, was the creation of Humphry, who used the organization as a vehicle to make himself a million dollars from the sale of his books."

Would There Be An October Surprise?

Late in the campaign, rumors trickled into the Proposition #119 headquarters that Dr. Kevorkian was preparing an "October surprise" by bringing a terminally ill patient to Washington to assist her in dying, an act that would sabotage the hopes for success of the proposition at the polls. When Mero called him on the phone to verify the rumor, Kevorkian denied that he was coming to Washington, but he did not rule out the possibility of another headline-making mercy killing somewhere in the country before the election.

On October 22, Kevorkian carried out the implied threat by helping Marjorie Wantz and Sherry Miller to die in a Michigan forest cabin (see chapter 9). The resulting front-page story helped to undermine the support for #119 with scare headlines about Dr. Death's latest escapade. Television coverage in the final weeks of the campaign often linked Kevorkian to #119, and by November 3 (on the eve of the election) a poll showed that 52 percent of the state's voters thought the Michigan pathologist would be able to bring his suicide device to Washington if the initiative passed. Significantly, only 28 percent of those polled approved of Kevorkian's actions. According to Dr. Linda Grombo, a pro-#119 family physician in Seattle, "Kevorkian gave a face to people's unspoken fears."

An Icon Appears on the TV Screen

Late in the campaign, the AMA pulled off a PR coup by putting former Surgeon General Dr. C. Everett Koop on statewide television with a thirty-second commercial. During the Reagan administration, the bearded, uniformed Dr. Koop had become known as the most forthright and visible Surgeon General in American history. As a pro-life, fundamentalist moralist, with an abiding reverence for the human body, he was thought of as America's family doctor. Koop had made a significant mark with the public as a result of his reports and campaigns on the effect of smoking, AIDs, and abortion on the nation's health. His stance against euthanasia was known in some quarters as "the Gospel according to Koop."

In his TV commercial, Koop implored his viewers to vote against the initiative because "it was against God," and it would be asking doctors to "murder their patients." He told his audience that the first victims of #119—if it passed—would be the "weak and the poor"! He stated that such an act would be sanctioning "medical homicide."

Unfortunately, the Hemlock Society could find no comparable celebrity physician, like a Dr. Jonas Salk, who could mount a credible counterattack to Koop's rantings. His commercial, along with two other AMA-sponsored TV commercials, which used actors representing a hospice nurse and an eye doctor "who could put you to death," tipped the scales in favor of the opposition.

A thirty-second countercommercial, sponsored by the pro-#119 forces, featured a real woman, Susan Baron, who had survived fourteen operations for terminal cancer. The dying patient said on camera: "I want a choice in the end to die in a dignified manner . . . with two doctors approving my wishes."

But this TV commercial was not enough to overcome the impact of the Koop aura on the electorate.

Election Day, 1991

In exit polls taken by the *Seattle Times* on election day, those voting against #119 gave the following reasons for their oppositon: they were morally opposed; disapproved of doctors taking a life; were concerned about the lack of safeguards; they would rather let nature take its course.

Those who voted for the measure had these responses: a person has a right to choose; it could end someone's pain; personal experiences had convinced them that this was a justifiable measure; it would allow death with dignity.

Since 1991 was an off-year election, the proponents of #119 felt that only 800,000 voters might cast their ballots. Besides #119 there were three other issues: a pro-abortion initiative legalizing the process for all women *if* the Supreme Court found *Roe* v. *Wade* to be unconstitutional; another limiting the terms of elected officials (which would directly affect Speaker of the U.S. House of Representatives, Tom Foley); and a third which would roll back the state's property taxes.

Beyond all expectations, the voters came out in droves because of the controversy surrounding both #119 and the abortion question. The total votes cast amounted to 1,400,000.

While the abortion initiative passed, #119 failed by 47,000 votes (701,818—yes and 811,104—no). Dr. Koop's thirty-second TV sound-bite helped to provide the "Koop-de-Grace" to drive the final nail into #119's coffin.

Post-Election Reaction

On November 13, the *Chicago Tribune* ran a story with this headline: "Catholics Rejoice in Prop. #119's Defeat." The article noted that, although the Bishop's Conference in Washington was happy with the defeat of the proposal, it warned that the issue would soon come up again in another state. On November 27, *The Journal of the American Medical Association* assessed the victory: "Medicine got lucky in Washington's historic vote this month to reject physician assisted suicide for the terminally ill." According to Dr. Peter McGough, the Washington State Medical Association spokesman against #119, "this time we were very lucky, but this is not the end of the debate; it's only the beginning" (Mero, January 1992).

Despite the defeat at the polls there was a clear message from the Washington voters; i.e., almost half of the people wanted to assert control over their own dying because they profoundly distrusted contemporary medicine's capacity to respond to terminal illness or protracted painful debilitation.

Ralph Mero concluded:

> We have tried to bring public attention to this issue and I think we succeeded in it. There simply must be a better way for people to face this last step in life. We know that mercy and compassion can be

widened. Our society's understanding of death and dying will not be the same from this day forward.

Mero summed up the end of the campaign to have #119 enacted into law, when he said:

> After two years of trying to have our little frail ship come into a safe harbor, and then to be torpedoed makes it difficult to cope with the results. But we almost made it. We must not stop our efforts. Let's use the knowledge that we gained, so desperate people will not have to take the law into their own hands in the future.

Mero also felt that because the initiative attracted 47 percent of the total vote, "our heads were held high since it legitimized our cause . . . and it showed the country that we [Hemlock] are now a strong movement and no longer to be looked upon as eccentric."

It was President Thomas Jefferson who said: "Democracy stands or falls on the education of the electorate." In the aftermath of the defeat of Initiative #119, it can be said that while its supporters did a credible job of educating the electorate, the effort was not good enough to persuade the majority of the voters.

Other states would have to take up the fight in future years.

Humphry's Assessment of the Defeat of #119

In a perceptive article published in *Newsday* on November 14 just over a week later, titled "Why Were They Beaten in Washington?" Derek Humphry presented an evaluation that could be of benefit to other states later on. Analyzing the role of the last-minute furor that Dr. Kevorkian unleashed by helping to end the lives of the two women in Michigan, Humphry observed:

> The specter of maverick doctors "on call" to assist the suicides of people whether or not they are judged terminally ill was potently raised.
>
> Kevorkian—the loose cannon of the euthanasia movement, not affiliated with any group—in my view, may have marginally affected the result, but not significantly.

But Humphry went on to outline what he felt were the two chief reasons for the Washington defeat. The first was *semantics:*

> The language of the campaigners was to the language of the media and the public as apples are to oranges. "Aid-in-dying"—as the campaigners called it—can mean anything from a physician's lethal injection all the way to holding hands with the dying patient and saying: "I love you."
>
> They avoided the words "suicide" and "euthanasia" as though they were obscenities. The media, ranging from the tabloids to the learned academic journals, along with the public, used the real words with relish.

The other failure, according to Humphry, was the lack of *safeguards:*

> [The Washington campaigners] "made the tactical mistake of painting their law with a broad brush, intending to sit down with the medical and legal professions after victory to hammer out the detailed guidelines under which euthanasia could be carried out.
>
> But the public did not want euthanasia laws on the books without built-in safeguards—a sign of the general distrust of the medical and legal professions.

Humphry hoped that these lessons could be learned in time to help California become the first state to legalize euthanasia.

15

California Here We Come: The Post-#119 Campaign to Legalize Death With Dignity

Go to the people at the top—that is my advice to anyone who wants to change the system, any system. Don't moan and groan with like minded souls. Don't write letters or place a few phone calls and then sit back and wait. Leave safety behind—even if your voice shakes. When you least expect it, someone may actually listen to what you have to say. Well-aimed slingshots can topple giants.

—Maggie Kuhn, eighty-six, the founder of the
Gray Panthers, in *No Stone Unturned:*
The Life and Times of Maggie Kuhn (1991)

Professor Hans Uffelmann of the University of Missouri, the American Humanist's Man of the Year, observed that the vote on Initiative #119 in Washington was not a defeat but the opening shot in a battle to attain nationwide approval for the concept. His assessment of the situation proved to be accurate, for the very next year, after the defeat of Initiative #119, the battle to decriminalize doctor-assisted suicide moved south from Washington to the largest state of the union. California became the next arena for the 1992 campaign to pass a meaningful death-with-dignity act.

There are some important lessons to be learned from the ups and downs of the six-year struggle in California to put a death-with-dignity proposition on the ballot. California was the first state to legally recognize living wills (1975) and the durable power of attorney for health care (1986), which empowers a designated agent to follow the desires of a terminally ill person who cannot make decisions because of coma or mental incapacitation regarding life-sustaining treatment. That state also recognized a directive to physicians which allowed individuals to make known their desires to withhold life-sustaining procedures. But this directive could be carried out only after a waiting period of fourteen days, starting from the day the doctor had told the patient that he or she was in a terminal condition. The statute was revised in 1991, permitting signing at any time.

Prospects of a #119 Successor in California

In 1986 Michael White and Robert Risley, two lawyers in Los Angeles, wrote the first proposed Humane and Dignified Death Act for our country's largest state. According to that bill, a dying person would be able to make a written request to a physician to help him or her to die. Furthermore, the doctor would have to consult with at least one other doctor who would also have to agree that the terminally ill suffering patient would probably die within six months or less. If both doctors agreed, then the primary physician would negotiate with the patient on how to die. A request to die would have to be in writing, unless the patient was comatose, and then the statute would have permitted a surrogate to act for the patient.

The original proposed bill stated that the doctor could always back out if he or she desired. Priority hospitals in California were given the right to decline to permit aid-in-dying in their facilities, and forgeries of patient's signatures would be made a crime. Finally, doctors could not be sued, prosecuted, or lose their license to practice for engaging in assisted dying.

That proposed initiative failed to get enough signatures to get on the ballot in 1988.

An Early Failed Attempt in the Golden State

In 1987, a Los Angeles–based group called Americans Against Human Suffering drafted a model piece of legislation titled, "The Humane and Dignified Death Act." The bill would have permitted an adult the right to request and receive a physician's aid in dying and was introduced through the initiative process. Public polls reported great support for the legislation and in San Francisco, where doctors polled their colleagues, the results showed that 60 percent of the doctors there stated that they would obey the law if it were passed. The Los Angeles Pharmaceutical Association also polled their members and found that 40 percent approved the intent of the referendum.

Nonetheless, the signature drive failed when the attempt to get the initiative on the ballot in 1988 garnered only 130,000 of the required 400,000 signatures. Americans Against Human Suffering attributed the failure mainly to organizational problems and lack of money. But Derek Humphry was of the opinion that something positive had been achieved:

> We shook the medical profession to the core and got their heads out of the sand. We got good press coverage there. . . .
>
> Furthermore, the California Medical Association objected to our attempt saying that no doctors were supporting us. They were wrong, since a poll conducted by the Hemlock Society showed that over 60 percent of the physicians in California were in favor of us. We were accused of rigging the referendum, which was also false.

But the California Medical Association had offered stiff opposition. They claimed that the people would no longer trust their doctors, that doctors would become "killers." They also charged that progress in medical science and the cure for cancer would be halted and that the initiative would legitimize suicide for the young.

High Hopes Again in California

Michael H. White, a California lawyer and president of Californians Against Human Suffering, which is advancing the current initiative there, is proud of the fact that his state was the first to legalize living wills by a statute passed in 1975, and to legalize the durable power of attorney for health care in 1986. White was one of the co-authors and leaders of the California Initiative campaign, made up of doctors, lawyers, psychologists, educators, and others trying to accomplish in that state what almost passed in Washington in November 1991.

White and attorney Robert Risley, founder and chariman of Californians Against Human Suffering, drew up the original legislation in 1986 and the revised initiative slated for the ballot in 1992. The proposed law calls for the request to die to be "enduring"—meaning made on more than one occasion. The family can be informed of the request to die, but can neither promote nor veto it. The bill remains faithful to the principle that while aid-in-dying is a basic right for all, it must be surrounded with safeguards against abuse. (See Appendix 7 for a copy of the California Death with Dignity Act.)

White knew that there were many doctors who were still reluctant to endorse the proposal, like one who said: "The California Initiative is defective for at least fifteen reasons, and if you succeed in eliminating them, I will still oppose it." White admitted that there were many problems ahead in organization, fund-raising, lobbying, and the negative connotations of the words "death with dignity." (He would have preferred to use "euthanasia," which comes from the Greek words *eu,* meaning "good," and *thanatos,* meaning "death." But the other phrase won out.)

The goal in California in 1992 was to obtain at least 600,000 signatures, which would ensure the initiative a place on the ballot in November 1992. The committee started out on October 7, 1991. While it is a grueling process to collect so many signatures and the initiative process is not the ideal way to legislate, this approach was taken in California because the California legislature would not consider the issue at all.

On April 9, 1992, the Secretary of State of California certified that there were enough signatures to put the measure on the November 3, 1992 ballot in that state.

Additional Safeguards in the California Initiative

Although Washington Initiative #119 had nine safeguards written into it, the opposition in that state effectively employed a lobbying campaign, in the print and electronics media, to claim that "there were no safeguards" in the proposal. The California proponents were aware of this ploy, so they made an effort to put additional safeguards into their initiative.

Even the opponents of the new initiative admitted that California's proposal contained some of the safeguards missing in Initiative #119, such as requiring hospitals and other health care providers to report the number of euthanasia cases annually, including the ages and illnesses of those who died. California also added a waiting period after a request for aid-in-dying was made, plus a mental competency check and family notification all of which Initiative #119 lacked.

The California initiative also differed from its predecessor in Washington in that it contained special protections for persons in skilled nursing facilities, prohibitions against intimidation and tampering, provisions for psychological consultation, limitation on fees, record-keeping requirements, and the notification of the family of a patient's intent. Besides these provisions, another safeguard in the act required that the written request be witnessed by two disinterested persons.

But there were other problems. On the one hand was the issue of the patients who have already lost the mental capacity to choose for themselves, and on the other, questions remained about those who are still able to choose, but are on the brink of what they or their families know will be an inexorable decline into both physical and mental helplessness. Creeping senility is a debilitating illness of the elderly and prevents such terminally mentally ill patients from signing a living will or power of attorney.

The highlights of the proposed California initiative are listed below (see the complete act in Appendix 7).

SUMMARY OF THE 1991–92
CALIFORNIA DEATH-WITH-DIGNITY ACT

- A licensed physician would be able to help a terminally ill patient to die. The patient must be a mentally competent adult and two physicians—one of whom must be the attending physician—must certify that the patient has an incurable or irreversible condition that will result in death within six months or less.

- The patient must have signed a directive requesting aid-in-dying that has been witnessed by two people. If the patient is in a nursing home, one of the witnesses must be a patient ombudsman.

- The request must have been communicated on more than one occasion.

- Aid-in-dying may be administered by the doctor or the appropriate means may be provided to the patient for self-administration.

- It is up to the patient to determine the time, place, and manner of death.

- Aid-in-dying means providing any medical procedure that will terminate the life of the qualified patient swiftly, painlessly, and humanely or providing the means to the patient for self-administration.

- The directive may be nullified orally or in writing by the patient.

- No health-care professional or private hospital is required to participate; their duty is only to transfer the patient upon request.

- Physicians are freed from civil, criminal, and administrative responsibility.

- A request for aid-in-dying, or talk of one, may not be used by insurance companies to alter any insurance benefit.

- Aid-in-dying cannot be deemed suicide, so insurance cannot be withheld if a person dies with assistance.

- A person cannot be required or forbidden to sign a directive; no medical service can be conditioned on the presence or absence of a directive.

- Forging a directive can be prosecuted as homicide if death results.

There was opposition from both the medical and the religious establishment in California to the initiative as there was in Washington. For example, Dr. Melvin Kirschner, co-chair of the Los Angeles County Medical Association and the Los Angeles County Bar Association Joint Committee on Biomedical Ethics, said he did not see the need for a law that would permit physicians to kill people. He believed it was not necessary to make euthanasia legal to assure terminally ill people a humane and dignified death. "Rather, we need to teach doctors to provide these patients *with better pain control and management,*" he said [emphasis added].

Opposition Begins

By mid-1992, the backers of the California death-with-dignity initiative were mounting an active campaign to garner support for the proposition. The new campaign asked volunteers to gather signatures and to solicit a financial contribution of $10 from each person willing to sign a fund-raising petition; the goal for the final push in the fall was $150,000. (This campaign device was an utter failure.)

Dark clouds appeared on the horizon when opposition to the initiative was expressed by the hierarchy of the Catholic Church and the California Medical Association. A coalition of fundamentalist religious groups was also believed to be marshalling forces to work against the approval of the proposition. The Scholl Institute of Bioethics, a division of International Life Services, Inc., organized a strategy session to defeat the initiative. A joint announcement by Scholl made on April 9, 1992, and signed by Sister Paula Vandegaer and Molly Grace Israel said:

> Polls show that the majority of Californians favor this initiative, so without a major effort on everyone's part, we will be the first state in the Union to legalize euthanasia.
>
> I am sure I do not need to remind you of the consequences for America and world society should California make this move.

The Semi-Secret Opposition to Proposition #161

In September 1992, the respected California Field Institute Poll produced the first reliable scientific survey during the campaign, which confirmed polling done earlier by others. After listening to a description by the pollsters of what the voter would read in the polling booth, 624 registered voters gave a ringing endorsement for Proposition #161 by a hefty margin of 68 percent yes as compared to 24 percent no and 8 percent undecided. Furthermore, Mike White, the president of Californians Against Human Suffering, revealed that 72 percent of lay Roman Catholics in the state were in favor of #161. "It has been the hierarchy of the church that has provided the chief opposition to our efforts," he said. Even the opposition conceded that there was overwhelming public support for Proposition #161 (White 1992).

By late in the 1992 campaign, it was clear that church-related organizations were paying for the bulk of the negative radio and TV ads throughout the state. Through a campaign committee called Californians Against the Euthanasia Initiative, the church attempted to impose its version of morality on the citizens of the Golden State by asking the voters to vote no. Supporters of the Death with Dignity Initiative labeled this politically offensive lobbying as "window dressing for a religious campaign orchestrated by the Catholic Church." While claiming the moral highground, the Roman Catholic Church was "operating in the shadows of political campaign law, violating the spirit, if not the letter, of reporting legal requirements" according to Death with Dignity. Although church officials refused to admit the hierarchy's dominant role, the supporters of Initiative #161 accused it of funding over 80 percent of the vote-no campaign against #161.

By the advent of the fall season, church-related entities had given over $800,000 direct from its treasuries to push for a no vote, and every parish priest was ordered to denounce the initiative and to give instructions about how to contribute during daily and Sunday services so as to keep the church from being listed with the Fair Employment Practices Commission. (In one California county, the local bishop boasted that he had collected over $150,000 from parishioners, none of which required the reporting of the involvement of the church.)

Although Proposition #161 leaders expected opposition from the church, based on the experience a year before in nearby Washington where the church played an active role in helping to defeat Initiative #119 there by a narrow margin, they did not expect the flurry of outright political speeches from the pulpits, the flood of checks from diocesan treasuries, the unprecedented collections of special right-to-life contribution envelopes at every mass, and the bevy of political placards instructing the parishioners how to vote on the issue. To cover up the "real" source of funds for the radio and TV ads, the church identified their vote-no messages as being sponsored by "health care providers and charitable organizations." The church appeared reluctant to reveal the true source of the money funding the drive against Proposition #161, which it considered sinful and against the laws of God.

The Church Plays Hardball

Near the end of the Fall campaign, in an unprecedented move, the Catholic bishops of California made a direct appeal to their parishioners for funds to fight Proposition #161. According to a report in the *Los Angeles Times* on September 15, 1992:

> In a letter being read at Mass throughout the state this month, the bishops are calling for volunteers and campaign contributions to oppose the initiative on the November 3rd ballot, charging that it condones suicide and portrays euthanasia as a "lethal and unacceptable way of terminating care."

The church literature also quoted from the *Declaration on Euthanasia* published by the Vatican in 1980, which reads: "We are confronted with a 'violation of the divine law, an offense against the dignity of the human person, a crime against life and an attack on humanity.' " The opposition ignored the fact that physicians are permitted under the present law to turn off respirators and withdraw food and hydration to allow people to suffocate or starve to death, and that they are also permitted to provide pain medications that may indirectly advance the time of death. They do not claim that terminally ill people are now being abused—*only starved to death.*

Appealing to fear, the opposition to Proposition #161 stated that "it cannot be contained. It will lead to involuntary euthanasia of people who are disabled, elderly or mentally ill." This statement misrepresented the initiative, which contained numerous safeguards as described above. Furthermore, involuntary euthanasia is presently permitted under law, for those terminally ill patients who are deemed mentally incompetent, through withdrawal of life support.

The Goal of #161

In retrospect, California's Humane and Dignified Death Act grew out of Robert Risley's experience of helping his late wife Darlene to die a dignified death back in 1984–85, after she had suffered from terminal ovarian cancer. When he and Michael White wrote the initiative to legalize physician-assisted aid-in-dying, their primary goal was to ensure that every human has a right to die as they choose. Their secondary goal after the passage of Proposition #161 was to encourage doctors to participate and cooperate once the proposition became law. If they didn't want to participate, they would have been given the option of declining.

Risley stated a reality when he said recently:

> #161 was not revolutionary since doctors do help patients to die today by turning up the morphine on terminally ill patients surreptitiously because it is currently illegal to do so, thus leading to cardiac arrest. Proposition #161, however, puts the final decision in the hands of the patient, and not the physicians where it does not belong.

California Voters Reject the Initiative—But Not by Much

When the votes were counted after the November 3, 1992, election, Initiative #161 had failed to pass by a 54 percent to 46 percent margin. Although the narrow defeat marked a temporary setback for Hemlock Society USA* and its supporters, the fact that 5,500,000 voters had marked yes on their ballots was encouraging for the future.

The 8 percent differential was attributed to the last-minute media assault by the Catholic Church with its $800,000 kitty contributed by its membership to oppose the initiative. That church was supported by fundamentalist religions of all faiths. The San Diego Ministerial Council (composed of Protestants, Catholics, and Jews) issued a joint statement summing up their position: "Our opposition was based on our belief on the sacred incomparable value of every human being."

The Hemlock Society USA put out a more positive statement, which looked ahead to the next steps:

---

*The new name for National Hemlock, coined by the Board at the end of 1992.

Despite the loss, a large number of voters clearly indicated a desire for such a law. The euthanasia movement will now concentrate on changing the laws in Oregon and Washington in 1994 [with new initiatives similar to #161]. The Hemlock Society USA anticipates the introduction of similar initiatives in other states throughout the nation in the months ahead.

Although the backers of #161 fell just short of the goal in 1992, they did provide an important education to the nation on the pressing need for similar legislation in *all* states.

16

Death-with-Dignity Legislation
in Other States

The right to die, with the help of doctor assisted suicide, is the next
major human rights issue in contemporary American society.
—Rev. Ralph Mero

Despite the setbacks in Washington and California, the aid-in-dying
issue will likely come to a head again in another state. In this chapter,
I will briefly review significant legislative action in other states that have
already begun to grapple with the dilemmas of dying.

Colorado

In 1991 there were five bills introduced into the Colorado state legislature, all of them dealing with some aspect of the death-with-dignity issue. One was created by antieuthanasia forces and attempted to disman-
tle the existing living-will law. But none of these bills passed because of
the lack of popular citizen and legislative support. In 1992, legislation
was introduced on specific directions for surrogacy; anyone who challenged
the surrogate's actions would have to bear the burden of proof. Another

bill proposed a bracelet to inform police or emergency ambulance services who answer telephone 911 calls that the bracelet wearer does not want any resuscitation if he or she is terminally ill or becomes comatose.

Colorado State Senator Bonnie Allison, who sponsored the living-will legislation, confessed that "many of us proponents of the legislation supporting doctor-assisted suicide have been afraid of retribution by the media if we stuck our necks out too far. This issue has not been dealt with fairly in the media." Senator Allison's bill stipulates that if a patient is comatose for at least seven days he or she has the option of having food and water continued or stopped, at a loved one's discretion. After an episcopal priest described her bill before the Colorado legislature's health committee as "the first step towards establishing a new Third Reich in the USA," Senator Allison was still able to get seven votes in the committee supporting her idea. She believes that those who support death with dignity need to shed their fears and "educate the legislators by lobbying for the right to individual choices on the issue of death. We should not be frightened by the opposition" (Allison 1991).

Florida

Florida, with its large number of retired senior citizens,* has the second largest membership in the Hemlock Society after California. Nonetheless, its local chapters have faced many roadblocks to passing meaningful death-with-dignity legislation. For example, in 1988, both houses of the legislature in Tallahassee passed the Life Prolonging Procedures Act, which would have permitted removal of passive IV feeding tubes, but the conservative Governor Bob Martinez vetoed the bill.

In recent years, several Florida legislators have submitted similar bills in the legislatures to allow life-support systems to be withdrawn (a form of passive euthanasia) from patients in a "persistent vegetative state," but they all failed to get out of committee, pass both houses, or obtain the governor's signature. Then several smaller bills were

---

*Since Florida's population is expected to soar from its present 13.2 million to over 16 million by 2001, petitioners seeking to place a referendum similar to Washington's #119 on the Florida ballot will need to acquire 363,000 names (equal to 8 percent of the voters in the 1991 election). Signatures must be obtained on a petition to approve the right to privacy in at least twelve of the twenty-three state election districts.

combined into one overall bill, and it passed both houses, but has not yet been signed into law.

When the legislature reconvened in January 1992, several amendments to the Life Prolonging Procedures Act were offered and it was hoped that positive action could be taken on the revised bill before the legislature adjourned on March 15, 1992. The amendments were aimed at removing the current restrictions on artificial feeding, making it easier to withdraw such feeding under certain circumstances, along with a new definition of the phrase "terminal condition." With a new governor, there was hope that passage could be achieved in 1992. The modified Florida bill setting out new rules for declining life-prolonging procedures and giving patients a broad choice in making advanced directives for health care finally passed the legislature and was signed into law by the new governor, Lawton Chiles, on April 10.

The new law, called "Health Care Advance Directives," gives patients the right to refuse unwanted medical treatment and the power to exercise such rights through a surrogate or proxy if the patient becomes mentally incompetent. The changes ensure the constitutional rights of the terminally ill to choose the time and manner of death while setting out rules to protect health care providers from unwarranted legal liability.

The new law defines and modifies some key terms and provisions. For example, "terminal condition" is defined as a persistent vegetative state in which the brain no longer functions (whether conscious or unconscious); the understanding of "life prolonging procedures" was revised to include nutrition and hydration feeding tubes; "emergency services" (911) will recognize and abide by "do not resuscitate" [DNR] directives; "the powers of the surrogate" include the authority to direct the withholding or withdrawing of life-prolonging procedures (unless the designation limits the authority of the surrogate), and they ensure that the surrogate is satisfied that the patient is terminal before making a final decision to recommend life-ending procedures. The law also allows the transference of the terminally ill patient to another health-care provider after seven days, if the first provider remains unwilling to carry out the patient's wishes.

All of these provisions, taken together, make the new Florida law one of the most advanced in the nation. However, it did not take the final step, to legalize doctor-assisted suicide, which was embodied in the California initiative.

New Hampshire

This state's bill would enable a mentally competent adult to obtain a lethal dose of prescription medicine from an attending physician and thus to control the time, place, and manner of death. The final decision to provide the lethal prescription would be made by both the attending and consulting physicians, along with a medical ethics committee. This joint group would first consider the nature and progress of the specific disease as well as the current physical and mental state of the patient. Prior history of mental illness, depression, or other influencing factors would also be considered. Other key issues such as immunity from prosecution for the physician, the nonobligatory status of the physician (allowing him to withdraw from the case if his conscience so dictates), and punishment for those who alter a patient's request are also included in the proposed bill to help forestall the dreaded malpractice suits. The vote on this comprehensive legislation was postponed on March 4, 1992, and it was sent back to committee for more study.

Iowa

This state's proposed bill describes the main issues in more general terms that leave open the possibility of future abuse. Although it requires that the patient be mentally competent (as the New Hampshire bill does), it has no provision for psychological evaluation when a patient requests aid in dying. It also does not make clear whether or not the physician would administer a lethal dose of drugs or merely provide the patient with the means by which the patient could end his or her life. The bill is careful to say, however, that anyone who works against the intent of the patient would be punished. But it does not have a penalty for people who coerce patients into signing a declaration for aid in dying.

Maine

The proposed bill in this state is also comprehensive and contains strong safeguards against abuses. There are penalties for noncompliance with the declaration, ranging from the failure to transfer a patient to another physician if the attending physician objects to aid in dying, to fraudulently inducing an individual to execute a declaration or forging a declaration.

But like Iowa's bill, this one is unclear about whether a medically assisted death includes injections or other invasive procedures by doctors or whether the physician needs only to provide a prescription. The definition of a medically competent person is also quite vague. Although the bill does specify that someone in a persistent vegetative state is ineligible, it does not make clear whether a person's psychological state should be taken into consideration. However, it does stipulate that the patient must be subjected to a thorough exam by two doctors. The medically assisted death is guaranteed to be humane, dignified, and painless.

Michigan

The proposed Michigan bill specifies that important conditions must be met before any aid-in-dying, particularly by intravenous injection, is carried out. These unique conditions work to protect both patient and doctor.

For example, each communication regarding the execution of the directive must be both videotaped and witnessed by two people, and the implementation of the directive must be videotaped as well. There is also a minimum sixty-day "cooling off" period between the time the directive is made and the time the doctor administers the fatal injection. The patient must also reaffirm at least twice, after each thirty-day period, that the directive still represents his or her real wishes. Finally, the bill requires mandatory counselling by both the attending physician and a social worker about all physical, emotional, and psychological issues surrounding the euthanasia procedures. The emphasis appears to be on a well informed, clearcut decision by the patient that will be respected by health-care providers, physicians, and insurance companies.

By early 1993, the bill had yet to come to a vote in the legislature.

A Post-#119 Victory in Washington

In mid-1991, a little noticed bill, HB #1481, was quietly introduced in the Washington State legislature (which had approved two of the three proposals of Initiative #119), but it was overshadowed by the publicity surrounding the "death with dignity" initiative. Its chief sponsor was Representative Fred May, a Republican from Mercer Island, Washington, and it stipulated that artificially supplied food and water would now be included under the definition of life-support machines in living wills that refused the use of life-support machines.

The second part of May's so called "Feeding Tubes Bill" would allow patients in irreversible comas or lying in a persistent vegetative state to be taken off life-support systems if they had previously requested this action in a living will. (Under the Natural Death Act of 1979, such supports could be removed only if death was "imminent," which was usually a judgment made by those who may not be in agreement with what the unconscious patient would have wished.) The third part of #119, authorizing the legalization of doctor-assisted-suicide, was left out of May's bill, however.

The bill passed the Democratically controlled house on February 13, 1992, by an overwhelming 82-14 vote and then moved to the Republican controlled Senate, where pro-life forces opposed the bill. Several Republican Senators, with the support of those who helped kill the #119 Initiative, spoke against the bill, saying that "artificial nutrition and hydration were basic necessities, and that people in comas sometimes wake up." But when certain religious groups withdrew their former opposition to the withdrawal of feeding tubes, the chance for final passage in the Senate brightened. That "miracle" occurred in mid-March 1992, when the Senate passed the House bill, and Governor Booth Gardner signed the legislation into law on April 1, 1992.

Washington was thus the first state in the country to enact a living-will law with these provisions. Although "passive" euthanasia was now legal in Washington, making "active euthanasia" part of the law would have to wait.

A Strong Motivating Factor:
Higher and Higher Hospital Costs

In addition to the political, medical, psychological, religious, and social ramifications of the drive to legalize doctor-assisted suicide in America, there are also *economic* factors to be considered. Increasingly high hospital and nursing-home costs, which can quickly bankrupt families with a loved one who is terminally ill on life support, have become an important consideration in the campaign for passage of this legislation. No American family wants to experience a situation comparable to the Nancy Cruzan case, in which medical expenses (not covered by insurance) can easily top $100,000 a year.

Economic considerations may also be motivating a part of the opposition forces against aid-in-dying, particularly the older members of the AMA power structure. However, younger doctors around the country have been showing signs of standing up to their elders in the profession. They can live without the high fees charged by some doctors to attend terminally ill patients. Furthermore, most hospital administrators have silently backed up the AMA, because they are profiting greatly ($500 to $1000 a day) from such patients, who require little personal care other than checking pulse rates regularly and ensuring that the nutrients in the IV bottles are full and that the respirators are working.

This is one of the prime reasons why Derek Humphry believes that the issue of voluntary euthanasia will be settled in the decade of the 1990s, not just in America but in the Western world. "The Netherlands already has it sanctioned by the courts," he pointed out in a recent speech, "but it has not yet been codified by statute law. In Britain, over 190 members of Parliament have signed a petition calling for it, and there is a similar voluntary euthanasia bill now in front of the French Parliament awaiting action" (Humphry, November 15, 1991).

Will the Medical Profession Wake Up Soon?

Rufus Miles, the former Assistant Secretary of Health, Education and Welfare in the 1980s and later a Senior Fellow at the Woodrow Wilson School of Princeton University, wrote about his personal enemies in a letter published in the June 1990 *New York Times* (Miles 1990). He said he was "deeply concerned about the tremendous lag in thinking about compassionate treatment for terminally ill patients, both on the part of the medical profession and the public." He stated that he was asked years ago by his wife—a victim of Alzheimer's disease—to help her find a way to end her life quickly and painlessly. He was not able to help her, and has felt a strong sense of responsibility about this. He wanted to tell his side of the story.

His late wife first showed signs of the Alzheimer's symptoms back in 1975 when she was sixty-six years old. Within two years she reached a stage when she was already very ill yet still able to make a rational and informed judgment about her future. A year later he wrote:

[She could] no longer make any judgment at all. She spent much of the last 5 years of her 14-year bout with Alzheimer's in a nursing home as a near vegetable. Her death, at 80, in December 1989, was a very delayed blessing, in contrast to the painless and pleasant death of Janet Adkins, just as she wanted it, a death with dignity.

Mr. Miles also made this important alternative point:

We abolished slavery less than a century and a half ago. Through constitutional and legislative change, we have made substantial progress in treating people of all races, people with mental and physical handicaps, more understandably and compassionately. It is now time that we permit voluntary ending of life by people who have had good, happy lives—or extremely unhappy lives—and who now have bleak prospects of the future. (Miles 1990)

Part V: A Question of Morality

ELEGY AT A BROTHER'S BEDSIDE

Like the hawks he knew as a boy
    His spirit swooped and soared here.
Now crushed, we see him supine,
    his face fixed in an empty gaze.

Our vigil is to no avail
    The wit is gone which
    sped the dance of laughter,
Gone the lambent lacework
    of the mind.

What savage civility impells us
    to prolong "life"—
When the fight for life is over?
When will we allow loving hands
    to close lives that have closed?

—Stewart Udall, former Secretary of the Interior
    (read during the March 1991
    National Health Care Protest march in
    Washington, D.C., in tribute to his dying brother,
    Representative Morris "Mo" Udall [Dem., Okla.],
    who was permanently disabled by
    Parkinson's Disease)

17

Abortion and Assisted Death*

Rape and incest are tragedies, but why visit on the second victim,
the unborn child . . . capital punishment?
                    —Illinois Republican Congressman Henry Hyde, 1990

At first glance there would appear to be only a tenuous link between
abortion and euthanasia. But on closer inspection there are certain moral
and legal dilemmas common to the death of a live embryo still in the
womb and the death of a comatose, incurable elderly patient lying
confined to a bed. An examination of the circumstances surrounding
both situations shows a number of parallels often overlooked by social
observers.

One significant parallel is that in both situations aid-in-dying is
provided by a doctor within a carefully defined legal framework. Doctor-
assisted suicide is supported by a living will and an abortion—a doctor-
assisted death of the fetus—is performed at the will of the mother-
to-be, with the support of the language of *Roe* v. *Wade*. A second
parallel is the quality-of-life issue. The right of the pregnant woman
in the first trimester to make a self-determination to end a second life

---

*The National Hemlock Society has made no policy decisions to date regarding any link
between abortion and doctor-assisted suicide of the fetus in a pregnant woman in any of the
three trimesters of pregnancy. The views expressed in this chapter are those of the author exclusively
and do not reflect those of any official spokesperson of the Hemlock Society USA.

emanating from her body can be justified morally on the grounds of maintaining the quality of her life, both mentally and physically. The decision to abort a deformed fetus in a later trimester can also be defended based on the lack of quality of the prospective life of the child. By the same token, the choice of ending the life of a suffering terminal patient may be based on the miserable quality of the patient's life.

The Supreme Court and the lower state courts seem to recognize some constitutional connection between the two controversial issues of abortion and aid-in-dying. For example, although the Cruzan case had reached the high court in May 1989, the justices waited until after the latest (Webster, Missouri) abortion decision on July 3, 1989, to announce that it would hear the euthanasia case, along with three new abortion cases, during the next term, beginning in October. That seemingly co-incidental case announcement was in itself an important link.

At the state level, there also appears to be some judicial connection of the two issues. State courts have sought to balance the state's interest in preserving life against the individual's right of free choice, which can be applied to either the right to die or the right to choose abortion.

Finally, in terms of technology, modern methods of safe, sterile, nonviolent abortions (i.e., the use of the suction tube technique) are paralleled by the semi-painless procedures involved in doctor-assisted suicide. The two contemporary methodologies are in stark contrast to the violent, old fashioned methods: using coathangers to perform back-alley abortions, or committing suicide by jumping off a bridge or taking a cyanide pill.

What America Thinks about Abortion

In 1990, both the Gallup and Harris polls independently found that 73 percent of Americans were in favor of abortion rights, but 77 percent also regarded abortion as a kind of killing. A minority of 49 percent saw the "killing" as outright "murder," while a smaller minority of 28 percent saw it as the "taking of a human life." These extreme views depended on whether a citizen was pro-life or pro-choice, and whether one viewed the issue as involving the rights of *one* individual or *two* individuals. This apparent dichotomy of opinion has led to divisiveness over whether the Supreme Court will abandon *Roe* v. *Wade,* with dire predictions of the consequences for American society if such an event occurs.

Linking Euthanasia and Abortion in the National Religious and Political Debate

Mary Senander, a speaker at an anti-abortion convention held in Chicago at the end of July 1990, invoked a familiar refrain. She condemned the "taking of innocent human life" and urged a passionate bipartisan battle against what she said history would record as the "most horrible story of the twentieth century."

But Ms. Senander was not talking about abortion. Her clarion call was meant to rally opposition in America against the growing notion of the "right to die." She represents the beginning of a new coalition of opponents of both abortion and euthanasia who wish to forge interlocking connections between the twin campaigns, at both state and federal levels, in order to create one coordinated effort to prevent the spread and legitimization of the right to an abortion and the right to die.

The basic philosophy of these two groups is that "life, no matter what its condition, is 'sacred.' " Mrs. Senander, a spokesperson for the International Anti-Euthanasia Task Force (IATF), a three-year-old umbrella organization based in Steubenville, Ohio, said: "Those of us in the pro-life movement are called to a second, the right-to-die movement. We are called once more to defend a group of vulnerable people." She and her cohorts are attempting to pour more gasoline on the fire of individual rights, to further polarize American politics regarding these now-linked issues. The new twist in their efforts is to get involved in the public debate over when a patient's life sustaining treatment should be ended (Suro 1990).

Doron Weber, a spokesperson for the Society for the Right to Die, commented on the Senander "declaration of war" on behalf of the opposition IATF: "The pro-life groups are very well organized. And they seem to exercise a disproportionate amount of power." (Backed by the long-armed tentacles of the Roman Catholic Church hierarchy, the IATF, as a front group, has the capacity to exert strong armed, political muscle in the halls of the fifty state legislatures and Congress.)

The opposition to both abortion and the right to die has argued that withdrawing a feeding tube or performing an abortion unjustly bestows the power to take another's life and that the government at all levels should uphold that belief. Although legal experts have pointed out that there is no direct legal link—as yet—between laws governing abortion and the withdrawal of medical life support, there are some implied connections. Geoffrey K. Stone, the Dean of the University of Chicago Law School, noted:

> In an indirect sense, the Supreme Court's recognition of a right to die legitimates *Roe* v. *Wade*. Neither of them are enumerated rights in the Constitution, unlike, say free speech. Rather, they are protected by the guarantee of privacy. So for those who want to see *Roe* v. *Wade* overturned, the last thing you'd want to see is the court creating or recognizing the right to die.
>
> This also highlights the extent to which the sanctity of the human life issue really has religious roots. It's not only a matter of protecting human life against murder, as these groups would consider abortion. It's also protecting human life against the will of the person who no longer wishes to have that life. (Lewin, June 20, 1991)

Clearly, the continuing debate is caught in the cross-currents of many complex religious, ethical, moral, medical, and legal considerations regarding the delicate matters of life and death in our society.

The Far Right Speaks Out

Anti-abortion and anti-euthanasia groups have conceded that the growing popularity of living wills, along with highly publicized cases like Cruzan, have brought the death-with-dignity issue to public attention. But they are not ready to make any further concessions.

Following the decision in the Cruzan case, Dr. John Wilke, the president of the National Right to Life Committee based in Washington, issued the statement: "I'm sorry to see that our predictions are coming true—that abortion was just the beginning of the slippery slope of the death ethic." His group claims to have three thousand local chapters around the nation, which have been mainly involved in fighting abortion clinics and the dismemberment of *Roe* v. *Wade*. But recently he has added euthanasia as a second enemy.

"You can expect the pro-life movement in the future to be speaking out more and more against forced starvation, and the other forms of euthanasia," commented Judie Brown, president of the American Life League, a national anti-abortion organization. Her group, based in Stafford, Virginia, claims 272,000 members and stresses religious themes.

Cardinal John O'Connor, bishop of the city of New York and chairman of the Roman Catholic Bishop's Pro-Life Committee, said in 1990 that his group's most recent meeting devoted "at least half of its time" to the moral questions raised by the withdrawal of feeding tubes in the Cruzan case. As of early 1993, the bishops had not yet taken a stand on the issue, although the church had not opposed the withdrawal of most life-support equipment, such as respirators for terminally ill patients. But most had opposed the withdrawal of intravenously fed nutrients (Goodman 1991).

Geraldine Ofteedahl, the head of the Right to Life State Committee of New York, opposed the recently enacted New York law allowing a competent person to designate a proxy to make health-care decisions in lieu of a living will. She said: "Just like abortion, this practice [of euthanasia] points to the devaluation of human life. One person should not make the judgment about another person's life."

A growing segment of the medical profession has allied itself with the anti-abortion movement and is quite vocal in its belief that all life is sacred. These doctors have formed the American Association of Pro-Life Obstetricians and Gynecologists, which numbers 650 members and is expanding fast. Most of them are of various fundamentalist Christian faiths, and many are located in rural areas which have few physicians. Thus, a farm woman can be denied any choice if there is only a single doctor in a rural area and his ideology is pro-life.

A Crossroad Looms on the Horizon

Abortion-rights and right-to-die proponents have now become aware of the barrier of absolutes hurled down by their opponents, who believe that taking life in any form—whether it be the life of a fetus or that of a terminally ill patient—is murder. Just as there have been challenges to *Roe* v. *Wade,* there will probably also be attempts to contest the Cruzan ruling.

Are Late Abortions Always "Murder"?

Although the Supreme Court sanctioned first trimester abortions in *Roe* v. *Wade* back in 1973, the technology and circumstances have changed radically in the ensuing nineteen years, and now a new look must be given to the morality of late mid-trimester and even final trimester abortions under certain circumstances.

A case in point involved a female lawyer who became pregnant, carried the fetus into the third trimester, and then discovered that the fetus had stumps for arms and legs, and possible brain damage. She and her husband agonized for a long period over whether to have an abortion, and she finally decided to terminate her pregnancy.

But when she informed her obstetrician of her decision, he was taken aback and informed her that her pregnancy was so far advanced that no one in the country would help her fulfill her desire. But he was wrong. She eventually found three doctors practicing at a Boulder, Colorado, abortion clinic who regularly abort severely deformed fetuses being carried by women in their last three months of pregnancy. (This is the delicate period at which a fetus can be expected to survive outside the womb after a premature or forced birth.)

With her mind made up, she flew to Boulder and had her abortion, saying later: "The point is, the technology has not gotten to the point where you can find out about the fetus. But the doctors say, 'Sorry, we'll tell you what's going to happen, but that's it.' To me, it's almost unconscionable" (*New York Times,* January 1992, p. 1).

The three doctors at the clinic, headed by Dr. Warren Hern, the director, all say that they are now doing more and more abortions in the third trimester as word spreads that they *can* and *will* do them. With the aid of sonograms, which doctors can suggest at any stage in the nine-month pregnancy cycle, the subtlest defects in fetuses can now be detected precisely. (A sonogram is a visual image produced by reflected sound waves in a diagnostic ultra-sound exam. The sonogram picture was developed in the late 1950s.) Each of the three obstetricians have done over a hundred abortions of this type, which are now legal in about half of the states. But most doctors in the country still simply refuse to do them at this stage for fear of malpractice suits.

To some people, Dr. Hern and the other two doctors—Dr. George Tiller, director of the Women's Health Care Services in Wichita, Kansas, and Dr. James McMahon, a clinic director in California—are "modern medical heroes" and their patients worthy of the deepest compassion. But others, including many who support abortion rights, feel that what they are doing is abhorrent and feel that such late abortions are akin to "murdering a child." The controversy over their practice of performing third-trimester abortions will continue as long as they remain open for business.

Pushing the Limits

Third-trimester abortions still remain highly unusual in the United States, representing just one-tenth of a percent of all the abortions done annually in this country. But because these near-term abortions push the limits of what many Americans are prepared to accept, they have brought into sharp focus serious questions of who should decide and how they should decide whether such abortions are morally permissible.

Although the Supreme Court ruled that the states could not restrict abortions in the first trimester in *Roe* v. *Wade* (1973), it did say that the states could prohibit abortions after the fetus was "viable," which has been interpreted to mean after the twenty-fourth week of pregnancy, except when the woman's life or health is endangered. Since the third trimester involves potentially viable fetuses, the great question then becomes: At what point, if any, do physicians and pregnant women believe that the fetus's right to life supersedes the right of the mother to decide if she wants to have the baby?

Doctors, like those in Boulder, who will perform third-trimester abortions admit that they are uncomfortable doing late abortions unless the fetus is abnormal or the woman's physical or mental health is endangered. They make their decisions, however, on a case-by-case basis and end up firmly on the side of the woman's right to decide for herself whether she wants to continue her pregnancy. They have established a set of informal guidelines, one of which is that the woman, and not the fetus, is their patient. Dr. Hern is adamant that it is up to the woman to decide whether to give birth, or not, to a child with medical problems. He says: "The idea that we have to salvage every individual no matter how impaired is really crazy. Some people feel that taking care of an impaired child is ennobling, and that is fine for them. But it's not for everybody. It's oppressive to say that everyone has to do this."

His colleague, Dr. Tiller, whose clinic was a target of anti-abortion protest in the summer of 1991, sees it as "a patient's rights issue, after you give women information about badly damaged babies [that they are carrying] late in the second trimester."

Dr. Hern acknowledged that this new procedure is a "very difficult area of medicine. You have to make a decision that's part ethical, part moral." He added that he would perform abortions on fetuses that have serious birth defects that are not necessarily lethal, including Downs syndrome and spina bifida, but that he would not perform them for "frivolous" reasons.

One of his patients was a twenty-nine-year-old woman who was told by her local doctor, based on a sonogram given at the end of the sixth month, that she was carrying a fetus with a huge tumor in its tailbone. If the tumor was benign, she was informed, it could be removed safely, but the baby would have no legs or buttocks. If it were malignant, the baby would die. After contacting twenty-five doctors, the woman and her husband got a reply from one doctor at 2 A.M., who gave them the name of Dr. Hern. She flew to Boulder and had an abortion, telling most friends and relatives that she had had a "miscarriage."

Another of Dr. Hern's patients discovered that her fetus had four holes in its heart, a missing kidney, a defective esophagus, and a cleft lip and palate. Her obstetrician warned her that it was not clear whether her baby would live, but that he would do his best to "patch him up." This frustrated woman was angry that "the medical profession leaves everyone high and dry. As parents you have no rights." Fortunately, she too heard about Dr. Hern after first frantically trying to induce a miscarriage by various means. But none of them worked, so she flew to Colorado and Dr. Hern terminated her pregnancy at eight months.

How It's Done

The technique used by the doctors at the Boulder abortion clinic is to inject the drug digoxin into the chest of the fetus to stop its heart from beating, which thus kills it. Then over a period of several days, the doctors gradually enlarge the cervix (the opening of the womb).

They perform this procedure by inserting sterilized seaweed suppositories, called laminaria, into the cervix, which then allows them to induce labor several days later. If this fails, they pull the intact fetus from the womb with forceps, or in some cases via dismemberment. According to Dr. McMahon, most embryologists claim that fetuses cannot feel pain until about thirty-two weeks into a pregnancy; but even if they could, they are so sedated by the medications given to the mother that they will not suffer.

Most of the women who go through these late abortions admit that the experiences are "devastating emotionally" and mark a "dark period of their lives." But most don't regret their decisions, knowing that if they bring a deformed baby into the world, that it would cast a shadow over both their waking lives for years to come.

The High Court Drops a Bombshell

On January 21, 1992, which ironically marked the eve of the nineteenth anniversary of the Supreme Court's landmark decision of *Roe* v. *Wade,* the high court announced that it would examine in its spring term the four abortion restrictions of the Pennsylvania Abortion Control Act, i.e., the *Planned Parenthood of Pennsylvania* v. *Casey* case. For twenty years, the Supreme Court's decision of *Roe* v. *Wade* has served as a partial, de facto substitute for the failed Equal Rights Amendment (ERA), which would have become the twenty-seventh Amendment to the Constitution had it passed. In this pinch-hitting role, *Roe* v. *Wade* has also served as a symbol of women's struggle for equal treatment as citizens until Congress, the White House, and/or the states recognize the remaining other sections of the ERA. But it is also a precursor of how we will finally deal with the right-to-die.

Roe Reaffirmed

In a surprising decision rendered on June 29, 1992, the U.S. Supreme Court backed the Constitutionality of the Pennsylvania Abortion Control Act by a seven to two vote, with the exception that the mother-to-be did not have to inform her husband. However, in a companion decision, a scant five-to-four majority of justices (Blackmun, O'Connor, Kennedy, Stevens, and Souter) voted to reaffirm Roe.

In a stinging rebuke to the minority, Justice Souter wrote that: "A decision to overrule Roe's essential holding under the existing circumstances would address error, if error there was, at the cost of both profound and unnecessary damage to the Court's legitimacy, and to the nation's commitment to the rule of law."

In reaffirming the heart of Roe and the women's right to choose at the beginning of life, there was a clear message in the wake of the Cruzan case that the citizen had a right to choose to die with dignity at the end of life. The parallel implications were obvious between the two cases.

One day in the not too distant future the highest court will be asked once again to reaffirm Cruzan on the right to die as it did in mid-1992 when it reaffirmed Roe after a nineteen-year test period.

18

The AIDS Factor

AIDS is a disease that for the most part can be controlled by individual behavior.
> —U.S. President George Bush at a White House
> News Conference (December 1991)

It is not a sin to die of AIDS, but it is to use condoms. It is more important to save the soul than the body.
> —Luis Cardinal Aponte Martinez, Roman Catholic
> Archbishop of San Juan, Puerto Rico (1991)

Acquired Immune Deficiency Syndrome (AIDS) continues to be an incurable, fast-spreading disease, which has expanded in the past five years to major epidemic proportions in many parts of the world. With the spread of the disease, the Hemlock Society has witnessed a change in its enrollment. Derek Humphry acknowledges that the tragedy of the AIDS epidemic has had an impact on Hemlock:

> It has been a boon to us, bringing many more young people into the movement. AIDS has changed the face of our organization. Up to 1984–85, we were predominantly an organization of elderly, gray-haired ladies.
>
> We don't ask people who come to us for help what they are dying of. That would be snooping. (Jamison 1992)

Humphry welcomes the infusion of AIDS and HIV-positive patients into the organization, because he feels they can make a positive contribution to the movement.

At the September 1991 meeting of the Hemlock Society chapter in San Diego, three professionals from the Owen Clinic at the University of California at San Diego (UCSD) came to share their experiences with AIDS with an overflow audience of 250. The most touching comments came from Dean Thomas, a Hemlock Support Group member, who described his five-year battle with AIDS. Because of the advanced state of his disease, and its psychological, social, and physical effects, Dean felt that self-deliverance was his most viable option. He shared his thoughts on a recent suicide attempt that failed.

Dr. Chris Matthews, the director of the Owen Clinic, an official UCSD AIDS treatment center where he has been dealing professionally with AIDS patients for ten years, described vividly how his clinic "had witnessed 90 deaths during the first three quarters of 1991 . . . of which at least 10 were suicides." So the direct link between Hemlock and AIDS victims was starkly dramatized by these statistics, which must have parallels in other clinics throughout the country.

How AIDS Groups Can Help Hemlock (and Vice Versa)

In many respects, AIDS-counselling organizations are way ahead of right-to-die organizations in their operations. They have better computerized libraries and information networks to assist their clients. In Philadelphia the Action AIDS organization (which has local, state, and federal funding) has the largest AIDS library in the country, including over 60,000 computerized entries consisting of case studies, articles, alternative treatments, procedures, and drugs. Such references provide an important bridge between Western and Eastern medical practices.

Kevin Burns, a Case Management Coordinator in the Philadelphia Action AIDS organization, points out that before the spread of the disease, most HIV-positive or full-blown AIDS pattients in the United States were not aware of the variety of techniques that can help to alleviate the suffering of those afflicted with the disease:

Before AIDS became an epidemic, AIDS doctors did not offer diet alternatives to their patients to try to stem the disease. . . . Most did not recommend acupuncture, an Oriental therapeutic/medical practice, which we know has been helpful to assist AIDS patients suffering from neuropathy [the sensation of pins and needles in the legs, arms, hands, and feet, in which feeling is lost in the extremities]. Massage is another technique, which we have found from experience gives relief to AIDS patients. (Burns 1991)

Right-to-Die groups can benefit from the social-service network that AIDS groups have perfected. AIDS counsellors have been trained in the correct amount of lethal drug doses that they can recommend to their clients who have descended into a terminal stage. Since many doctors presently do *not* know the amount of drugs to prescribe to end a patient's life (witness the Humphry and Rosier cases), the research that AIDS counsellors have accumulated on this touchy subject can be most helpful to patients as well as physicians.

Is the ACT-UP Approach the Answer for Right-to-Die Forces?

AIDS groups, through their activist lobbying organizations like the five-year-old ACT-UP (AIDS Coalition to Unleash Power), are far in front of right-to-die organizations in their lobbying, in the art of mounting effective public protest demonstrations, and in obtaining grassroots support for their cause.*

A national network of ACT-UP is already in place in every major city in the country and is able—if asked—to assist right-to-die groups in organizing, fund-raising, lobbying, and education. ACT-UP groups currently help Planned Parenthood, the Campaign for Human Rights, and other groups who are like-minded on the right of privacy and choice. Action AIDS and ACT-UP have found that working alone is not half as successful as the power of joining forces in coalition with other groups who can then outnumber the right-to-life forces, which are older and better financed.

---

*To some observers, if the Initiative #119 forces in Washington had obtained the help of ACT-UP in that state in organizing a more potent educational campaign to pass the proposal, they might have won a great victory instead of losing by a small plurality of votes.

Coming to Terms with Death from AIDS

Because AIDS is still incurable and largely untreatable, AIDS patients are forced to face the realities of dying and the issues surrounding the dying process. Kevin Burns, of the Philadelphia Action AIDS organization, describes the various forms of the terminal illness:

> Terminally ill AIDS patients have different symptoms in each individual case. Some fall into a coma, while others become bedridden and incontinent, requiring round-the-clock custodial care. Some keep most of their mental capacities to the end, while others lose theirs gradually, like Alzheimer's patients. Some are unable to eat, and must be fed with tubes intravenously. Most need medications of one or more drugs to keep them from suffering major pain. Some AIDS patients resist medication and sedatives at the end, since they want to remain alert and be with their loved ones in a conscious state whether they be a homo- or heterosexual by choice. (Burns 1991)

Burns, who is a social worker, points out that the Code of Ethics of the National Council of Social Workers, stresses a commitment to the self-determination of all their patients, whether they are AIDS victims or terminally ill older citizens. "That is why, many of us try to become aware, that when an incurable AIDS client has a living will, which identifies a lover or family member important in his or her life, we then find at least two doctors who will be willing to recommend making the final determination in the case," he says.

Psychologist Stephen Levine's book *Healing into Life and Death* (New York, 1986) has helped AIDS victims to cope with living with a terminal illness and dealing with an early death. He points out that we can resolve our fear of death by deepening our understanding of healing, including forgiveness to better prepare ourselves for death when it comes.

He tells a story of a man with AIDS named Bill, who had been feeling so judged, mistreated, and in so much pain that he was envious of people in his discussion group who "only had cancer." To Bill, these people didn't have to suffer from the subtle and not-so-subtle messages that "you have made your bed, now go lie in it." He was also feeling embarrassed and ashamed because there were visible signs of illness showing on his body. During a meditation retreat with others, he began to understand the process of sending love and kindness into his illness, after which he went through a final period of near ecstasy, when all kinds of old angers and judgments fell away, despite periods of depression. Shortly before his death, however, Bill described the remarkable sense of being healed:

> For many months, my idea of healing was that of curing my body. I gave it my best shot and I am proud of the fact . . . but then I reached a point where I recognized the need to accept my own impending death. . . . Among other things, I realized that self-compassion meant feeling in my heart that even physical death was not a sign of weakness and failure. This seems to be the ultimate act of self-acceptance. I thank God for it. . . .
>
> Soon my body will drop away from me like a cocoon and my spirit will fly like a butterfly—beautiful and perfect. I don't claim to know exactly where it is that I am going, but my heart tells me it is filled with light and love. An open heart is a much greater blessing than death is a tragedy. Let us all take comfort in this knowledge. (Levine 1986)

Bill's passing was truly a "death with dignity."

AIDS and Euthanasia

Anna Forbes, the director of Community Relations for Action AIDS—an organization that provides direct services for people living with AIDS, their families, and loved ones—confessed that AIDS has forced counselors to deal with the concept of death among young people because of the short projected life span for those contracting the disease.

> We're talking about choosing death or not choosing death at a point when the person's still early in life and clinging to the feeling that something good will happen. My guess would be that there's a much greater understanding of euthanasia here and sympathy for why someone would make that decision than there might be in other settings, because all of us have seen what the endstages of AIDS looks like. (AIDS Action Network 1987)

Forbes and others involved with counseling AIDS patients have discovered that most of them tend to be at greatest risk of suicide between the time they test positive and the time they become symptomatic, when the fear of pain is greatest.

Dr. Dan Estes, a gay psychotherapist who has tested HIV positive and counsels dozens of AIDS patients in his work, has noted that the suicide rate among HIV-positive people is sixty times the rate of non-HIV-positive populations in our culture, and more than thirty times the rate of those diagnosed with some form of terminal cancer:

> The reason is multifaceted. There is a stigma that comes with having an HIV diagnosis, of being an "AIDS" victim. There is social pressure, work pressure, financial pressure. Will your family hate you? Will you be fired from your job? Will you lose your housing? Will you be able to go to a restaurant and be served? Will your friends desert you? (Estes 1991)

Fear, anxiety, and depression are never reasons for suicide, in Estes' opinion. "The only reason to commit suicide for me," he says, "would be the expectation of death soon, with protracted pain and suffering and greatly diminished quality of life."

Although he is bound by professional ethics always to counsel against suicide, he personally espouses the philosophy of "self-deliverance" for himself: he keeps "a 'suicide kit' and in that 'suicide kit' I have the means that would deliver me from suffering."

Dr. Benjamin Verdile, a retired New Jersey supervising school principle, who was HIV positive, points out that the gay community had a suicide-prevention counseling program in operation (similar to abortion-counseling programs for pregnant women), but local religious forces undermined their efforts and funding to expand and legitimize this constructive program.

> [They] won't let us gays go to our deaths with dignity. The Christian power structure won't allow us to do preventive counselling in the gay and lesbian communities. Furthermore, the federal government suppressed a recent medical research report conducted by Dr. Louis Sullivan, the Secretary of Health and Human Services, on the high suicide rates among our teens. His 1989 report's statistics showed that

over 30 percent of teen suicides are performed by gay and lesbian youths. (Verdile 1992)

(Verdile, a neighbor friend of the author, died of AIDS in mid-January 1993.)

The still controversial issue of euthanasia is now rapidly coming into focus as part of the complex AIDS dilemma facing the nation and the world. The escalating incidence of the disease and the lack of effective treatments suggest that more and more AIDS sufferers will consider euthanasia as a way of ending their pain.

The Real Truth About AIDS

Stephen Jamison, Ph.D., the regional director of the Hemlock Society in San Francisco, has recently conducted research into the AIDS epidemic with anonymity of interviewees guaranteed. He discovered that many physicians who treat AIDS patients do not fully investigate or even want to know the true cause of death. "I was told," he related, "that many deaths officially listed as AIDS were actually caused by a deliberate overdose or a combination of overdose and asphyxiation. In one instance, a mother told her son's doctor that he had taken his life. The doctor replied, 'You shouldn't have told me; I now have to report it.' " Jamison concludes that rational, assisted suicides are often inaccurately reported as "accidental overdoses."

Because the final stages of AIDS often consist of multiple, severely painful conditions, the use of morphine frequently comes into play. Says Jamison: "AIDS, more than any other disease, has led to widescale use of rational and assisted suicide as an accepted means of death for many victims." But heroin appears to be the preferred drug of self-deliverance in one part of the AIDS community, comprised of former IV drug users where more than 9000 documented AIDS deaths have occurred since July 1981. Several AIDS victims have also been taught how to use a painter's mask under a plastic bag to allow final asphyxiation when the time arrives to take one's life.

As one AIDS victim stated:

We think of birth as a miracle and we all want to be there, but we have looked at death as ugly and undignified. Death is honorable and holy and to be there, to support them emotionally by calming or reassuring them, to help physically with a hug or a back rub, or to assist them in dying by securing the means or by helping to administer the drugs—all of this is a gift. In this way, death is as holy as birth. (Jamison 1992)

AIDS may yet become the catalyst for America to do something positive to confront the whole comprehensive issue of death with dignity.

19

The Ethical-Medical Issue

Death is a great way of cutting expenses.

—Woody Allen

The Doctors' Dilemma

In a 1991 interview Dr. C. Everett Koop, the former Surgeon General of the Reagan administration (1981–89), expressed his worries about the surge of interest in physician-assisted suicide: "We are pulling the plug on a great medical history. If you ask your doctor to be both the killer and the healer, then when you get sick you won't know which doctor is approaching your bed." But Dr. Koop doesn't seem to understand that the long-held tenets of traditional medical ethics, based on the Hippocratic Oath, may no longer apply to the contemporary medical problems facing America and the world in the last decade of the twentieth century. The challenges of abortion, AIDS, and assisted death cry out for new ethical approaches.

The Ethics of the Right to Die

Dr. Frederick R. Abrams, associate director of the Center for Health Ethics and Policy at the University of Colorado's Graduate School of Public Affairs in Denver, has become a respected voice on the controversial issue of death with dignity. As the longtime chairman (1970–1990) of the ethics committee of the American College of Gynecologists, Abrams has spent the past two decades debating the pros and cons of this once back-burner medical issue, which is now moving into the public arena. Abrams is one of the handful of courageous doctors who have challenged the conservative position of the American Medical Association (AMA) on this topic, but he is extremely cognizant of the underlying doctors' mission to heal and preserve life. Instead of following the old version of the Golden Rule in practicing medicine, Abrams would follow a new version, i.e., "Do unto others what they would have you do unto them," which means simply keeping in mind their best interests and respecting the right of self-determination.

He is concerned about the theologians and doctors who believe in the "moral absolutes," i.e., that "all killing is immoral" and that "life is but a stewardship of God to supervise and dispose of as he sees fit" (Abrams 1991).

Today, according to Abrams, physicians have three alternatives if they are faced with a request to terminate the life of an incurable patient. They are: (1) do nothing; (2) order the tubes and respirators to be removed (a form of passive euthanasia); or (3) administer a lethal drug dose, either orally if the patient is conscious or intravenously if the patient is comatose. After telling the patient the alternatives, it must be the patient who does the final choosing, or loved ones with the aid of the living will, if it is available.

Dr. Abrams points out that if all terminal patients had equal and ready access to a lethal drug dosage, there would be no need for physicians to get involved with aid-in-dying. This would eliminate the dilemma that doctors currently face when an incurably ill patient is in their care. But "our society has checks and balances to restrict the dispensing of these potent drugs only to licensed medical doctors."

Medical research has shown us that there is little prospect for the discovery of a "magic bullet" to give us a "quick cure" for any of the diseases of the elderly. So, the initiative must always come from the patient alone, or collectively through the ballot. Once aid-in-dying is approved, rigid guidelines must be established to protect society from abuses. The medical profession in America is already worried about who will write the guidelines and close the loopholes once such an initiative becomes law. That is a challenge still to be overcome, and this is where the bioethicists enter the picture.

The philosophers and sociopsychologists who make up the core of this relatively new profession (the term *bioethics* entered the English language in 1971) are attempting to codify medical ethics and to help doctors make tough life and death decisions regarding their patients. When medical doctors found themselves embroiled in a quagmire of problems involving euthanasia, abortion, and the desires of terminally ill patients and loved ones, they were forced to turn to people outside their profession for help. Most physicians are not trained in medical schools in how to differentiate what is and is not "ethically correct," particularly in regard to the issue of pain and the quality of life; yet until recently, most hospitals were adamant in the belief that *only* physicians should be a party to medical discussions about ethics. But now there appears to be a new realization on the part of doctors that bioethicists can help them with the dilemmas posed by advancing technology. For example, Dr. Mark Seigler, the director of the Center for Clinical Medical Ethics at the University of Chicago's Hospital, regularly invites professional ethicists and philosophers to meet with his staff on life and death problems involving the choices of the hospital's patients.

The Intrusion of Technology in Life and Death Decisions

By 1990, the American Hospital Association has estimated, 70 percent of the 6,000 deaths that occurred in the United States each day were already somehow timed or negotiated; i.e., medical technology was either not applied at all or was withdrawn. For instance, every year some 12,000 of the 80,000 patients on artificial kidney machines voluntarily quit, thus ensuring a self-determined death through passive-euthanasia within two weeks.

Our need to come to grips with technology's advances and to decide if and when it is to be used or discontinued will only grow more acute in the future. Expensive new technology continues to evolve and come into wide use. "They're developing an artificial liver machine," said Arthur Caplan, the director of the Center of Biomedical Ethics at the University of Minnesota. "There's a sophisticated new respirator for infants in the pipeline. The possibilities are endless. *But no one is writing the rules* [emphasis added]."

This unsolved, national medical and ethical dilemma has frightened both families with loved ones on the brink of death and doctors who may lose their licenses to practice because of the failure of state legislatures to legalize doctor-assisted suicide. While people have the right to do everything to prolong their own lives as long as possible, the question has arisen: Does society have the obligation to pay for all the costs— as Missouri did during the last four years of Nancy Cruzan's life?

Is a "Good Death" Possible

In a penetrating essay in the March 1989 issue of the *New England Journal of Medicine* (NEJM), several physicians explored the question: "Is there such a thing as a good death?" Their analysis showed:

> The concept of a "good death" does not mean simply the withholding of technological treatments that would serve only to prolong the act of dying. A good death requires the art of deliberately creating an environment that allows a peaceful death. This involves a level of care that optimizes comfort and dignity. This may involve increasing the dosage of narcotics to whatever level is needed to negate pain even though such medication may contribute to the dulling of consciousness or even death, providing the goal of the physician is to relieve suffering. ("Sounding Board" 1989)

The physicians in the NEJM piece also attempted to define that "fine line" between using all possible means to sustain a dying person's life and just providing comfort while nature takes its course. The summary of a reasonable objective and ethical approach concludes:

> One of the basic ethical assumptions upon which medicine and efforts to nurse and feed people is based, is that life should be prolonged

because living enables us to pursue the purpose of life, but does that obligation ever cease?

Clearly it would cease if prolonging life does not contribute to striving for the purpose of life. If efforts to prolong life are useless or result in a severe burden for the patient insofar as pursuing the purpose of life is concerned, then the ethical obligation to prolong life is no longer present and life prolonging therapy becomes useless.

Based on the above criteria, there is a reasonable expectation that most physicians can make an objective decision whether or not to treat the patient.

Unless those doctors, theologians, and others who oppose euthanasia can show that human suffering has some deep meaning that transcends its endurance and that it has a *moral* good, as some have claimed, then it is nothing but cruelty to impose their beliefs on suffering patients. But up until now those who believe in the positive aspects of the "theology of suffering" have been in the driver's seat in our culture.

The modern dilemma of finding the dividing line between prolonging suffering through technology and allowing patients to die is like the question posed by Herman Melville in his novel *Billy Budd:* "Who can draw the line in viewing a rainbow as to where the purple tint ends and the orange tint begins?" In a democracy, can the common sense of the majority outweigh the religious taboos of a powerful minority? Before assisted suicide is condoned or even considered, it will be necessary for society to make these delicate distinctions.

The Mounting Pocketbook Issue

Many doctors are now quietly recognizing that the prospect of keeping incurable patients alive at a cost of $50,000 to $150,000 a year is wrong, particularly when it is known that Medicare and most private medical insurance plans do not cover such patients after sixty days in a hospital or a nursing home. This escalation to bankruptcy in numerous families of terminally ill patients, many of whom have some form of cancer (which now afflicts one out of three Americans), is a specter that haunts both the medical profession and the people at large.

Rational decision making is required to avoid turning the tragedy of a dying loved one into a catastrophe. A case in point involved the Reverend Clair Frederick Yohe, a retired eighty-seven-year-old Methodist minister, who was involved in a life-threatening automobile accident. His right leg, pelvis, and ribs were injured and he also suffered from a collapsed lung and lacerated internal organs. His wife, Louise, eighty-one, had also been seriously injured. At his advanced age and with so many injuries, the doctors knew that the minister had a scant chance of surviving. Yet, they had the best of modern high-tech devices at their disposal and in theory, all of the injuries could be repaired. "But theoretically everything is reversible," said Dr. W. Fein, the attending surgeon, "so we just trudge along and see what happens."

After two weeks, Rev. Yohe was still hanging in there and being wheeled daily into a special room for daily orthopedic procedures. But his long-term prognosis was exceedingly slim, according to his doctor. A week later, his liver and kidneys declined under the cumulative strain, even though his lungs had recovered, despite three complete blood transfusions. Hospital infections then started to set in to his injury-wracked body. Rev. Yohe's doctor reluctantly informed Mrs. Yohe how ill her husband was, but said that he could be kept alive longer on a dialysis machine.

She decided against this option: "No, we don't want that. We had decided a long time ago that neither of us wanted to be on life support." She had to sign a special form that allowed the doctors to discontinue any further extraordinary measures to keep him alive. "That was very hard," she said. Mrs. Yohe made the decision for her husband, which ultimately saved the family thousands of dollars in needless medical care and her husband pointless suffering.

"I wasn't surprised," Louise said later, "when the doctor came into my room on the 28th day [while she was in another room at the hospital on physical therapy] and told me that 'he just went to sleep.' "

Dr. Thomas Smith, chief of Albany's medical intensive care unit, commented on this and similar cases: "Doctors can't decide these things. *Society has to tell us what to do* [emphasis added]." But society has not been ready—so far—to signal this change through their fifty state legislatures or through Congress.

A Florida Nightmare: An Abuse of a Patient's Rights

Sometimes the arrogance of the medical profession knows no bounds and tramples over a patient's rights. Nan Billings, the president of the Suncoast Hemlock Society in Florida, has related this bizarre story about one of her constituents. It reflects the conservatism on the part of a member of the medical profession, who seemed to show little concern for his patient's medical rights (Billings 1992):

> Ann S., an attractive middle-aged widow, living in Lake County [Fla.] had long suffered from emphysema, bronchial asthma, and a mild nervous disorder. Like many of us, she had discovered some medicines to be more effective than others and wanted to be an active participant in her own medical care.
>
> Recently, when Ann found herself considerably on edge, she recalled going to see Dr. C. five years ago and that he had helped her then. She had not gone to him since then because he had relocated to another town. However, she felt he could help her again with what she considered to be a problem of "chemical imbalance" combined with trouble sleeping.
>
> During the course of her fifteen minute interview with Dr. C., she mentioned the names of several medications such as Seconal. She felt this might overcome the bad effects of the Prednisone she was taking. He asked her where she had learned of these medications, and she told him from reading *Final Exit*. He then told her he thought she was "suicidal." She pointed out that she wouldn't be worrying about the side-effects of her medications if she were. After paying her $35 bill for the consultation, she returned home.
>
> Later that day, a deputy sheriff visited her at home, having been told by the doctor that she was "suicidal." After she told her story to the officer, he finally left, saying that the incident "appeared to be a misunderstanding."
>
> Some time later, the deputy returned with his supervisor and they both announced that Ann must go to the mental hospital with them. If she did not go voluntarily, she was told she would be handcuffed. They refused to show her any commitment papers, but she was reassured that it was a formality and that she would be released in short order. After a long wait at the hospital, she was interviewed by a counselor who also felt that there had been a misunderstanding. Two phone calls were immediately put through to Dr. C., but he did not return the calls.

What followed became a nightmare for Ann. She was denied the right to call another physician or lawyer. "It felt worse than jail!" she said later. She was not allowed to have any visitors. Finally after two days of incarceration, she was released, followed by a hospital bill for $1600!

It seems incredible to believe that a commitment to an area mental hospital was made by a doctor who failed to consult earlier records of his former patient, failed to consult another physician, and then interviewed her for only fifteen minutes. His diagnosis, apparently based on an allusion to the book his patient claimed to have read, appears to be both laughable and unprofessional, to say the least. Ann's case should serve as a warning to other senior citizens who may become victims of charlatans masquerading behind the guise of a doctor's certificate.

The Dilemma of Dying in a High-Tech Age

Four hundred years ago, the French skeptic and essayist Montaigne wrote: "If you do not know how to die, don't worry; nature herself will teach you in the proper time; she will discharge that work for you; don't trouble yourself." Without question Montaigne's advice of "not to worry" was both sage and sensible at a time when people died of contagious diseases, like tuberculosis, and the Black Plague, famine, and other natural catastrophes over which humans had little or no control. But with modern advances in technology and medical research, man can now interfere with nature to the point that he no longer needs to wait for nature to take her course.

The late Dr. Joseph Fletcher, ethicist, moral theologian, and professor of Theological Ethics at the Episcopal Theological Seminary in Cambridge, Massachusetts, wrote a pioneering and prescient article in *Harpers* back in the fifties called "The Patient's Right to Die." In this seminal effort to address what was then the beginning of a growing public concern over the dilemma of active and passive euthanasia, Dr. Fletcher wrote,

> Death control like birth control is a matter of human dignity. Without it persons become puppets. . . . Some claim to see a moral difference,

between deciding to end a life by deliberately doing something and deciding to end a life by deliberately not doing something. . . . What, morally, is the difference between doing nothing to keep [a] patient alive and [giving] a fatal dose of a pain killing or other lethal drug? The intention is the same either way. A decision not to keep a patient alive is as morally deliberate as a decision to [actively] end a life. (Nichols 1991)

In the present age, we have made little progress in making moral deliberations that are in the patient's best interest, as the following shows.

Have We Lost Our Humanity? A Doctor's Dilemma

In a September 7, 1992, column in *Newsweek* titled "We Have Lost Our Humanity," Dr. Sam Brody, a Long Island, N.Y., physician, described a visit with a nurse to see an eighty-year-old Alzheimer's patient in his hospital. The nurse informed him before entering the patient's room that the patient was a "DNR" (Do Not Resuscitate) and that she "came that way from the nursing home." Dr. Brody guessed that "the patient's family, with the advice of the doctor at the nursing home had made that decision rather than subject her to extensive, expensive, and ultimately fruitless measures. But our health care system won't allow this. And I've allowed myself to be made a pawn in the game."

He admitted that he had seen similar situations time and time again and that the family or the nursing home does not wish to be put to the trouble because there might be an investigation.

So they ship the poor soul, often comatose and "pretzeled," as medical staff sometimes say—in the fetal position—to the hospital. The hospital calls in a specialist (like me) to protect itself from any possible malpractice charges. The specialist in turn orders all sorts of expensive tests, procedures, maybe even surgery. All of which gets billed to Medicaid, i.e., the taxpayers. It's a horror for the family and it's costing us all a fortune, money that could be better spent on lives that can be saved.

He goes on to explain why this irrational behavior has become the order of the day in a system that has gone berserk:

> We've got to cover our asses or they will sue us or worse. The family wants anything done. . . . [Doctors] repeat this mantra of self-serving paranoia as we put our patients through paces that frequently serve only our own interests. . . . I have become inured to a health care system gone crazy because I have to function within it. I realize that if DNR meant "Do Not Reimburse" instead of "Do Not Resuscitate," far fewer of the terminally and hopelessly ill would receive pointless treatment.

After looking at the patient in question and being informed by the nurse that she was already near death, Dr. Brody thought of the many terminally ill patients lying like "human loaves of bread in the health care supermarket," each attached to at least "one piece of technology, *modern medicine's bulwark against death, replacing prayer, kindness and compassion. . . . Why do we accept this expensive, inhuman set of circumstances?* In coming so far, it seems we have left some very important things behind." (emphasis added)

A Poet's View of Death

Arthur Lundkvist was a prominent contemporary Swedish poet, linguist, essayist, and influential member of the Nobel Prize Committee, who died in 1991 at age eighty-five. He left behind a lyrical expression of his feelings about life and death in his slender volume *Journeys in Dream and Imagination* (1991). Lundkvist describes his return from clinical death in 1981 (a decade before he finally died), recalling the sensation of traveling down a long tunnel toward a blinding source of light. An avowed secularist, he showed his readers his view of the death experience:

> I have met imperceptible death, without recognizing it,
> as an ever so rapidly passing pain,
> not a moment of suffocation or anxiety,
> now I know that death is nothing once it has arrived,
> . . . a repose like an extinguished flame, leaving no trace,

there is no meaning to your having lived . . .
but we are bound to the concept that nothing has a meaning unless
    it is transformed into something else,
a consequence of our incorrigible overestimation of ourselves.

Aware of the blasphemy that he wrote, Lundkvist anticipated the voice of his accusers: "You have been unconscious for two months, and if you haven't seen God in that time, you are beyond hope."

Coming back from the edge of the abyss after suffering a near fatal heart attack in 1981, he reported on adventurous excursions filled with vivid detail and hallucinatory travels into a land of dreams, including a return to the landscape of his boyhood—all this a decade before he finally attained his final good death. Lundkvist's tribute to human courage marks an approach to death that most of us might seek. As he wrote, "Our awareness of humanity is our innermost self."

20

Where Do We Go from Here?

We do not leave birth to God. We space births. We prevent births.
We arrange births. Man should learn to become the lord of death
as well as master of birth.
                    —Rev. Leslie Whitehead, late British Methodist clergyman

A Taboo Breached

For most of the decade of the eighties, there was an unwritten taboo
that doctors did not discuss with their colleagues the largely underground
issue of doctor-assisted suicide for the terminally ill. After the Cruzan
case and the Supreme Court decision of June 1990, doctors began to
consult one another regarding the pros and cons of writing lethal
prescriptions for certain patients under their care. But there is perhaps
no other topic that provokes such angry debates among physicians.

In 1988, the *Journal of the American Medical Association* created
a furor within the profession when it published an essay entitled "It's
Over, Debbie!" It was written by a doctor-in-training who gave a lethal
injection of morphine to a patient dying of ovarian cancer whom he
had never met previously. Because it was by an anonymous doctor and
several medical facts appeared to be peculiar, some readers suspected

220

it was a hoax.

But even before the publicity generated by the actions of Dr. Quill and Dr. Kevorkian in 1990–1993, doctors of America could not have been shocked at what some of their colleagues might do in the gray area of euthanasia. Arthur Caplan, an ethicist at the University of Minnesota, has confessed that over a dozen physicians had consulted with him about their role in responding to requests from conscious, mentally clear patients to help them die. All spoke to him, sub rosa, because they told him they believed that both public policy and medical practice were out of step with the needs of the dying, and they felt professionally helpless in trying to bridge the gap.

To date, there have been no adequate nationwide research studies to assess the extent of doctor-assisted suicides, because most doctors who have participated in one or more of these cases fear the loss of their licenses and their practices, which take so long to build up. One issue that needs clarification is the percentage of patients who feel they are in control of their own destinies and give their assent to doctor-assisted suicide, yet then back out at the last minute. Until such clarification has been conducted to clear the air on this and attendant issues, the profession remains largely in the dark as to which direction to go in formulating a viable policy and to establish workable guidelines.

The Multiple Problems of Legalizing Doctor-Assisted Suicide

There are four major factors that proponents of the legalization of doctor-assisted suicide for terminally ill citizens need to take into consideration. They are as follows:

1. *The Political Factor.* No state (as of February 1993) has yet approved active euthanasia with physician assistance, despite the fact that suicide is no longer viewed as a crime. Supporters of death-with-dignity proposals are banking on the Fourteenth Amendment's rule of the "guarantee of life, liberty and due process of law" for all citizens. But this specific dictum has yet to be tested in the Supreme Court in a relevant case (like that of Dr. Quill, which never got beyond a local grand jury). The right to privacy for the individual also has to be considered here.

2. *The Economic Factor.* The increasingly high costs of keeping incurable patients alive are bringing greater pressures on legislators to do something to meet this daunting burden.

3. *The Religious Factor.* The informal alliance of the various right-to-life groups (backed by the fundamentalist Christian and the Roman Catholic Church) has been able to stave off any progress so far at the state level. These groups vehemently believe that since "God created life, only God can end a life," and have conducted strong protests against any proposed legislation that departs from this maxim.

4. *The Sociological Factor.* Society has to decide by majority rule whether the price of keeping "zombies" alive is more important than letting them go to a pain-free death with dignity.

Together, the country must seek and find a solution to the problems raised by these interrelated factors before the individual problems collectively escalate into a national crisis. A reform of the law will be necessary sooner than later.

Hemlock's Views on the Future

Derek Humphry believes that both the legal and medical professions need to "be pushed" into drastic reform in the area of responsible euthanasia. Universities must offer better training in the legal and medical options available to combat the Catch-22 dilemmas posed by high-tech machines that can keep human bodies alive indefinitely.

> We've got to educate the medical profession that they are not the only ones who can make a final decision on the quality of life for their patients. We also have to clarify the roles of hospital management and the physicians on what information is imparted to patients and their families . . . who are suffering from an incurable disease. (Humphry, November 15, 1991)

The younger doctors whom Humphry has addressed all appear in favor of his approach to the problem. One young physician from the

Denver General Hospital put it well in November 1991, when he told a Hemlock conference: "It's up to Hemlock to take the complacent doctors by their balls and shake them up. That's the way to do it."

William Delaman, the president of Organizational Resources Inc. and a former hospital administrator, has observed that "nursing is the conscience of the medical profession," and that nurses are quietly, individually and collectively, helping to motivate their doctors, hospitals, medical insurance companies, and pharmaceutical houses to set standards in a profession that has become corrupted by greed and excess profits. Most of the nurses—particularly the younger ones— are the ones who live with the terminally ill patients all day and night, while the others in the health profession have only peripheral or little contact with them. The nurses are the quiet heroines and heroes of the surge to pass legislation to make doctor-assisted suicide legal (Delaman 1993).

Humphry believes that there should be a presidential inquiry with a special task force to examine the legal, ethical, and medical implications of doctor-assisted suicide and that Congressman Henry Waxman's health committee in the House of Representatives should look into the alternatives. "It's no good just to pass laws in the area of doctor-assisted suicide unless the public wants them to be implemented and respected. We will no longer stand for the ignorance of the doctors on these options," asserts Humphry. A thrust to increase the enrollment of the Hemlock Society, above the current (mid-1992) fifty thousand members, is also needed. (This is only one out of seventy-two thousand Americans based on the 1990 census of 360 million). Such growth is needed to obtain the necessary money to lobby fifty state legislatures and Congress into passing acts similar to the state of Washington's Initiative #119.

In answer to the brickbats of such celebrity critics as Drs. Koop and Kevorkian, Humphry says:

> Our aim is the legalization of the process. While Dr. Kevorkian's freelance activities make his point by the way he approaches the problem of euthanasia, I'd say there is a genuine difference of opinion in how best to do it. We don't expect a consensus, but the strength of our support groups is to find more physicians like Dr. Frederick Abrams to crush our opposition. We have finally disproved the notion that all doctors [in the AMA] are against us. If celebrities beyond the medical

profession—like Magic Johnson—will endorse our efforts, that will be fine, but I don't look for it to happen anytime soon. (Humphry November 5, 1991)

The Hemlock Society has been able to survive and flourish. As a skilled chief executive, Derek has been the driving force in the movement and the revenue from his books has brought in big money to nourish the expansion of Hemlock during its first decade of life.

Humphry has also been successful at damage control in the wake of his personal family tragedies. His hallmark has always been his ability to bounce back from life's problems and to move on to new horizons. As a survivor he has learned to elevate himself by directing his own inner drives into a passion for his life's goal. He has thus been able to witness major accomplishments in the protection of the people's right to die.

If Derek ever writes his autobiography, he says it will be called "Seesaw," because of his up-and-down life of "deep valleys, but also moments of incredible joy." But now as he campaigns for the people's right to die peacefully and painlessly, he says, "The roots of life are in the dying process. It can be very beautiful." For a man who has witnessed the deaths of loved ones up close, this mission is one that has consumed him for the past decade and will undoubtedly be the centerpiece of the rest of his life.

Humphry does not seem to have tired of the campaign that he helped to found. "I won't stop until I've made a significant change," he said. "I will go on writing about it, shouting about it. Put it this way: I won't shut up until the law is changed." Death with dignity is a worthy goal, and a good death should follow a good life wherever possible, he believes.

Au Revoir—Humphry Retires

After twelve years at the helm of the Hemlock Society, Humphry tendered his resignation to the board, effective May 8, 1992. On May 15, the board chose Cheryl Smith, the society's deputy director and staff attorney, as the interim director, while a national search was conducted to find a permanent successor to the founder of the organization.

Humphry stated that he would spend his "retirement" writing, lecturing, and promoting the goals of Hemlock, particularly by helping to get the California Initiative passed into law in the Fall of 1992.

Hemlock Selects a New Leader for the 1990s

In October 1992, Hemlock's board of directors appointed John A. Pridinoff, Ph.D., as executive director. With an extensive background in both psychology and theology, Dr. Pridinoff has been involved in the area of death and dying for the past twenty-five years. Starting in 1968, he had been the administrator of the Counselling Center in San Diego, California, a nonprofit organization providing counseling to medical professionals and other caregivers on dealing with patient trauma, grief, pastoral needs, and crisis intervention. He has participated in public debates on the ethical and moral perspectives of patient autonomy and has presented numerous papers at national conferences on death and dying. He has also served as editor of the *Forum,* the national newsletter of the Association for Death Education and Counseling.

Dr. Pridinoff represents a pioneer in the recent wave of professional, multitalented people who are carving out a new field by becoming qualified to deal with *all* the complex problems in the euthanasia movement, and he is especially qualified to lead the struggle to legalize doctor-assisted suicide in America.

Is a Presidential Commission Now in the Offing?

In early 1993 Derek Humphry, in his new post as the editor of the *World Right-to-Die Newsletter* (the chief organ of thirty global euthanasia organizations), once again suggested that the "wisest solution" to the complex problem of legal reform in the area of modern euthanasia, including the legalization of doctor-assisted suicide for the terminally ill, would be a special "President's Commission," appointed by President Bill Clinton, which would make recommendations on how to solve the present impasse on both the state and federal levels. He feels that the panel must include strong patient representation, along with doctors and ethicists to give it a proper balance.

Since Clinton emphasized in his campaign his deep concerns for improving the nation's health-delivery systems for all Americans, such a commission would appear to be a much needed early move by his administration. The clock is ticking and the new president can use the "bully pulpit" of the White House to show his commitment in this area of the nation's health, not only for the sake of our senior citizens, but also for the growing numbers of younger HIV and AIDS victims.

The Netherlands Becomes the First Nation to Pass Euthanasia Legislation

On February 9, 1993, the Dutch Parliament in the Hague passed the first modern euthanasia law in the civilized world establishing the least restrictive policies for "mercy killing" of terminally ill patients. Specific rules were spelled out that would allow a doctor to assist in a suicide of a terminally ill patient at the patient's explicit request. Although ending a patient's life or helping in a suicide remained illegal under the new law, secions of the law approve what the Netherlands' courts had already condoned as sanctioned medical practices for the past decade (Simons 1993)

The new law marks a giant step in protecting doctors from prosecution if they notify the local coroner of any death that they deliberately brought on, but it does require them to provide a detailed account of their actions following the strictures of an official checklist. Prosecutions had been rare under the previously existing law in the Netherlands, which called for a three-to-twelve-year prison term in the case of a conviction. But no doctor had been sent to prison in any of the cases that had gone to court.

Voluntary euthanasia, which has become an accepted practice in Dutch health circles, is not legal anywhere else in Europe. Nowhere else on the continent has the public debate over the legality and morality of the practice been so passionate as has been occurring in the Netherlands. Lawyers, physicians, theologians, and euthanasia educators have come from abroad to study the open medical practice in that country.

Unlike the United States, where the economic factor has been playing an increasing role in the resolution of terminally ill cases because of the uninsured financial burdens heaped on the families of such patients, the Dutch people do not face similar anxieties because the Netherlands provides its citizens with virtually universal insurance coverage through various health plans that cover *all* medical costs.

One factor that acted as an impetus to the voluntary euthanasia movement in the Netherlands was the results of a January 1993 public opinion poll on the subject: 78 percent of those questioned supported the right of the terminally ill to ask for euthanasia. Only 10 percent said they were opposed, while 71 percent said doctors who proceed according to rules should not have to justify themselves before a court (ibid.).

The powerful American Medical Association might learn a lesson from the Royal Dutch Medical Association, which (unlike its American counterpart) has been vocal in pressing the government for euthanasia legislation to end the legal jeopardy that its members have had to face, despite the fact that there have been no malpractice suits by the next of kin in the Netherlands in such cases. In this county, the AMA has been reluctant to come forward to endorse responsible doctor-assisted suicide propositions and legislation. They have ignored the challenge and the plea of a seventy-five-year-old dying AIDS patient's, who on a network television show in 1992 said, "When are you doctors going to come forward and take the leadership in this health-care controversy instead of whispering in the ears of right-to-die organizations telling them: 'You lead, we'll follow'?"

On the day that the Dutch parliament approved the new law sanctioning euthanasia by a ninety-one to forty-five vote, Dr. Herbert Cohen, sixty-two, a family doctor who had been practicing for ten years in the village of Capelle, reflected the views of the 89 percent of the physicians in the Netherlands who signified that they would go along with the new act. Cohen announced that he had brought on the end for some of his patients and helped others to kill themselves to relieve their suffering. He said he had cooperated with his patients' request to die for the past decade because:

> We need a counterweight for the enormous technology of present medicine. We are talking mostly about older people, who in other times would have died from their condition. If we can keep people alive but give them a life that is no life, we must be consistent and

give them the choice to end it. . . . It gives the patient the chance to take leave openly of his children, his grandchildren, a nurse, household help, perhaps neighbors, the people in his world. (ibid.)

Saying goodbye is painful, he said, but it can be of great benefit. "It is dignified to say, 'I'm leaving.' It creates moments of great intimacy between people . . . *and makes the mourning process easier*" (emphasis added).

Appendices

Appendix 1

Planning for Death with Dignity—
A Checklist*

Being with the Dying: Part I: Talking and Listening

- If the patient is in a wheelchair or bed, lower yourself to his or her eye level.

- Never assume that because a person can't talk or appears asleep, that he or she can't hear you.

- Ask the patient if he or she feels like talking at all. If the answer is "yes," ask if there is something specific he or she wants to talk about.

- Be comfortable with silences. You can be with the person without talking; your touch and presence show you care.

- Even admitting, "I don't know what to say, but I'm thinking of you," will give a message of support to the patient.

- Don't dominate the conversation. Give the patient openings for discussion.

- Don't say, "I know just how you feel." We can't possibly know, and the patient will feel it's hollow, insincere, and unsympathetic.

- If the patient looks terrible, don't say, "You look great." Your lie will make the patient suspicious of everything else you say. It isn't necessary to comment on looks.

---

*Printed by permission of the Hemlock Society of Washington State.

- Don't try to cheer the patient up by saying that things could be worse or he or she could have had a worse disease.

- Let the patient bring up the subject of death. Be honest. If the patient says he or she is dying, don't say, "Of course you're not. You'll be up and about in no time." If the patient expresses a wish to die, ask: "Is there anything that would make life more bearable and meaningful now?" or "What makes you feel that way today?" If the dying person expresses a fear of death, ask what the specific fear is. If he or she wants to talk about funeral plans or a will, carry out those wishes.

- Be nonjudgmental. This is not the time to push your views.

- Talk about what the two of you used to talk about—politics, religion, books, the office, children, in-laws. Speak of the good times the patient has had—the high points in a career, family, community work, or avocation. Let the patient talk about his or her early years. Chat about your own life. Keep your old style: If you used to laugh together, inject humor into the conversation. Use affectionate nicknames.

- Mention the names of deceased loved ones: the patient may find comfort in believing he or she will see them again.

- A dying person is often confused about place, time, and who people are. If that is the case, calmly and gently remind the patient who and where you are and what day it is.

- If the patient is too weak to talk, use a soft, gentle voice to say comforting things like: "I love you. You're the best husband anyone could want," or "I'm so proud of you. You've shown such courage." If what you are saying is kind and supportive, keep repeating it.

- If the patient responds favorably, you are saying the right thing.

Being with the Dying:
Part II: Giving Physical and Emotional Comfort

- Because sleeping increases as death approaches, plan your conversation for when the person seems most alert. Let the patient sleep as needed.

- Just sitting quietly in a hospital room while a patient naps is helpful. So is showing concern and affection. One patient said of her husband, "He let me know he loved me even if my hair fell out."

- A gentle, loving touch is often comforting.

- Avoid excessive, bubbly cheerfulness—you will not fool the patient. On the other hand, try not to be around the patient when you are extremely upset or feeling negative.

- Let the patient make as many decisions as possible. It is essential for everyone, but especially for a dying person to retain dignity and self-worth.

- Ask if there is anything you can do. Be specific. Ask, "Would you like me to read from your favorite book?" or "Would you like to listen to some music together?"

- Ask if there is someone he or she would like to see and arrange for a visit. (One of the most painful experiences for dying patients is to have loved ones abandon them. Yet many people avoid those with a serious illnses.)

- Unless the patient indicates otherwise, don't bring articles about other doctors, hospitals, or methods of treatment.

- A dying person is so physically vulnerable that all stimuli seem magnified. Try to minimize every negative influence possible. Walk softly, gently put dishes on the meal tray, do not drag chairs, try not to cough, and beware of a loud stereo or television.

- Ask the patient which smells are nauseating and which are pleasant. Also find out likes and dislikes in colors and adjust the environment accordingly. Place the patient's favorite objects nearby.

- As the desire for food decreases, offer small servings of a favorite food or beverage. Do not force the patient to eat or drink.

- If the patient has developed a dry mouth, use Vaseline on the lips and swab the mouth with water or a saline solution of salt dissolved in water. Some patients get relief from ice chips or sucking on a moist washcloth.

- A damp cloth put gently on the patient's forehead can be soothing, as can a back rub and fresh powder on the skin.

- As circulation slows, the body trunk may become warmer than usual while the legs and arms may become cool and pale. Keep warm, nonelectric blankets on the patient.

Appendix 2

Eleven Doctors Prosecuted for Euthanasia in the U.S.A. (1950-1991)*

Eleven medical doctors have been accused of killing a terminally ill patient or family member. None, however, has been sent to prison. The cases are:

1935

A general practitioner in Montevista, Colorado, **Harold Blazer,** was accused of the murder of his thirty-year-old daughter, Hazel, a victim of cerebral spinal meningitis. Evidence was given that she had the mind of a baby and her limbs were the size of a five-year-old child.

Dr. Blazer, together with his wife and another daughter, had taken care of Hazel for thirty years. One day he placed a handkerchief soaked in chloroform over her face and kept it in place until she died.

At his trial, the doctor was acquitted.

1950

New Hampshire doctor **Hermann N. Sanders** was charged with first-degree murder of a terminally ill patient, Abbie Borroto. At the request of Borroto's husband, Sanders injected Borroto with 40 cc's of air and she died within ten minutes. When he logged

---

*Printed with the author's emendations by permission of the Hemlock Society.

the fatal injection into the hospital record, Sanders was reported to authorities.

At the close of a three-week trial, the jury deliberated an hour and ten minutes before returning a verdict of innocent.

1972

Long Island doctor **Vincent Montemarano,** chief surgical resident at the Nassau County Medical Center, was indicted on a charge of willful murder in the death of fifty-nine-year-old Eugene Bauer.

Bauer, suffering with cancer of the throat, had been given two days to live. Bauer died within five minutes of Montemarano's injection of potassium chloride.

The defense argued that the state didn't prove Bauer was alive prior to the injection. The jury deliberated fifty-five minutes before returning an innocent verdict.

1981

California doctors **Robert Nedjil** and **Neil Barber** were charged with murder for discontinuing mechanical ventilation and intravenous fluids to Clarence Herbert, fifty-five.

The patient had a heart attack after surgery to correct an intestinal obstruction. Herbert stayed in a coma for three days before his condition was declared hopeless.

Following the wishes of Herbert's wife and eight children, he was taken off life-support systems but continued to breathe. Five days later the intravenous fluid was discontinued. Herbert died six days later.

In October 1983, a court of appeals dismissed the charges.

1985

Dr. John Kraai, an old-time physician from a small New York town, was charged with second-degree murder in the death of his patient and friend Frederick Wagner, eighty-one. Wagner suffered from Alzheimer's disease for five years and had gangrene of the foot.

On the morning of Wagner's death, Kraai injected three large doses of insulin into Wagner's chest. As Wagner's condition worsened, a nurse called the State Department of Patient Abuse. Kraai was charged with murder.

Three weeks after his arrest, Kraai killed himself with a lethal injection.

1986

New Jersey doctor **Joseph Hassman** was charged with murder in connection with the death of his mother-in-law, Esther Davis.

Davis, eighty, suffered from Alzheimer's disease. At the family's request, Hassman injected Davis with a lethal dose of Demerol.

Hassman cried several times in court during the trial. He was found guilty and sentenced to two years probation, fined $10,000, and ordered to perform four hundred hours of community service.

1987

Fort Myers doctor **Peter Rosier** was acquitted of first-degree murder in the death of his wife, Patricia. Pat tried to end her life with an overdose of Seconal, but when the powerful sedative didn't take hold, Rosier began injecting her with morphine.

The morphine wasn't lethal. Rosier didn't then know it, but Pat's stepfather Vincent Delman smothered her. See Stanley Rosenblatt, *Murder of Mercy* (Prometheus Books, 1992) for the full story of the Rosier case.

1989

Dr. Donald Caraccio, thirty-three, of Troy, Michigan, was charged in Detroit with the murder of a seventy-four-year-old woman hospital patient who was terminally ill and comatose.

Dr. Caraccio gave the patient a lethal injection of potassium chloride in the presence of other medical staff.

In court, the doctor said he did it to terminate her pain and suffering. Evidence was given that he was overworked and stressed-out by the recent lengthy and painful death of his father. Accepting Dr. Caraccio's guilty plea, the judge imposed five years probation with community service.

1990

Dr. Richard Schaeffer, sixty-nine, was arrested under suspicion of having caused the death by injection at home of a patient, Melvin Seifert, seventy-five, of Redondo Beach, California, who was suffering from the effects of a stroke and other ailments.

The dead man's wife, Mary, seventy-five, was also arrested. Both were released pending further investigation. One year later the District Attorney dropped all charges.

1990-1991

Dr. Jack Kevorkian was charged in December with the first-degree murder of Hemlock Society member Janet Adkins who died on June 4. Suffering from early-stage Alzheimer's disease, Mrs. Adkins flew from her home in Portland, Oregon, to Michigan, where Dr. Kevorkian connected her to his so-called "suicide machine." She chose the time to press a button which resulted in lethal drugs entering her body. On December 13, 1990, a judge dismissed the murder charge.

In November 1991, the state of Michigan rescinded his license to practice medicine for assisting in the death of two terminally ill women a month before in a Michigan forest cabin. (See chapters 8-10 for details of his four cases).

Appendix 3

Excerpts from U.S. Supreme Court Majority and Minority Opinions on *Cruzan* v. *Director, Missouri Dept. of Health* (June 25, 1990)

From the Opinion

JUSTICE REHNQUIST

Petitioner Nancy Beth Cruzan was rendered incompetent as a result of severe injuries sustained during an automobile accident. Co-petitioners Lester and Joyce Cruzan, Nancy's parents and co-guardians, sought a court order directing the withdrawal of their daughter's artificial feeding and hydration equipment after it became apparent that she had virtually no chance of recovering her cognitive faculties. The Supreme Court of Missouri held that because there was no clear and convincing evidence of Nancy's desire to have life-sustaining treatment withdrawn under such circumstances, her parents lacked authority to effectuate such a request. We granted certiorari, (1989), and now affirm.

* * *

After it became apparent that Nancy Cruzan had virtually no chance of regaining her mental faculties her parents asked hospital employees to terminate the artificial nutrition and hydration procedures. All agree that such a removal would cause her death.

238

The employees refused to honor the request without court approval. The parents then sought and received authorization from the state trial court for termination. The court found that a person in Nancy's condition had a fundamental right under the State and Federal Constitutions to refuse or direct the withdrawal of "death prolonging procedures." The court also found that Nancy's "expressed thoughts at age 25 in somewhat serious conversation with a housemate friend that if sick or injured she would not wish to continue her life unless she could live at least halfway normally suggests that given her present condition she would not wish to continue on with her nutrition and hydration."

The Supreme Court of Missouri reversed by a divided vote. The court recognized a right to refuse treatment embodied in the common-law doctrine of informed consent, but expressed skepticism about the application of that doctrine in the circumstances of this case. . . . The court also declined to read a broad right of privacy into the State Constitution which would "support the right of a person to refuse medical treatment in every circumstance," and expressed doubt as to whether such a right existed under the United States Constitution. It then decided that the Missouri Living Will statute, Mo. Rev. Stat. embodied a state policy strongly favoring the preservation of life. The court found that Cruzan's statements to her roommate regarding her desire to live or die under certain conditions were "unreliable for the purpose of determining her intent," "and thus insufficient to support the co-guardians claims to exercise substituted judgment on Nancy's behalf." . . .

We granted certiorari to consider the question of whether Cruzan has a right under the United States Constitution which would require the hospital to withdraw life-sustaining treatment from her under these circumstances.

At common law, even the touching of one person by another without consent and without legal justification was a battery. See W. Keeton, D. Dobbs, R. Keeton, & D. Owen, Prosser and Keeton on Law of Torts 9, pp. 39–42 (5th ed. 1984). . . .

The logical corollary of the doctrine of informed consent is that the patient generally possesses the right not to consent, that is, to refuse treatment. Until about 15 years ago and the seminal decision in In re Quinlan, 70 N.J. 10, the number of right-to-refuse-treatment decisions were relatively few. . . . More recently, however, with the advance of medical technology capable of sustaining life well past the point where natural forces would have brought certain death in earlier times, cases involving the right to refuse life-sustaining treatment have burgeoned. . . .

As these cases demonstrate, the common-law doctrine of informed consent is viewed as generally encompassing the right of a competent individual to refuse medical treatment. Beyond that, these decisions demonstrate both similarity and diversity in their approach to decision of what all agree is a perplexing question with unusually strong moral and ethical overtones. State courts have available to them for decision a number of sources—state constitutions, statutes, and common law—which are not available to us.

In this Court, the question is simply and starkly whether the United States Constitution prohibits Missouri from choosing the rule of decision which it did. This is the first case in which we have been squarely presented with the issue of whether the

United States Constitution grants what is in common parlance referred to as a "right to die." We follow the judicious counsel of our decision in Twin City Bank v. Nebeker, (1897), where we said that in deciding "a question of such magnitude and importance . . . it is the [better] part of wisdom not to attempt, by any general statement, to cover every possible phase of the subject."

The 14th Amendment provides that no state shall "deprive any person of life, liberty, or property, without due process of law." The principle that a competent person has a constitutionally protected liberty interest in refusing unwanted medical treatment may be inferred from our prior decisions. . . .

Just this term, in the course of holding that a state's procedures for administering antipsychotic medication to prisoners were sufficient to satisfy due process concerns, we recognized that prisoners possess "a significant liberty interest in avoiding the unwanted administration of antipsychotic drugs under the Due Process Clause of the 14th Amendment." Washington v. Harper, (1990) . . .

But determining that a person has a "liberty interest" under the Due Process Clause does not end the inquiry; (footnote—Although many state courts have held that a right to refuse treatment is encompassed by a generalized constitutional right of privacy, we have never so held. We believe this issue is more properly analyzed in terms of a 14th Amendment liberty interest.) "whether respondent's constitutional rights have been violated must be determined by balancing his liberty interests against the relevant state interests."

Petitioners insist that under the general holdings of our cases, the forced administration of life-sustaining medical treatment, and even of artificially delivered food and water essential to life, would implicate a competent person's liberty interest. Although we think the logic of the cases discussed above would embrace such a liberty interest, the dramatic consequences involved in refusal of such treatment would inform the inquiry as to whether the deprivation of that interest is constitutionally permissible. But for purposes of this case, we assume that the United States Constitution would grant a competent person a constitutionally protected right to refuse life-saving hydration and nutrition.

Petitioners go on to assert that an incompetent person should possess the same right in this respect as is possessed by a competent person. . . .

The difficulty with petitioners' claim is that in a sense it begs the question: an incompetent person is not able to make an informed and voluntary choice to exercise a hypothetical right to refuse treatment or any other right. Such a "right" must be exercised for her, if at all, by some sort of surrogate. Here, Missouri has in effect recognized that under certain circumstances a surrogate may act for the patient in electing to have hydration and nutrition withdrawn in such a way as to cause death, but it has established a procedural safeguard to assure that the action of the surrogate conforms as best it may to the wishes expressed by the patient while competent.

Missouri requires that evidence of the incompetent's wishes as to the withdrawal of treatment be proved by clear and convincing evidence. The question, then, is whether the United States Constitution forbids the establishment of this procedural requirement by the state. We hold that it does not.

Whether or not Missouri's clear and convincing evidence requirement comports with the United States Constitution depends in part on what interests the state may properly seek to protect in this situation. Missouri relies on its interest in the protection and preservation of human life, and there can be no gainsaying this interest. As a general matter, the states—indeed, all civilized nations—demonstrate their commitment to life by treating homicide as serious crime. Moreover, the majority of states in this country have laws imposing criminal penalties on one who assists another to commit suicide. We do not think a state is required to remain neutral in the face of an informed and voluntary decision by a physically able adult to starve to death.

But in the context presented here, a state has more particular interests at stake. The choice between life and death is a deeply personal decision of obvious and overwhelming finality. We believe Missouri may legitimately seek to safeguard the personal element of this choice through the imposition of heightened evidentiary requirements. It cannot be disputed that the Due Process Clause protects an interest in life as well as an interest in refusing life-sustaining medical treatment. Not all incompetent patients will have loved ones available to serve as surrogate decision makers. . . .

In our view, Missouri has permissibly sought to advance these interests through the adoption of a "clear and convincing" standard of proof to govern such proceedings. . . .

In sum, we conclude that a state may apply a clear and convincing evidence standard in proceedings where a guardian seeks to discontinue nutrition and hydration of a person diagnosed to be in a persistent vegetative state. . . .

The Supreme Court of Missouri held that in this case the testimony adduced at trial did not amount to clear and convincing proof of the patient's desire to have hydration and nutrition withdrawn. . . .

No doubt is engendered by anything in this record but that Nancy Cruzan's mother and father are loving and caring parents. If the state were required by the United States Constitution to repose a right of "substituted judgment" with anyone, the Cruzans would surely qualify. But we do not think the Due Process Clause requires the state to repose judgment on these matters with anyone but the patient herself. Close family members may have a strong feeling—a feeling not at all ignoble or unworthy, but not entirely disinterested, either—that they do not wish to witness the continuation of the life of a loved one which they regard as hopeless, meaningless and even degrading. But there is no automatic assurance that the view of close family members will necessarily be the same as the patient's would have been had she been confronted with the prospect of her situation while competent. All of the reasons previously discussed for allowing Missouri to require clear and convincing evidence of the patient's wish lead us to conclude that the state may choose to defer only to those wishes, rather than confide the decision to close family members.

JUSTICE O'CONNOR, CONCURRING

I agree that a protected liberty interest in refusing unwanted medical treatment may be inferred from our prior decisions, and that the refusal of artificially delivered food and water is encompassed within that liberty interest. I write separately to clarify why I believe this to be so.

As the Court notes, the liberty interest in refusing medical treatment flows from decisions involving the states's invasions into the body. Because our notions of liberty are inextricably entwined with our idea of physical freedom and self-determination, the Court has often deemed state incursions into the body repugnant to the interests protected by the Due Process Clause. . . . Our Fourth Amendment jurisprudence has echoed this same concern. . . . The state's imposition of medical treatment on an unwilling competent adult necessarily involves some form of restraint and intrusion. A seriously ill or dying patient whose wishes are not honored may feel a captive of the machinery required for life-sustaining measures or other medical interventions. Such forced treatment may burden that individual's liberty interests as much as any state coercion. . . .

The state's artificial provision of nutrition and hydration implicates identical concerns. Artificial feeding cannot readily be distinguished from other forms of medical treatment. . . .

I also write separately to emphasize that the Court does not today decide the issue whether a state must also give effect to the decisions of a surrogate decision maker. In my view, such a duty may well be constitutionally required to protect the patient's liberty interest in refusing medical treatment. Few individuals provide explicit oral or written instructions regarding their intent to refuse medical treatment should they become incompetent. States which decline to consider any evidence other than such instructions may frequently fail to honor a patient's intent. Such failures might be avoided if the state considered an equally probative source of evidence: the patient's appointment of a proxy to make health care decisions on her behalf. . . .

Today's decision, holding only that the Constitution permits a state to require clear and convincing evidence of Nancy Cruzan's desire to have artificial hydration and nutrition withdrawn, does not preclude a future determination that the Constitution requires the states to implement the decisions of a patient's duly appointed surrogate. Nor does it prevent states from developing other approaches for protecting an incompetent individual's liberty interest in refusing medical treatment. As is evident from the Court's survey of state court decisions, no national consensus has yet emerged on the best solution for this difficult and sensitive problem. Today we decide only that one state's practice does not violate the Constitution; the more challenging task of crafting appropriate procedures for safeguarding incompetents' liberty interests is entrusted to the "laboratory" of the states, . . . in the first instance.

JUSTICE SCALIA, CONCURRING

The various opinions in this case portray quite clearly the difficult, indeed agonizing, questions that are presented by the constantly increasing power of science to keep the human body alive for longer than any reasonable person would want to inhabit it. The states have begun to grapple with these problems through legislation. I am concerned, from the tenor of today's opinions, that we are poised to confuse that enterprise as successfully as we have confused the enterprise of legislating concerning abortion—requiring it to be conducted against a background of Federal constitutional imperatives that are unknown because they are being newly crafted from term to term. That would be a great misfortune.

While I agree with the Court's analysis today, and therefore join in its opinion, I would have preferred that we announce, clearly and promptly, that the Federal courts have no business in this field; . . .

What I have said above is not meant to suggest that I would think it desirable, if we were sure that Nancy Cruzan wanted to die, to keep her alive by the means at issue here. I assert only that the Constitution has nothing to say about the subject. To raise up a constitutional right here we would have to create out of nothing (for it exists neither in text nor tradition) some constitutional principle whereby, although the state may insist that an individual come in out of the cold and eat food, it may not insist that he take medicine; and although it may pump his stomach empty of poison he has ingested, it may not fill his stomach with food he has failed to ingest.

Are there, then, no reasonable and humane limits that ought not to be exceeded in requiring an individual to preserve his own life? There obviously are, but they are not set forth in the Due Process Clause. What assures us that those limits will not be exceeded is the same constitutional guarantee that is the source of most of our protection—what protects us, for example, from being assessed a tax of 100 percent of our income above the subsistence level, from being forbidden to drive cars, or from being required to send our children to school for 10 hours a day, none of which horribles is categorically prohibited by the Constitution. Our salvation is the Equal Protection Clause, which requires the democratic majority to accept for themselves and their loved ones what they impose on you and me. This Court need not, and has no authority to, inject itself into every field of human activity where irrationality and oppression may theoretically occur, and if it tries to do so it will destroy itself.

From Dissenting Opinions

JUSTICE BRENNAN

Nancy Cruzan has dwelt in that twilight zone for six years. She is oblivious to her surroundings and will remain so.

*   *   *

Today the Court, while tentatively accepting that there is some degree of constitutionally protected liberty interest in avoiding unwanted medical treatment, including life-sustaining medical treatment such as artificial nutrition and hydration, affirms the decision of the Missouri Supreme Court. The majority opinion, as I read it, would affirm that decision on the ground that a state may require "clear and convincing" evidence of Nancy Cruzan's prior decision to forgo life-sustaining treatment under circumstances such as hers in order to insure that her actual wishes are honored. Because I believe that Nancy Cruzan has a fundamental right to be free of unwanted artificial nutrition and hydration, which right is not outweighed by any interests of the state, and because I find that the improperly biased procedural obstacles imposed by the Missouri Supreme Court impermissibly burden that right, I respectfully dissent. Nancy Cruzan is entitled to choose to die with dignity.

[T]he timing of death—once a matter of fate—is now a matter of human choice. . . . Of the approximately two million people who die each year, 80 percent die in hospitals and long-term care institutions, and perhaps 70 percent of those after a decision to forgo life-sustaining treatment has been made. Nearly every death involves a decision whether to undertake some medical procedure that could prolong the process of dying. Such decisions are difficult and personal. They must be made on the basis of individual values, informed by medical realities, yet within a framework governed by law. The role of the courts is confined to defining that framework, delineating the ways in which government may and may not participate in such decisions.

The question before this Court is a relatively narrow one: whether the Due Process Clause allows Missouri to require a now-incompetent patient in an irreversible persistent vegetative state to remain on life-support absent rigorously clear and convincing evidence that avoiding the treatment presents the patient's prior, express choice. If a fundamental right is at issue, Missouri's rule of decision must be scrutinzed under the standards the Court has always applied in such circumstances. . . .

There are also affirmative reasons why someone like Nancy might choose to forgo artificial nutrition and hydration under these circumstances. Dying is personal. And it is profound. For many, the thought of an ignoble end, steeped in decay, is abhorrent. A quiet, proud death, bodily integrity intact, is a matter of extreme consequence. . . .

Although the right to be free of unwanted medical intervention, like other constitutionally protected interests, may not be absolute, no state interest could outweigh the rights of an individual in Nancy Cruzan's position. Whatever a state's possible interests in mandating life-support treatment under other circumstances, there is no good to be obtained here by Missouri's insistence that Nancy Cruzan remain on life-support systems if it is indeed her wish not to do so. Missouri does not claim, nor could it, that society as a whole will be benefited by Nancy's receiving medical treatment. No third party's situation will be improved and no harm to others will be averted.

The only state interest asserted here is a general interest in the preservation of life. But the state has no legitimate general interest in someone's life, completely abstracted from the interest of the person living that life, that could outweigh the person's choice to avoid medical treatment. . . . Thus, the state's general interest in life must accede to Nancy Cruzan's particularized and intense interest in self-determination in her choice of medical treatment. There is simply nothing legitimately within the state's purview to be gained by superseding her decision.

*   *   *

JUSTICE STEVENS

Our Constitution is born of the proposition that all legitimate governments must secure the equal right of every person to "life, liberty, and the pursuit of happiness." In the ordinary case we quite naturally assume that these three ends are compatible, mutually enhancing and perhaps even coincident.

The Court would make an exception here. It permits the state's abstract, undifferentiated interest in the preservation of life to overwhelm the best interests of Nancy Beth Cruzan, interests which would, according to an undisputed finding, be served by allowing her guardians to exercise her constitutional right to discontinue medical treatment.

Ironically, the Court reaches this conclusion despite endorsing three significant propositions which should save it from any such dilemma. First, a competent individual's decision to refuse life-sustaining medical procedures is an aspect of liberty protected by the Due Process Clause of the 14th Amendment. Second, upon a proper evidentiary showing, a qualified guardian may make that decision on behalf of an incompetent ward. Third, in answering the important question presented by this tragic case, it is wise "not to attempt by any general statement, to cover every possible phase of the subject." Together, these considerations suggest that Nancy Cruzan's liberty to be free from medical treatment must be understood in light of the facts and circumstances particular to her.

I would so hold: in my view, the Constitution requires the state to care for Nancy Cruzan's life in a way that gives appropriate respect to her own best interests.

This case is the first in which we consider whether, and how, the Constitution protects the liberty of seriously ill patients to be free from life-sustaining medical treatment. So put, the question is both general and profound. We need not, however, resolve the question in the abstract. Our responsibility as judges both enables and compels us to treat the problem as it is illuminated by the facts of the controversy before us.

*   *   *

The portion of this Court's opinion that considers the merits of this case is similarly unsatisfactory. It, too, fails to respect the best interests of the patient. It, too, relies on what is tantamount to a waiver rationale: the dying patient's best interests are put to one side and the entire inquiry is focused on her prior expressions of intent.

An innocent person's constitutional right to be free from unwanted medical treatment is thereby categorically limited to those patients who had the foresight to make an unambiguous statement of their wishes while competent. The Court's decision affords no protection to children, to young peole who are victims of unexpected accidents or illnesses, or to the countless thousands of elderly persons who either fail to decide, or fail to explain, how they want to be treated if they should experience a similar fate.

Because Nancy Cruzan did not have the foresight to preserve her constitutional right in a living will, or some comparable "clear and convincing" alternative, her right is gone forever and her fate is in the hands of the state Legislature instead of in those of her family, her independent natural guardian ad litem, and an impartial judge—all of whom agree on the course of action that is in her best interests. The Court's willingness to find a waiver of this constitutional right reveals a distressing misunderstanding of the importance of individual liberty.

*   *   *

Only because Missouri has arrogated to itself the power to define life, and only because the Court permits this usurpation, are Nancy Cruzan's life and liberty put into disquieting conflict. If Nancy Cruzan's life were defined by reference to her own interests, so that her life expired when her biological existence ceased serving any of her own interests, then her constitutionally protected interest in freedom from unwanted treatment would not come into conflict with her constitutionally protected interest in life.

Conversely, if there were any evidence that Nancy Cruzan herself defined life to encompass every form of biological persistence by a human being, so that the continuation of treatment would serve Nancy's own liberty, then once again there would be no conflict between life and liberty. The oppositions of life and liberty in this case are thus not the result of Nancy Cruzan's tragic accident, but are instead the artificial consequence of Missouri's effort, and this Court's willingness, to abstract Nancy Cruzan's life from Nancy Cruzan's person. . . .

Appendix 4

A LIVING WILL*
AND
DURABLE POWER OF ATTORNEY
FOR HEALTH CARE

To my family, my relatives, my friends, my physicians, my employers, and all others whom it may concern:

Directive made this _____ day of ____ 198 __ I, _____ (name), being of sound mind, willfully, and voluntarily make known my desire that my life shall not be prolonged artificially under the circumstances set forth below, do hereby declare:

1. If at any time I should have an incurable injury, disease, illness or condition certified to be terminal by two medical doctors who have examined me, and where the application of life-sustaining procedures of any kind would serve only to prolong artificially the moment of my death, and where a medical doctor determines that my death is imminent, whether or not life-sustaining procedures are utilized, I direct that such procedures be withheld or withdrawn and that I be permitted to die naturally, and that I receive whatever quantity of whatever drugs may be required to keep me free of pain or distress even if the moment of death is hastened.

2. I hereby appoint _____ (name) currently residing at _____ , as my attorney-in-fact (i.e., proxy or agent) for the making of decisions relating to my health care in my place; and it is my intention that this appointment shall be honored by him/her, by my family, relatives, friends, physicians and lawyer as the final expression of my legal right to refuse medical or surgical treatment; and I accept the consequences of such a decision. I have duly executed a Durable Power of Attorney for health care decisions on this date.[1]

3. In the absence of my ability to give further directions regarding my treatment, including life-sustaining procedures, it is my intention that this directive shall be honoured by my family and physicians as the final expression of my legal right to refuse or accept medical and surgical treatment, and I accept the consequences of such refusal.

4. If I have been diagnosed as pregnant and that diagnosis is known to any interested person, this directive shall have no force during the course of my pregnancy.[2]

5. I have been diagnosed, and notifed at least 14 days ago, as being in a terminal condition by _____ , M.D., whose address is _____ and whose telephone number is _____ . I understand that if I have not filled in the physician's name and address, it shall be presumed that I did not have a terminal condition when I made out this directive.[3]

6. This directive shall have no force and effect after five years from the date (above) of its execution, nor, if sooner, after revocation by me, either orally or in writing.[1]

7. I understand the full importance of this directive and am emotionally and mentally competent to make this directive. No participant in the making of this directive or in its being carried into effect, whether it be a medical doctor, my spouse, a relative, friend or any other person shall be held responsible in any way, legally, professionally or socially, for complying with my directions.

Signed _____ .

City, county and state of residence _____

The declarant has been known to me personally and I believe her/him to be of sound mind.

Witness _____ Witness _____

address _____ address _____

_____

Notes appear on page 6.   ©The National Hemlock Society

1.

---

*Reprinted by permission of the Hemlock Society. This sample varies from state to state, depending on the strictures of specific state laws.

A DURABLE POWER OF ATTORNEY FOR HEALTH CARE

This is California's legal document. If you live in another state fill in that state's name.

Before signing you must first read and sign the warning printed on page 5 of this document.

1. DESIGNATION OF HEALTH CARE AGENT.

I, _____

(Insert your name and address)

_____

do hereby designate and appoint _____

_____

_____

(Insert name, address, and telephone number of one individual only as your agent to make health care decisions for you. None of the following may be designated as your agent: (1) your treating health care provider, (2) a nonrelative employee of your treating health care provider, (3) an operator of a community care facility, or (4) a nonrelative employee of an operator of a community care facility).

as my attorney in fact (agent) to make health care decisions for me as authorized in this document. For the purposes of this document, "health care decision" means consent, refusal of consent, or withdrawal of consent to any care, treatment, service, or procedure to maintain, diagnose, or treat an individual's physical or mental condition.

2. CREATION OF DURABLE POWER OF ATTORNEY FOR HEALTH CARE. By this document I intend to create a durable power of attorney for health care. (Under Sections 2430 to 2443, inclusive, of the California Civil Code. This power of attorney is authorized by the Keene Health Care Agent Act and shall be construed in accordance with the provisions of Sections 2500 to 2506, inclusive, of the California Civil Code.) This power of attorney shall not be affected by my subsequent incapacity.

3. GENERAL STATEMENT OF AUTHORITY GRANTED. Subject to any limitations in this document, I hereby grant to my agent full power and authority to make health care decisions for me to the same extent that I could make such decisions for myself if I had the capacity to do so. In exercising this authority, my agent shall make health care decisions that are consistent with my desires as stated in this document or otherwise made known to my agent, including, but not limited to, my desires concerning obtaining or refusing or withdrawing life-prolonging care, treatment, services, and procedures.

(If you want to limit the authority of your agent to make health care decisions for you, you can state the limitations in paragraph 4

("Statement of Desires, Special Provisions, and Limitations") below. You can indicate your desires by including a statement of your desires in the same paragraph.)

4. STATEMENT OF DESIRES, SPECIAL PROVISIONS, AND LIMITATIONS.

(Your agent must make health care decisions that are consistent with your known desires. You can, but are not required to, state your desires in the space provided below. You should consider whether you want to include a statement of your desires concerning life-prolonging care, treatment, services, and procedures. You can also include a statement of your desires concerning other matters relating to your health care. You can also make your desires known to your agent by discussing your desires with your agent or by some other means. If there are any types of treatment that you do not want to be used, you should state them in the space below. If you want to limit in any other way the authority given your agent by this document, you should state the limits in the space below. If you do not state any limits, your agent will have broad powers to make health care decisions for you, except to the extent that there are limits provided by law.)

In exercising the authority under this durable power of attorney for health care, my agent shall act consistently with my desires as stated below and is subject to the special provisions and limitations stated below:

(a) Statement of desires concerning life-prolonging care, treatment, services, and procedures:

_____
_____
_____
_____
_____
_____
_____
_____
_____
_____
_____
_____

(b) Additional statement of desires, special provisions, and limitations: _____

_____
_____
_____
_____

_____
_____
_____
_____
_____
_____
_____
_____
_____
_____
_____

(You may attach additional pages if you need more space to complete your statement. If you attach additional pages, you must date and sign *each* of the additional pages at the same time you date and sign this document.)

5. INSPECTION AND DISCLOSURE OF INFORMATION RELATING TO MY PHYSICAL OR MENTAL HEALTH. Subject to any limitations in this document, my agent has the power and authority to do all of the following:

(a) Request, review, and receive any information, verbal or written, regarding my physical or mental health, including, but not limited to, medical and hospital records.

(b) Execute on my behalf any releases or other documents that may be required in order to obtain this information.

(c) Consent to the disclosure of this information.
[If you want to limit the authority of your agent to receive and disclose information relating to your health, you must state the limitations in paragraph 4 ("Statement of Desires, Special Provisions, and Limitations") above.]

6. SIGNING DOCUMENTS, WAIVERS, AND RELEASES. Where necessary to implement the health care decisions that my agent is authorized by this document to make, my agent has the power and authority to execute on my behalf all of the following:

(a) Documents titled or purporting to be a "Refusal to Permit Treatment" and "Leaving Hospital Against Medical Advice."

(b) Any necessary waiver or release from liability required by a hospital or physician.

7. UNIFORM ANATOMICAL GIFT ACT. Subject to any limitations in this document, my agent has the power and authority to make a disposition of a part or parts of my body under the Uniform Anatomical Gift Act (Chapter 3.5 (commencing with Section 7150) of Part 1 of Division 7 of the Health and Safety Code).
(If you want to limit the authority of your agent to make a disposition under the Uniform Anatomical Gift Act, you must state the limitations in paragraph 4 ("Statement of Desires, Special Provisions, and Limitations") above.)

8. DURATION.
(Unless you specify a shorter period in the space below, this power of attorney will exist for seven years from the date you execute this document and, if you are unable to make health care decisions for yourself at the time when this seven-year period ends, the power will continue to exist until the time when you become able to make health care decisions for yourself.)

This durable power of attorney for health care expires on _____ .
(Fill in this space ONLY if you want the authority of your agent to end *earlier* than the seven-year period described above.)

9. DESIGNATION OF ALTERNATE AGENTS.
(You are not required to designate any alternate agents but you may do so. Any alternate agent you designate will be able to make the same health care decisions as the agent you designated in paragraph 1, above, in the event that agent is unable or ineligible to act as your agent. If the agent you designated is your spouse, he or she becomes ineligible to act as your agent if your marriage is dissolved.)

If the person designated as my agent in paragraph 1 is not available or becomes ineligible to act as my agent to make a health care decision for me or loses the mental capacity to make health care decisions for me, or if I revoke that person's appointment or authority to act as my agent to make health care decisions for me, then I designate and appoint the following persons to serve as my agent to make health care decisions for me as authorized in this document, such persons to serve in the order listed below:

A. First Alternate Agent _____
_____
_____
_____
(Insert name, address, and telephone number
of first alternate agent)

B. Second Alternate Agent _____
_____
_____
_____
(Insert name, address, and telephone number
of second alternate agent)

10. NOMINATION OF CONSERVATOR OF PERSON.
(A conservator of the person may be appointed for you if a court decides that one should be appointed. The conservator is responsible for your physical care, which under some circumstances includes making health care decisions for you. You are not required to nominate a conservator but you may do so. The court will appoint the person you nominate unless that would be contrary to your best interests. You may, but are not required to, nominate as your conservator the same persons you named in paragraph 1 as your health care agent. You can nominate an individual as your conservator by completing the space below.)

If a conservator of the person is to be appointed for me, I nominate the following individual to serve as conservator of the person

_____
_____
_____
(Insert name and address of person nominated as
conservator of the person)

11. PRIOR DESIGNATIONS REVOKED. I revoke any prior durable power of attorney for health care.

3.

DATE AND SIGNATURE OF PRINCIPAL
(You Must Date and Sign This
Power of Attorney)

I sign my name to this Statutory Form Durable Power of Attorney for Health Care on _____
(Date)

at _____   _____
(City)   (State)

_____
(You sign here)

(This Power of Attorney will not be valid unless it is signed by two qualified witnesses who are present when you sign or acknowledge your signature. If you have attached any additional pages to this form, you must date and sign each of the additional pages at the same time you date and sign this Power of Attorney.)

STATEMENT OF WITNESSES

(This document must be witnessed by two qualified adult witnesses. None of the following may be used as a witness: (1) a person you designate as your agent or alternate agent, (2) a health care provider, (3) an employee of a health care provider, (4) the operator of a community care facility, (5) an employee of an operator of a community care facility. At least one of the witnesses must make the additional declaration set out following the place where the witnesses sign.)

I declare under penalty of perjury under the laws of California _____ that the person who signed
other state

or acknowledged this document is personally known to me (or proved to me on the basis of convincing evidence) to be the principal, that the principal signed or acknowledged this durable power of attorney in my presence, that the principal appears to be of sound mind and under no duress, fraud, or undue influence, that I am not the person appointed as attorney in fact by this document, and that I am not a health care provider, an employee of a health care provider, the operator of a community care facility, nor an employee of an operator of a community care facility.

Signature: _____
Print name: _____
Date: _____
Residence address: _____
_____
_____

Signature: _____
Print name: _____
Date: _____
Residence address: _____
_____
_____

(AT LEAST ONE OF THE ABOVE WITNESSES MUST ALSO SIGN THE FOLLOWING DECLARATION.)

I further declare under penalty of perjury under the laws of California _____ that I am not related
other state

to the principal by blood, marriage, or adoption, and, to the best of my knowledge, I am not entitled to any part of the estate of the principal upon the death of the principal under a will now existing or by operation of law.

Signature: _____
Signature: _____

STATEMENT OF PATIENT ADVOCATE OR OMBUDSMAN
(If you are a patient in a skilled nursing facility, one of the witnesses must be a patient advocate or ombudsman. The following statement is required only if you are a patient in a skilled nursing facility—a health care facility that provides the following basic services: skilled nursing care and supportive care to patients whose primary need is for availability of skilled nursing care on an extended basis. The patient advocate or ombudsman must sign both parts of the "Statement of Witnesses" above AND must also sign the following statement.)

I further declare under penalty of perjury under the laws of California _____ that I am a patient
other state

advocate or ombudsman as designated by the State Department of Aging and that I am serving as a witness as required by subdivision (f) of Section 2432 of the Civil Code.

Signature: _____

NOTARY

(Signer of instrument may either have it witnessed as above or have his/her signature notarized as below, to legalize this instrument.)

State of California _____
other state

County of _____ ss
On this _____ day of _____ 198 ___
before me personally appeared _____
(full name of signer of instrument)

to me known (or proved to me on basis of satisfactory evidence) to be the person whose name is subscribed to this instrument, and acknowledged that he/she executed it. I declare under penalty of perjury that the person whose name is subscribed to this instrument appears to be of sound mind and under no duress, fraud or undue influence.

_____
(Signature of Notary)

NOTARY SEAL

4.

Warning to Person Executing this Document

This is an important legal document. It creates a durable power of attorney for health care. Before executing this document, you should know these important facts:

This document gives the person you designate as your attorney in fact the power to make health care decisions for you, subject to any limitations or statement of your desires that you include in this document. The power to make health care decisions for you may include consent, refusal of consent, or withdrawal of consent to any care, treatment, service, or procedure to maintain, diagnose, or treat a physical or mental condition. You may state in this document any types of treatment or placements that you do not desire.

The person you designate in this document has a duty to act consistent with your desires as stated in this document or otherwise made known or, if your desires are unknown, to act in your best interests.

Except as you otherwise specify in this document, the power of the person you designate to make health care decisions for you may include the power to consent to your doctor not giving treatment or stopping treatment which would keep you alive.

Unless you specify a shorter period in this document, this power will exist for seven years from the date you execute this document and, if you are unable to make health care decisions for yourself at the time when this seven-year period ends, this power will continue to exist until the time when you become able to make health care decisions for yourself.

Notwithstanding this document, you have the right to make medical and other health care decisions for yourself so long as you can give informed consent with respect to the particular decision. In addition, no treatment may be given to you over your objection, and health care necessary to keep you alive may not be stopped if you object.

You have the right to revoke the appointment of the person designated in this document by notifying that person of the revocation orally or in writing.

You have the right to revoke the authority granted to the person designated in this document to make health care decisions for you by notifying the treating physician, hospital, or other health care provider orally or in writing.

The person designated in this document to make health care decisions for you has the right to examine your medical records and to consent to their disclosure unless you limit this right in this document.

If there is anything in this document that you do not understand, you should ask a lawyer to explain it to you.

(b) The printed form described in subdivision (a) shall also include the following notice: "This power of attorney will not be valid for making health care decisions unless it is either (1) signed by two qualified witnesses who are personally known to you and who are present when you sign or acknowledge your signature or (2) acknowledged before a notary public in California."

(c) A durable power of attorney prepared in this state that permits the attorney in fact to make health care decisions and that is not a printed form shall include one of the following:

(1) The substance of the statements provided for in subdivision (a) in capital letters.

(2) A certificate signed by the principal's lawyer stating: "I am a lawyer authorized to practice law in the state where this power of attorney was executed, and the principal was my client at the time this power of attorney was executed. I have advised my client concerning his or her rights in connection with this power of attorney and the applicable law and the consequences of signing or not signing this power of attorney, and my client, after being so advised, has executed this power of attorney."

(d) If a durable power of attorney includes the certificate provided for in paragraph (2) of subdivision (c) and permits the attorney in fact to make health care decisions for the principal, the applicable law of which the client is to be advised by the lawyer signing the certificate includes; but is not limited to, the matters listed in subdivision (a).

SEC. 6. Section 2434 of the Civil Code is amended to read:

2434. (a) Unless the durable power of attorney provides otherwise, the attorney in fact designated in a durable power of attorney for health care who is known to the health care provider to be available and willing to make health care decisions has priority over any other person to act for the principal in all matters of health care decisions, but the attorney in fact does not have authority to make a particular health care decision if the principal is able to give informed consent with respect to that decision.

(b) Subject to any limitations in the durable power of attorney, the attorney in fact designated in a durable power of attorney for health care may make health care decisions for the principal, before or after the death of the principal, to the same extent as the principal could make health care decisions for himself or herself if the principal had the capacity to do so, including; (1) making a disposition under the Uniform Anatomical Gift Act, Chapter 3.5 (commencing with Section 7150.5) of Part 1 of Division 7 of the Health and Safety Code, (2) authorizing an autopsy under Section 7113 of the Health and Safety Code, and (3) directing the disposition of remains under Section 7100 of the Health and Safety Code. In exercising the authority under the durable power of attorney for health care, the attorney in fact has a duty to act consistent with the desires of the principal as expressed in the durable power of attorney or otherwise made known to the attorney in fact at any time or, if the principal's desires are unknown, to act in the best interests of the principal.

(c) Nothing in this article affects any right the person designated as attorney in fact may have, apart from the durable power of attorney for health care, to make or participate in the making of health care decisions on behalf of the principal.

Read on (date) _____

Signed _____

5.

Natural Death Act, 1976
Guidelines for Signers

The DIRECTIVE allows you to instruct your doctor not to use artificial methods to extend the natural process of dying.

Before signing the DIRECTIVE, you may ask advice from anyone you wish, but you do not have to see a lawyer or have the DIRECTIVE certified by a notary public.

If you sign the DIRECTIVE, talk it over with your doctor and ask that it be made part of your medical record.

The DIRECTIVE must be WITNESSED by two adults who 1) are not related to you by blood or marriage, 2) are not mentioned in your will, and 3) would have no claim on your estate.

The DIRECTIVE may NOT be witnessed by your doctor or by anyone working for your doctor. If you are in a HOSPITAL at the time you sign the DIRECTIVE, none of its employees may be a witness. If you are in a SKILLED NURSING FACILITY, one of your two witnesses MUST be a "patient advocate" or "ombudsman" designated by the State Department of Aging.

You may sign a DIRECTIVE TO PHYSICIANS if you are at least 18 years old and of sound mind, acting of your own free will in the presence of two qualified witnesses.

No one may force you to sign the DIRECTIVE. No one may deny you insurance or health care services because you have chosen *not* to sign it. If you *do* sign the DIRECTIVE, it will not affect your insurance or any other rights you may have to accept or reject medical treatment.

Your doctor is bound by the DIRECTIVE only 1) if he/she is satisfied that your DIRECTIVE is valid, 2) if another doctor has certified your condition as terminal, and 3) at least 14 days have gone by since you were informed of your condition. (California only.)

If you sign a DIRECTIVE while in good health, your doctor may respect your wishes but is not bound by the DIRECTIVE.

The DIRECTIVE is valid for a period of five years, at which time you may sign a new one.

The DIRECTIVE is not valid during pregnancy.

Revocation
You may revoke the DIRECTIVE *at any time,* even in the final stages of a terminal illness, by 1) destroying it, 2) signing and dating a written statement, or 3) by informing your doctor. No matter how you revoke the DIRECTIVE, be sure your doctor is told of your decision.

NOTES FOR A LIVING WILL

1. Under California law, for such an appointment to be as fully effective as the law will permit, it must be in the form included on page one under the title "DURABLE POWER OF ATTORNEY FOR HEALTH CARE DECISIONS." Persons living in other states and executing this "Living Will" also might wish to execute that form (Durable Power of Attorney), as it might well be honored by the medical practitioners and courts of any particular state. If you do not in fact execute a Durable Power of Attorney, strike out the last sentence of this paragraph.

2. This is an explicit requirement of the California statute.

However, even a woman of child-bearing age in another state should leave it in, in order to avoid the implication that this problem has not been considered, with the possible effect of voiding the instrument.

3. If you are *not* a resident of California, strike out Paragraph 5 in its entirety.

4. The five-year limit is a California legal requirement. If a different one exists in your state, strike out the 5 and insert the proper limit. If no limit is imposed in your state, strike out Paragraph 6 entirely.

THE NATIONAL
HEMLOCK SOCIETY
P.O. Box 11830
Eugene, OR 97440-3900
503/342-5748
A Nonprofit Corporation Founded in 1980

6.

Appendix 5

Death and Dignity*
A Case of Individualized Decision Making

Diane was feeling tired and had a rash. A common scenario, though there was something subliminally worrisome that prompted me to check her blood count. Her hematocrit was 22, and the white-cell count was 4.3 with some metamyelocytes and unusual white cells. I wanted it to be viral, trying to deny what was staring me in the face. Perhaps in a repeated count it would disappear. I called Diane and told her it might be more serious than I had initially thought—that the test needed to be repeated and that if she felt worse, we might have to move quickly. When she pressed for the possibilities, I reluctantly opened the door to leukemia. Hearing the word seemed to make it exist. "Oh, shit!" she said. "Don't tell me that." Oh, shit! I thought, I wish I didn't have to.

Diane was no ordinary person (although no one I have ever come to know has been really ordinary). She was raised in an alcoholic family and had felt alone for much of her life. She had vaginal cancer as a young woman. Through much of her adult life, she had struggled with depression and her own alcoholism. I had come to know, respect, and admire her over the previous eight years as she confronted these problems and gradually overcame them. She was an incredibly clear, at times brutally honest, thinker and communicator. As she took control of her life, she developed a strong sense of independence and confidence. In the previous 3½ years, her hard work had paid off. She was completely abstinent from alcohol, she had established much

---

*Printed by permission of the *New England Journal of Medicine,* where the article originally appeared in the "Sounding Board" section (vol. 324, no. 10, March 7, 1991), written by Timothy Quill, M.D..

deeper connections with her husband, college-age son, and several friends, and her business and her artistic work were blossoming. She felt she was really living fully for the first time.

Not surprisingly, the repeated blood count was abnormal, and detailed examinations of the peripheral-blood smear showed myelocytes. I advised her to come into the hospital, explaining that we needed to do a bone marrow biopsy and make some decisions relatively rapidly. She came to the hospital knowing what we would find. She was terrified, angry, and sad. Although we knew the odds, we both clung to the thread of possibility that it might be something else.

The bone marrow confirmed the worst: acute myelomonocytic leukemia. In the face of this tragedy, we looked for signs of hope. This is an area of medicine in which technological intervention has been successful, with cures 25 percent of the time—long-term cures. As I probed the costs of these cures, I heard about induction chemotherapy (three weeks in the hospital, prolonged neutropenia, probable infectious complications, and hair loss; 75 percent of patients respond, 25 percent do not). For the survivors, this is followed by consolidation chemotherapy (with similar side effects; another 25 percent die, for a net survival of 50 percent). Those still alive, to have a reasonable chance of long-term survival, then need bone marrow transplantation (hospitalization for two months and whole-body irradiation, with complete killing of the bone marrow, infectious complications, and the possibility for graft-versus-host disease—with a survival of approximately 50 percent, or 25 percent of the original group). Though hematologists may argue over the exact percentages, they don't argue over the outcome of no treatment—certain death in days, weeks, or at most a few months.

Believing that delay was dangerous, our oncologist broke the news to Diane and began making plans to insert a Hickman catheter and began induction chemotherapy that afternoon. When I saw her shortly thereafter, she was enraged at his presumption that she would want treatment, and devastated by the finality of the diagnosis. All she wanted to do was go home and be with her family. She had no further questions about treatment and in fact had decided that she wanted none. Together we lamented her tragedy and the unfairness of life. Before she left, I felt the need to be sure that she and her husband understood that there was some risk in delay, that the problem was not going to go away, and that we needed to keep considering the options over the next several days. We agreed to meet in two days.

She returned in two days with her husband and son. They had talked extensively about the problem and the options. She remained very clear about her wish not to undergo chemotherapy and to live whatever time she had left outside the hospital. As we explored her thinking further, it became clear that she was convinced she would die during the period of treatment and would suffer unspeakably in the process (from hospitalization, from lack of control over her body, from the side effects of chemotherapy, and from pain and anguish). Although I could offer support and my best effort to minimize her suffering if she chose treatment, there was no way I could say any of this would not occur. In fact, the last four patients with acute leukemia at our hospital had died very painful deaths in the hospital during various stages of treatment (a fact I did not share with her). Her family wished she would choose treatment but sadly accepted her decision. She articulated very clearly that it was she who would be experiencing all the side effects of treatment and that odds of 25 percent were not good enough for her to undergo so toxic a course of therapy, given her expectations of chemotherapy and hospitalization and the absence of a closely matched bone marrow donor. I had her repeat her understanding of the treatment, the odds, and what to expect if there were no treatment. I clarified a few misunderstandings, but she had a remarkable grasp of the options and implications.

I have been a longtime advocate of active, informed patient choice of treatment or nontreatment, and of a patient's right to die with as much control and dignity as possible. Yet there was something about her giving up a 25 percent chance of long-term survival in favor of almost certain death that disturbed me. I had seen Diane fight and use her considerable inner resources to overcome alcoholism and depression, and I half expected her to change her mind over the next week. Since the window of time in which effective treatment can be initiated is rather narrow, we met several times that week. We obtained a second hematology consultation and talked at length about the meaning and implications of treatment and nontreatment. She talked to a psychologist she had seen in the past. I gradually understood the decision from her perspective and became convinced that it was the right decision for her. We arranged for home hospice care (although at that time Diane felt reasonably well, was active, and looked healthy), left the door open for her to change her mind, and tried to anticipate how to keep her comfortable in the time she had left.

Just as I was adjusting to her decision, she opened up another area that would stretch me profoundly. It was extraordinarily important to Diane to maintain control of herself and her own dignity during the time remaining to her. When this was no longer possible, she clearly wanted to die. As a former director of a hospice program, I know how to use pain medicines to keep patients comfortable and lessen suffering. I explained the philosophy of comfort care, which I strongly believe in. Although Diane understood and appreciated this, she had known of people lingering in what was called relative comfort, and she wanted no part of it. When the time came, she wanted to take her life in the least painful way possible. Knowing of her desire for independence and her decision to stay in control, I thought this request made perfect sense. I acknowledged and explored this wish but also thought that it was out of the realm of currently accepted medical practice and that it was more than I could offer or promise. In our discussion, it became clear that preoccupation with her fear of a lingering death would interfere with Diane's getting the most out of the time she had left until she found a safe way to ensure her death. I feared the effects of a violent death on her family, the consequences of an ineffective suicide that would leave her lingering in precisely the state she dreaded so much, and the possibility that a family member would be forced to assist her, with all the legal and personal repercussions that would follow. She discussed this at length with her family. They believed that they should respect her choice. With this in mind, I told Diane that information was available from the Hemlock Society that might be helpful to her.

A week later she phoned me with a request for barbiturates for sleep. Since I knew that this was an essential ingredient in a Hemlock Society suicide, I asked her to come to the office to talk things over. She was more than willing to protect me by participating in a superficial conversation about her insomnia, but it was important to me to know how she planned to use the drugs and to be sure that she was not in despair or overwhelmed in a way that might color her judgment. In our discussion, it was apparent that she was having trouble sleeping, but it was also evident that the security of having enough barbiturates available to commit suicide when and if the time came would leave her secure enough to live fully and concentrate on the present. It was clear that she was not despondent and that in fact she was making deep, personal connections with her family and close friends. I made sure that she knew how to use the barbiturates for sleep, and also that she knew the amount needed to commit suicide. We agreed to meet regularly, and she promised to meet with me before taking her life, to ensure that all other avenues had been exhausted. I wrote the prescription with an uneasy feeling about the boundaries I was exploring—spiritual, legal, professional, and personal. Yet I also felt strongly that I was setting her free to get the most out of the time she had left, and to maintain dignity and control on her own terms until her death.

The next several months were very intense and important for Diane. Her son stayed home from college, and they were able to be with one another and say much that had not been said earlier. Her husband did his work at home so that he and Diane could spend more time together. She spent time with her closest friends. I had her come into the hospital for a conference with our residents, at which she illustrated in a most profound and personal way the importance of informed decision making, the right to refuse treatment, and the extraordinary personal effects of illness and interaction with the medical system. There were emotional and physical hardships as well. She had periods of intense sadness and anger. Several times she became very weak, but she received transfusions as an outpatient and responded with marked improvement of symptoms. She had two serious infections that responded surprisingly well to empirical courses of oral antibiotics. After three tumultuous months, there were two weeks of relative calm and well-being, and fantasies of a miracle began to surface.

Unfortunately, we had no miracle. Bone pain, weakness, fatigue, and fevers began to dominate her life. Although the hospice workers, family members, and I tried our best to minimize the suffering and promote comfort, it was clear that the end was approaching. Diane's immediate future held what she feared the most—increasing discomfort, dependence, and hard choices between pain and sedation. She called up her closest friends and asked them to come over to say goodbye, telling them that she would be leaving soon. As we had agreed, she let me know as well. When we met, it was clear that she knew what she was doing, that she was sad and frightened to be leaving, but that she would be even more terrified to stay and suffer. In our tearful goodbye, she promised a reunion: in the future at her favorite spot on the edge of Lake Geneva, with dragons swimming in the sunset.

Two days later her husband called to say that Diane had died. She had said her final goodbyes to her husband and son that morning, and asked them to leave her alone for an hour. After an hour, which must have seemed an eternity, they found her on the couch, lying very still and covered by her favorite shawl. There was no sign of struggle. She seemed to be at peace. They called me for advice about how to proceed. When I arrived at their house, Diane indeed seemed peaceful. Her husband and son were quiet. We talked about what a remarkable person she had been. They seemed to have no doubts about the course she had chosen or about their cooperation, although the unfairness of her illness and the finality of her death were overwhelming to us all.

I called the medical examiner to inform him that a hospice patient had died. When asked about the cause of death, I said, "acute leukemia." He said that was fine and that we should call a funeral director. Although acute leukemia was the truth, it was not the whole story. Yet any mention of suicide would have given rise to a police investigation and probably brought the arrival of an ambulance crew for resuscitation. Diane would have become a "coroner's case," and the decision to perform an autopsy would have been made at the discretion of the medical examiner. The family or I could have been subject to criminal prosecution, and I to professional review, for our roles in support of Diane's choices. Although I truly believe that the family and I gave her the best care possible, allowing her to define her limits and directions as much as possible, I am not sure the law, society, or the medical profession would agree. So I said "acute leukemia" to protect all of us, to protect Diane from an invasion into her past and her body, and to continue to shield society from the knowledge of the degree of suffering that people often undergo in the process of dying. Suffering can be lessened to some extent, but in no way eliminated or made benign, by the careful intervention of a competent, caring physician, given current social constraints.

Diane taught me about the range of help I can provide if I know people well and if I allow them to say what they really want. She taught me about life, death, and honesty and about taking charge and facing tragedy squarely when it strikes. She taught me that I can take small risks for people that I really know and care about. Although I did not assist in her suicide directly, I helped indirectly to make it possible, successful, and relatively painless. Although I know we have measures to help control pain and lessen suffering, to think that people do not suffer in the process of dying is an illusion. Prolonged dying can occasionally be peaceful, but more often the role of the physician and family is limited to lessening but not eliminating severe suffering.

I wonder how many families and physicians secretly help patients over the edge into death in the face of such severe suffering. I wonder how many severely ill or dying patients secretly take their lives, dying alone in despair. I wonder whether the image of Diane's final aloneness will persist in the minds of her family, of if they will remember more the intense, meaningful months they had together before she died. I wonder whether Diane struggled in that last hour, and whether the Hemlock Society's way of death by suicide is the most benign. I wonder why Diane, who gave so much to so many of us, had to be alone for the last hour of her life. I wonder whether I will see Diane again, on the shore of Lake Geneva at sunset, with dragons swimming on the horizon.

Timothy E. Quill, M.D.
The Genesee Hospital
Rochester, NY 14607

Appendix 6

U.S. Congress
Patient Self-Determination
Act Provision in OBRA 1990
(Public Law 101-508) signed
November 5, 1990, by President Bush

SEC. 420C. MEDICARE PROVIDER AGREEMENTS ASSURING THE IMPLEMENTATION OF A
PATIENT'S RIGHT TO PARTICIPATE IN AND DIRECT HEALTH CARE DECISIONS
AFFECTING THE PATIENT.

    (a) IN GENERAL—Section 1866(a)(1) (42 U.S.C. 1395cc(a)(1)) is amended—

        (1) in subsection (a)(1)—

            (A) by striking "and" at the end of subparagraph (O),

            (B) by striking the period at the end of subparagraph (P) and
inserting ", and", and

            (C) by inserting after subparagraph (P) the following new subparagraph:

    "(Q) in the case of hospitals, skilled nursing facilities, home health agencies,
and hospice programs, to comply with the requirement of subsection (f) (relating to
maintaining written policies and procedures respecting advance directives)"; and

        (2) by inserting after subsection (e) the following new subsection:

    "(f)(1) For purposes of subsection (a)(1)(Q) and sections 1819(c)(2)(E), 1833(r),
1876(c)(8), and 1891 (a)(6), the requirement of this subsection is that a provider of
services or prepaid or eligible organization (as the case may be) maintain written policies
and procedures with respect to all adult individuals receiving medical care by or through
the provider or organization—

"(A) to provide written information to each individual concerning—

"(i) an individual's rights under State law (whether statutory or as recognized by the courts of the State) to make decisions concerning such medical care, including the right to accept or refuse medical or surgical treatment and the right to formulate advance directives (as defined in paragraph (3)), and

"(ii) the written policies of the provider or organization respecting the implementation of such rights;

"(B) to document in the individual's medical record whether or not the individual has executed an advance directive;

"(C) not to condition the provision of care or otherwise discriminate against an individual based on whether or not the individual has executed an advance directive;

"(D) to ensure compliance with requirements of State law (whether statutory or as recognized by the courts of the State) respecting advance directives at facilities of the provider or organization; and

"(E) to provide (individually or with others) for education for staff and the community on issues concerning advance directives.

Subparagraph (C) shall not be construed as requiring the provision of care which conflicts with an advance directive.

"(2) The written information described in paragraph (1)(A) shall be provided to an adult individual—

"(A) in the case of a hospital, at the time of the individual's admission as an inpatient,

"(B) in the case of a skilled nursing facility, at the time of the individual's admission as a resident,

"(C) in the case of a home health agency, in advance of the individual coming under the care of the agency,

"(D) in the case of a hospice program, at the time of initial receipt of hospice care by the individual from the program, and

"(E) in the case of an eligible organization (as defined in section 1876(b)) or an organization provided payments under section 1833(a)(1)(A), at the time of enrollment of the individual with the organization.

"(3) In this subsection, the term 'advance directive' means a written instruction, such as a living will or durable power of attorney for health care, recognized under State law (whether statutory or as recognized by the courts of the State) and relating to the provision of such care when the individual is incapacitated."

(b) APPLICATION TO PREPAID ORGANIZATIONS—

(1) ELIGIBLE ORGANIZATIONS.—Section 1876(c) of such Act (42 U.S.C. 1395mm(c)) is amended by adding at the end the following new paragraph:

"(8) A contract under this section shall provide that the eligible organization shall meet the requirement of section 1866(f) (relating to maintaining written policies and procedures respecting advance directives)."

(2) OTHER PREPAID ORGANIZATIONS.—Section 1833 of such Act (42 U.S.C. 13951) is amended by adding at the end the following new subsection:

"(r) The Secretary may not provide for payment under subsection (a)(1)(A) with respect to an organization unless the organization provides assurances satisfactory to the Secretary that the organization meets the requirement of section 1866(f) (relating to maintaining written policies and procedures respecting advance directives."

(c) EFFECT ON STATE LAW.—Nothing in subsections (a) and (b) shall be construed to prohibit the application of a State law which allows for an objection on the basis of conscience for any health care provider or any agent of such provider which, as a matter of conscience, cannot implement an advance directive.

(d) CONFORMING AMENDMENTS.—

(1) Section 1819(c)(1) of such Act (42 U.S.C. 1395i-3(c)(1)) is amended by adding at the end the following new subparagraph:

"(E) INFORMATION RESPECTING ADVANCE DIRECTIVES.—A skilled nursing facility must comply with the requirement of section 1866 (f) (relating to maintaining written policies and procedures respecting advance directives)."

(2) Section 1891(a) of such Act (42 U.S.C. 1395bbb(a)) is amended by adding at the end the following:

"(6) The agency complies with the requirement of section 1866(f) (relating to maintaining written policies and procedures respecting advance directives)."

(e) EFFECTIVE DATES.—

(1) The amendments made by subjections (a) and (d) shall apply with respect to services furnished on or after the first day of the first month beginning more than 1 year after the date of the enactment of this Act.

(2) The amendments made by subsection (b) shall apply to contracts under section 1876 of the Social Security Act and payments under section 1883(a)(1)(A) of such Act as of first day of the first month beginning more than 1 year after the date of the enactment of this Act.

SEC. 4571. REQUIREMENTS FOR ADVANCED DIRECTIVES UNDER STATE PLANS FOR MEDI-
    CAL ASSISTANCE.

(a) IN GENERAL.—Section 1902 (42 U.S.C. 1396a(a)), as amended by sections 4401(a)(2), 4601(d), 4711(a), and 4722 of this title, is amended—

(1)in subsection (a)—

(A) by striking "and" at the end of paragraph (55),

(B) by striking the period at the end of paragraph (56) and inserting "; and", and

(C) by inserting after paragraph (56) the following new paragraphs:

"(57) provide that each hospital, nursing facility, provider of home health care or personal care services, hospice program, or health maintenance organization (as defined in section 1903(m)(1)(A)) receiving funds under the plan shall comply with the requirements of subsection (w);

"(58) provide that the State, acting through a State agency, association, or other private nonprofit entity, develop a written description of the law of the State (whether statutory or as recognized by the courts of the State) concerning advance directives that would be distributed by providers or organizations under the requirements of subsection (w).”; and

(2) by adding at the end the following new subsection:

“(u)(1) For purposes of subsection (a)(57) and sections 1903(m)(1)(A) and 1919(c)(2)(E), the requirement of this subsection is that a provider or organization (as the case may be) maintain written policies and procedures with respect to all adult individuals receiving medical care or through the provider or organization—

“(A) to provide written information to each such individual concerning—

“(i) an individual’s rights under State law (whether statutory or as recognized by the courts of the state) to make decisions concerning such medical care, including the right to accept or refuse medical or surgical treatment and the right to formulate advance directives (as defined in paragraph (3)), and

“(ii) the provider’s or organization’s written policies respecting the implementation of such rights;

“(B) to document in the individual’s medical record whether or not the individual has executed an advance directive;

“(C) not to condition the provision of care or otherwise discriminate against an individual based on whether or not the individual has executed an advance directive;

“(D) to ensure compliance with requirements of State law (whether statutory or as recognized by the courts of the State) respecting advance directives; and

“(E) to provide (individually or with others) for education for staff and the community on issues concerning advance directives.

Subparagraph (C) shall not be construed as requiring the provision of care which conflicts with an advance directive.

“(2) The written information described in paragraph (1)(A) shall be provided to an adult individual—

“(A) in the case of a hospital, at the time of the individual’s admission as an inpatient,

“(B) in the case of a nursing facility, at the time of the individual’s admission as a resident,

“(C) in the case of a provider of home health care or personal care services, in advance of the individual coming under the care of the provider,

“(D) in the case of a hospice program, at the time of initial receipt of hospice care by the individual from the program, and

“(E) in the case of a health maintenance organization, at the time of enrollment of the individual with the organization.

“(3) Nothing in this section shall be construed to prohibit the application of a State law which allows for an objection on the basis of conscience for any health care provider or any agent of such provider which as a matter of conscience cannot implement an advance directive.”

"(4) In this subsection, the term 'advance directive' means a written instruction, such as a living will or durable power of attorney for health care, recognized under State law (whether statutory or as recognized by the courts of the State) and relating to the provision of such care when the individual is incapacitated.

(b) CONFORMING AMENDMENTS.—

(1) Section 1903(m)(1)(A)(42) U.S.C. 1396b(m)(1)(A) is amended—

(A) by inserting "meets the requirement of section 1902(a) and" after "which" the first place it appears, and

(B) by inserting "meets the requirement of section 1902(a) and" after "which" the second place it appears.

(2) Section 1919(c)(2) of such Act (42 U.S.C. 1396r(c)(2)) is amended by adding at the end of the following new subparagraph:

"(E) INFORMATION RESPECTING ADVANCE DIRECTIVES.—A nursing facility must comply with the requirement of section 1902(w) (relating to maintaining written policies and procedures respecting advance directives)."

(c) EFFECTIVE DATE.—The amendments made by this section shall apply with respect to services furnished on or after the first day of the first month beginning more than 1 year after the date of the enactment of this Act.

(d) PUBLIC EDUCATION CAMPAIGN.—

(1) IN GENERAL.—The Secretary, no later than 6 months after the date of enactment of this section, shall develop and implement a national campaign to inform the public of the option to execute advance directives and of a patient's right to participate and direct health care decisions.

(2) DEVELOPMENT AND DISTRIBUTION OF INFORMATION.—The Secretary shall develop or approve nationwide informational materials that would be distributed by providers under the requirements of this section, to inform the public and the medical and legal profession of each person's right to make decisions concerning medical care, including the right to accept or refuse medical or surgical treatment, and the existence of advance directives.

(3) PROVIDING ASSISTANCE TO STATES.—The Secretary shall assist appropriate State agencies, associations, or other private entities in developing the State-specific documents that would be distributed by providers under the requirements of this section. The Secretary shall further assist appropriate State agencies, associations, or other private entities in ensuring that providers are provided a copy of the documents that are to be distributed under the requirements of the section.

(4) DUTIES OF SECRETARY.—The Secretary shall mail information to Social Security recipients, add a page to the medicare handbook with respect to the provisions of this section.

Appendix 7

The 1992 California
Death with Dignity Act
(Proposition #161)*

California Civil Code, Title 10.5

SEC. 1. Title 10.5 (commencing with Section 2525.) is added to Division 3 of part 4 of the Civil Code, to read:

2525 Title

This title shall be known and may be cited as the Death With Dignity Act.

22525.1 Declaration of Purpose

The people of California declare:

Current state laws do not adequately protect the rights of terminally ill patients. The purpose of this Act is to provide mentally competent terminally ill adults the legal right to voluntarily request and receive physician aid-in-dying. This Act protects physicians who voluntarily comply with the request and provides strong safeguards against

---

*On November 3, 1992, the voters cast 4,562,010 (46 percent) yes ballots and 5,348,947 (54 percent) no ballots.

abuse. The Act requires the signing of a witnessed revocable Directive in advance and then requires a terminally ill patient to communicate his or her request directly to the treating physician.

Self-determination is the most basic of freedoms. The right to choose to eliminate pain and suffering, and to die with dignity at the time and place of our own choosing when we are terminally ill is an integral part of our right to control our own destinies. That right is hereby established in law, but limited to ensure that the rights of others are not affected. The right should include the ability to make a conscious and informed choice to enlist the assistance of the medical profession in making death as painless, humane, and dignified as possible.

Modern medical technology has made possible the artificial prolongation of human life beyond natural limits. This prolongation of life for persons with terminal conditions may cause loss of patient dignity and unnecessary pain and suffering, for both the patient and the family, while providing nothing medically necessary or beneficial to the patient.

In recognition of the dignity which patients have a right to expect, the State of California recognizes the right of mentally competent terminally ill adults to make a voluntary revocable written Directive instructing their physician to administer aid-in-dying to end their life in a painless, humane and dignified manner.

The Act is voluntary. Accordingly, no one shall be required to take advantage of this legal right or to participate if they are religiously, morally or ethically opposed.

2525.2 Definitions

The following definitions shall govern the construction of this title:

(a) "Attending physician" means the physician selected by, or assigned to, the patient who has primary responsibility for the treatment and care of the patient.

(b) "Directive" means a revocable written document voluntarily executed by the declarant in accordance with the requirements of Section 2525.3 in substantially the form set forth in Section 2525.24.

(c) "Declarant" means a person who executes a Directive, in accordance with this title.

(d) "Life-sustaining procedure" means any medical procedure or intervention which utilizes mechanical or other artificial means to sustain, restore, or supplant a vital function, including nourishment and hydration which, when applied to a qualified patient, would serve only to prolong artificially the moment of death. "Life-sustaining procedure" shall not include the administration of medication or the performance of any medical procedure deemed necessary to alleviate pain or reverse any condition.

(e) "Physician" means a physician and surgeon licensed by the Medical Board of California.

(f) "Health care provider" and "Health care professional" mean a person or facility or employee of a health care facility licensed, certified, or otherwise authorized by the law of this state to administer health care in the ordinary course of business or practice of a profession.

(g) "Community care facility" means a community care facility as defined in Section 1502 of the Health and Safety Code.

(h) "Qualified patient" means a mentally competent adult patient who has voluntarily executed a currently valid revocable Directive as defined in this section, who has been diagnosed and certified in writing by two physicians to be afflicted with a terminal condition, and who has expressed an enduring request for aid-in-dying. One of said physicians shall be the attending physician as defined in subsection (a). Both physicians shall have personally examined the patient.

(i) "Enduring request" means a request for aid-in-dying, expressed on more than one occasion.

(j) "Terminal condition" means an incurable or irreversible condition which will, in the opinion of two certifying physicians exercising reasonable medical judgment, result in death within six months or less. One of said physicians shall be the attending physician as defined in subsection (a).

(k) "Aid-in-dying" means a medical procedure that will terminate the life of the qualified patient in a painless, humane, and dignified manner whether administered by the physician at the patient's choice or direction or whether the physician provides means to the patient for self-administration.

2525.3 Witnessed Directive

A mentally competent adult individual may at any time voluntarily execute a revocable Directive governing the administration of aid-in-dying. The Directive shall be signed by the declarant and witnessed by two adults who, at the time of witnessing, meet the following requirements:

(a) Are not related to the declarant by blood or marriage, or adoption;

(b) Are not entitled to any portion of the estate of the declarant upon his/her death under any will of the declarant or codicil thereto then existing, or, at the time of the Directive, by operation of law then existing;

(c) Have no creditor's claim against the declarant, or anticipate making such claims against any portion of the estate of the declarant upon his or her death;

(d) Are not the attending physician, an employee of the attending physician, a health care provider, or an employee of a health care provider;

(e) Are not the operator of a community care facility or an employee of a community care facility.

The Directive shall be substantially in the form contained in Section 2525.24.

2525.4 Skilled Nursing Facilities

A Directive shall have no force or effect if the declarant is a patient in a skilled nursing facility as defined in subdivision (c) of Section 1250 of the Health and Safety Code and intermediate care facility or community care facility at the time the Directive is executed unless one of the two witnesses to the Directive is a Patient Advocate or Ombudsman designated by the Department of Aging for this purpose pursuant to any other applicable provision of law. The Patient Advocate or Ombudsman shall have the same qualifications as a witness under Section 2525.3.

The intent of this paragraph is to recognize that some patients in skilled nursing facilities may be so insulated from a voluntary decision-making role, by virtue of the custodial nature of their care, as to require special assurance that they are capable of willingly and voluntarily executing a Directive.

2525.5 Revocation

A Directive may be revoked at any time by the declarant, without regard to his or her mental state or competency, by any of the following methods:

(a) By being canceled, defaced, obliterated, burned, torn, or otherwise destroyed by or at the direction of the declarant with the intent to revoke the Directive.

(b) By a written revocation of the declarant expressing his or her intent to revoke the Directive, signed and dated by the declarant. If the declarant is in a health care facility and under the care and management of a physician, the physician shall record in the patient's medical record the time and date when he or she received notification of the written revocation.

(c) By a verbal expression by the declarant of his or her intent to revoke the Directive. The revocation shall become effective only upon communication to the attending physician by the declarant. The attending physician shall confirm with the patient that he or she wishes to revoke, and shall record in the patient's medical record the time, date, and place of the revocation.

There shall be no criminal, civil or administrative liability on the part of any health care provider following a Directive that has been revoked unless that person has actual knowledge of the revocation.

2525.6 Term of Directive

A Directive shall be effective unless and until revoked in the manner prescribed in Section 2525.5. This title shall not prevent a declarant from re-executing a directive at any time in accordance with Section 2525.3, including re-execution subsequent to a diagnosis of a terminal condition.

2525.7 Administration of Aid-in-Dying

When, and only when, a qualified patient determines that the time for physician aid-in-dying has arrived and has made an enduring request, the patient will communicate that determination directly to the attending physician who will administer aid-in-dying in accordance with this Act.

2525.8 No Compulsion

Nothing herein requires a physician to administer aid-in-dying, or a licensed health care professional, such as a nurse, to participate in administering aid-in-dying under the direction of a physician, if he or she is religiously, morally, or ethically opposed. Neither shall privately owned hospitals be required to permit the administration of physician aid-in-dying in their facilities if they are religiously, morally, or ethically opposed.

2525.9 Protection of Health Care Professionals

No physician, health care facility or employee of a health care facility who, acting in accordance with the requirements of this title, administers aid-in-dying to a qualified patient shall be subject to civil, criminal, or administrative liability therefore. No licensed health care professional, such as a nurse, acting under the direction of a physician, who participates in the administration of aid-in-dying to a qualified patient in accordance with this title shall be subject to any civil, criminal, or administrative liability. No physician, or licensed health care professional acting under the direction of a physician, who acts in accordance with the provisions of this chapter, shall be guilty of any criminal act or of unprofessional conduct because he or she administers aid-in-dying.

2525.10 Transfer of Patient

No physician, or health care professional or health care provider acting under the direction of a physician, shall be criminally, civilly, or administratively liable for failing to effectuate the Directive of the qualified patient, unless there is willful failure to transfer the patient to any physician, health care professional, or health care provider upon request of the patient.

2525.11 Fees

Fees, if any, for administering aid-in-dying shall be fair and reasonable.

2525.12 Independent Physicians

The certifying physicians shall not be partners or shareholders in the same medical practice.

2525.13 Consultations

An attending physician who is requested to give aid-in-dying may request a psychiatric or psychological consultation if that physician has any concern about the patient's competence, with the consent of a qualified patient.

2525.14 Directive Compliance

Prior to administering aid-in-dying to a qualified patient, the attending physician shall take reasonable steps to determine that the Directive has been signed and witnessed, and all steps are in accord with the desires of the patient, expressed in the Directive and in their personal discussions. Absent knowledge to the contrary, a physician or other health care provider may presume the Directive complies with this title and is valid.

2525.15 Medical Standards

No physician shall be required to take any action contrary to reasonable medical standards in administering aid-in-dying.

2525.16 Not Suicide

Requesting and receiving aid-in-dying by a qualified patient in accordance with this title shall not, for any purpose, constitute a suicide.

2525.17 Insurance

(a) No insurer doing business in California shall refuse to insure, cancel, refuse to renew, re-assess the risk of an insured, or raise premiums on the basis of whether or not the insured has considered or completed a Directive. No insurer may require or request the insured to disclose whether he or she has executed a Directive.

(b) The making of a Directive pursuant to Section 2525.3 shall not restrict, inhibit, or impair in any manner the sale, procurement, issuance or rates of any policy of life, health, or disability insurance, nor shall it affect in any way the terms of an existing policy of life, health or disability insurance. No policy of life, health, or disability insurance shall be legally impaired or invalidated in any manner by the administration of aid-in-dying to an insured qualified patient, notwithstanding any term of the policy to the contrary.

(c) No physician, health care facility, or other health care provider, and no health care service plan, insurer issuing disability, insurance, other insurer, self-insured employee welfare benefit plan, or non-profit hospital service plan shall require any person to execute or prohibit any person from executing a Directive as a condition for being insured for, or receiving, health care services, nor refuse service because of the execution, the existence, or the revocation of a Directive.

(d) A person who, or a corporation, or other business which requires or prohibits the execution of a Directive as a condition for being insured for, or receiving, health care services is guilty of a misdemeanor.

(e) No life insurer doing business in California may refuse to pay sums due upon the death of the insured whose death was assisted in accordance with this Act.

2525.18 Inducement

No patient may be pressured to make a decision to seek aid-in-dying because that patient is a financial, emotional, or other burden to his or her family, other persons, or the state. A person who coerces, pressures, or fraudulently induces another to execute a Directive under this chapter is guilty of a misdemeanor, or if death occurs as a result of said coercion, pressure or fraud, is guilty of a felony.

2525.19 Tampering

Any person who willfully conceals, cancels, defaces, obliterates, or damages the Directive of another without the declarant's consent shall be guilty of a misdemeanor. Any person who falsifies or forges the Directive of another, or willfully conceals or withholds personal knowledge of a revocation as provided in Section 2525.5, with the intent to induce aid-in-dying procedures contrary to the wishes of the declarant, and thereby, because of such act, directly causes aid-in-dying to be administered, shall be subject to prosecution for unlawful homicide as provided in Chapter 1 (commencing with Section 187) of Title 8 of Part 1 of the Penal Code.

2525.20 Other Rights

This Act shall not impair or supersede any right or legal responsibility which any person may have regarding the withholding or withdrawal of life-sustaining procedures in any lawful manner.

2525.21 Reporting

Hospitals and other health care providers who carry out the Directive of a qualified patient shall keep a record of the number of these cases, and report annually to the State Department of Health Services the patient's age, type of illness, and the date the Directive was carried out. In all cases, the identity of the patient shall be strictly confidential and shall not be reported.

2525.22 Recording

The Directive, or a copy of the Directive, shall be made a part of a patient's medical record in each institution involved in the patient's medical care.

2525.23 Mercy Killing Disapproved

Nothing in this Act shall be construed to condone, authorize, or approve mercy killing.

2525.24 Form of Directive

In order for a Directive to be valid under this title, the Directive shall be in substantially the following form:

VOLUNTARY DIRECTIVE TO PHYSICIAN

Notice to Patient:

This document will exist until it is revoked by you. This document revokes any prior Directive to administer aid-in-dying but does not revoke a durable power of attorney for health care or living will. You must follow the witnessing procedures described at the end of this form or the document will not be valid. You may wish to give your doctor a signed copy.

INSTRUCTIONS FOR PHYSICIANS

Administration of a Medical Procedure to End My Life in a Painless, Humane, and Dignified Manner

This Directive is made this _____ day of _____ (month) _____ (year). I, _____, being of sound mind, do voluntarily make known my desire that my life shall be ended with the aid of a physician in a painless, humane, and dignified manner when I have a terminal condition or illness, certified to be terminal by two physicians, and they determine that my death will occur within six months or less.

When the terminal diagnosis is made and confirmed, and this directive is in effect, I may then ask my attending physician for aid-in-dying. I trust and hope that he or she will comply. If he or she refuses to comply, which is his or her right, then I urge that he or she assist in locating a colleague who will comply.

Determining the time and place of my death shall be in my sole discretion. The manner of my death shall be determined jointly by my attending physician and myself.

This Directive shall remain valid until revoked by me. I may revoke this Directive at any time.

I recognize that a physician's judgment is not always certain, and that medical science continues to make progress in extending life, but in spite of these facts, I nevertheless wish aid-in-dying rather than letting my terminal condition take it natural course.

I will endeavor to inform my family of this Directive, and my intention to request the aid of my physician to help me to die when I am in a terminal condition, and take those opinions into consideration. But the final decision remains mine. I acknowledge that it is solely my responsibility to inform my family of my intentions.

(continued)

I have given full consideration to and understand the full import of this Directive, and I am emotionally and mentally competent to make this Directive. I accept the moral and legal responsibility for receiving aid-in-dying.

This Directive will not be valid unless it is signed by two qualified witnesses who are present when you sign or acknowledge your signature. The witness must not be related to you by blood, marriage, or adoption; they must not be entitled to any part of your estate or at the time of execution of the Directive have no claim against any portion of your estate, nor anticipate making such claim against any portion of your estate; and they must not include: your attending physician; an employee of the attending physician; a health care provider; an employee of a health care provider; the operator of the community care facility or an employee of an operator of a community care facility.

If you have attached any additional pages to this form, you must sign and date each of the additional pages at the same time you date and sign this Directive.

Signed:

_____

_____

City, County, and State of Residence

(continued)

STATEMENT OF WITNESSES

I declare under penalty of perjury under the laws of California that the person who signed or acknowledged this document is personally known to me (or proved to me on the basis of satisfactory evidence to be the declarant of this Directive); that he or she signed and acknowledged this Directive in my presence, and that he or she appears to be of sound mind and under no duress, fraud, or undue influence; that I am not the attending physician, an employee of the attending physician, a health care provider, an employee of a health care provider, the operator of a community care facility, or an employee of an operator of a community care facility.

I further declare under penalty of perjury under the laws of California that I am not related to the declarant by blood, marriage, or adoption, and, to the best of my knowledge, I am not entitled to any part of the estate of the principal upon the death of the principal under a will now existing or by operation of law, and have no claim nor anticipate making a claim against any portion of the estate of the declarant upon his or her death.

Dated: _____

Witness's Signature: _____

Print Name: _____

Residence Address: _____

Dated: _____

Witness's Signature: _____

Print Name: _____

Residence Address: _____

STATEMENT OF PATIENT ADVOCATE
OR OMBUDSMAN

(If you are a patient in a skilled nursing facility, one of the witnesses must be a Patient Advocate or Ombudsman. The following statement is required only if you are a patient in a skilled nursing facility, a health care facility that provides the following basic services: skilled nursing care and supportive care to patients whose primary need is for availability of skilled nursing care on an extended basis. The Patient Advocate or Ombudsman must sign the "Statement of Witnesses" above AND must also sign the following statement.)

I further declare under penalty of perjury under the laws of California that I am a Patient Advocate or Ombudsman as designated by the State Department of Aging and that I am serving as a witness as required by Section 2525.4 of the California Civil Code.

Signed: _____

SEC. 2 PENAL CODE AMENDMENT

Section 401 of the Penal Code is amended to read:

401. Suicide, aiding, advising or encouraging. Every person who deliberately aids, or advises, or encourages another to commit suicide, is guilty of a felony. Death resulting from a request for aid-in-dying pursuant to Title 10.5 (commencing with Section 2525) of Division 3 of Part 4 of the Civil Code shall not constitute suicide, nor is a licensed physician who lawfully administers aid-in-dying or a health care provider or licensed health care professional acting under the direction of a physician, liable under this section. Death resulting from aid-in-dying pursuant to a directive in accordance with the Death With Dignity Act does not, for any purpose, constitute a homicide.

SEC. 3 AMENDMENT OF INITIATIVE

This Act may be amended only by a statute passed by a two-thirds vote of each house of the legislature and signed by the Governor.

Appendix 8

Care of the Hopelessly III*

In the article referenced below, three doctors recommend a new public policy to allow physician-assisted suicide and offer six guidelines to help their colleagues understand and follow such a policy. They urge both doctors and lawyers to "create public policy that fully recognizes irreversible suffering" for the benefit of "competent patients who met carefully defined criteria." In their judgment, the hidden practices of the estimated 3 to 37 percent of the doctors who secretly help their patients to commit suicide are risky for the patients and can damage the reputation of the doctors.

The six test guidelines that they propose all doctors follow before participating in an assisted suicide are:

1. "The patient must have a condition that is incurable and associated with severe, unrelenting suffering" and must understand the medical problem.

2. Doctors must be sure patients are not asking for death only because they are not getting treatment that would relieve their suffering.

3. The patient must "clearly and repeatedly" ask to die to avoid suffering, yet it is important not to force the patient to "beg" for assistance.

4. A doctor must be sure a patient's judgment is not distorted or resulting from a treatable problem like depression.

---

*This is a synopsis, with excerpts, of an article by the same name published in the *New England Journal of Medicine* (November 5, 1992) and authored by Dr. Timothy Quill, School of Medicine, University of Rochester; Dr. Christine K. Cassel, University of Chicago; and Dr. Diane E. Meier, Mt. Sinai School of Medicine, New York City. See also "Suicide Assistance Gains New Backing," *New York Times,* November 5, 1992, p. A32. (reproduced by permission of NEJM)

5. The doctor who assists in the suicide should be the patient's physician unless he or she has moral objections.

6. An independent doctor should give a second opinion in the case, and finally, all three should sign some kind of document showing informed consent.

Dr. Quill and his colleagues also make clear that, although family members should be involved, "under no circumstances should the family's wishes and request override those of a competent patient."

If the doctor provides the medicine, they say, the overdose should be taken in the doctor's presence. "It is of the utmost importance not to abandon the patient at this critical moment." Any laws that would allow suicide assisted by doctors, they stress, must "not require that the patient be left alone at the moment of death in order for the assisters to be safe from prosecution." They also note that "terminally ill patients who do choose to take their lives often die alone so as not to place their families or care givers in legal jeopardy."

Appendix 9

World Right-to-Die Federation Members*

Australia

South Australian Voluntary Euthanasia
Society (SAVES)
P O Box 2151, Kent Town Centre 5071,
South Australia

Voluntary Euthanasia Society of New
South Wales, Inc. (VES of NSW)
P O Box 25, Broadway, NSW 2007
Australia

Voluntary Euthanasia Society of
Victoria, Inc. (VESV)
Unit 1/71 Riversdale Road
Hawthorn, Victoria 3122, Australia

West Australian Voluntary Euthanasia
Society, Inc., (WAVES)
P O Box 7243, Cloisters Square
Perth 6580, Western Australia

Belgium

Association pour le Droit de Mourir
dans la Dignite
rue du President, 55, B-1050
Bruxelles, Belgium

Recht op Waardig Sterven (RWS)
Constitutiestraat 33,B 2060
Antwerpen, Belgium

Britain

Voluntary Euthanasia Society (VES)
13 Prince of Wales Terrace
London W8 5PG, England

Voluntary Euthanasia Society of Scotland
17 Hart Street
Edinburgh, EH1 3RN, Scotland, UK

---

*Printed by permission of the World Federation of Right-to-Die Societies (1992).

Canada
Dying with Dignity (DWD)
600 Eglinton Ave. East, Suite 401
Toronto, ON M4P 1P3, Canada

Fondation Responsable jusqu'a la fin
10150 de Bretagne, Quebec,
PQ, G2B 2R1, Canada

Goodbye—A Right to Die Society
P O Box 39149, Point Grey RPO
Vancouver, BC, V6R 4P1,
Canada

The Right to Die Society of Canada
P O Box 39018
Victoria, BC, V8V 1B1, Canada

Colombia
Fundación Pro Derecho a
     Morir Dignamente (DMD)
A.A. 88900
Bogotá, Colombia, South America

Denmark
Landsforeningen Mit Livstestamente-
     retten til en vaerdig dod
Brondstrupvej 5, DK-8500
Grena, Denmark

France
Association pour el Droit de Mourir
     dans la Dignite (ADMD)
103 rue Lafayette
75011 Paris, France

India
The Society for the Right to Die
     with Dignity (SRDD)
Maneckji Wadia Building, 4th Floor
127 Mahatma Gandhi Road,
Fort, Bombay 400 023, India

Israel
The Israeli Society for the Right to Die
     with Dignity (DWD)
P O Box 21751
Tel Aviv, Israel 61217

Japan
Japan Society for Dying with
     Dignity (JSDD)
Watanabe Building 202
2-29-1 Hongou Bunkyo-ku
Tokyo 113, Japan

Luxembourg
Association pour le Droit de Mourir dans
     la Dignite (ADMD-L)
50 bd. J F Kennedy
L-4170 Esch-sur-Alzette, Luxembourg

Netherlands
Nederlandse Vereniging voor Vrijwillige
     Euthanasie (NVVE)
Postbus 75331
1070 AH Amsterdam, Nederland

New Zealand
Voluntary Euthanasia Society
     (Auckland) Inc.
PO Box 10-351, Dominion Road,
Wellington 2, New Zealand

Voluntary Euthanasia Society (VES)
95 Melrose Road, Island Bay
Wellington 2, New Zealand

South Africa
SAVES—The Living Will Society
     (SAVES)
P O Box 1460, Wandsbeck 3630
Republic of South Africa

Spain
Derecho a Morir dignamente (DMD)
Apartado 31.134
08080 Barcelona, Spain

Sweden
Ratten Till Var Dod (RTVD)
Hoganasgatan 20
753 30, Uppsala, Sweden

Switzerland
EXIT (Deutsche Schweiz)
Vereinigung für humanes Sterben
Ch-2450 Grenchen, Switzerland

EXIT Association pour le Droit de Mourir
    dans la Dignite (EXIT—ADMD)
C.P. 100, 1222 Vesenaz
Genève, Switzerland

United States of America
Americans Against Human Suffering
    (AAHA)
87 East Green Street, #303
Pasadena, CA 91105, USA

Choice in Dying (CID)
200 Varick Street
New York, NY 10014, USA

Hemlock Society U.S.A.
P O Box 11830
Eugene, OR 97440-4030, USA

Reference List*

Introduction

Associated Press. March 25, 1992. "Alzheimers Patient Dumped at Dog Track," *Philadelphia Inquirer,* p. 1.

Egan, Tim. March 26, 1991. "Robbed by Alzheimers, A Man is Cast Away." *New York Times,* pp. 1A–B12.

Pence, Gregory. 1990. *Classical Cases of Medical Ethics.* New York: McGraw-Hill, p. 134.

Chapter 1: The Dramatic Entrance of *FINAL EXIT* and
Chapter 2: The Impact of *FINAL EXIT*

Altman, Lawrence. August 9, 1991. "A How-to Book on Suicide Surges to the Top of the Best-Seller Lists in a Week." *New York Times,* pp. 1–10.

Ames, Katherine, et al. August 26, 1991. "Choosing Death." *Newsweek,* pp. 40–45.

---

*References cited in each of the twenty chapters and the introduction are listed here in alphabetical order. Also included are general background references to each chapter, which are not specifically cited in the text and are here marked with an asterisk.

Angelo, Bonnie. November 18, 1991. "Assigning the Blame for a Man's Suicide." *Time,* pp. 12–74.

Clarke, David. July 1991. "Shop Manual for Self-Deliverence." *Hemlock Quarterly,* p. 6.

"Donahue" (ABC-TV show), Dec. 8, 1991.

Hamel, Ron. September 9, 1991. "Overcoming the Suicide Option." *Philadelphia Inquirer,* p. 11A.

Henry, III, William. August 15, 1991. "Do It Yourself Death Lessons." *Time,* p. 55.

Humphry, Derek. April 29, 1990. Lecture to Hemlock Society of the Delaware Valley, Beaver College, Glenside, Pa.

———. *Final Exit.* 1991. New York: Carol Publishing Co.

———. "*Final Exit* Bombshell." October 1991. *Hemlock Quarterly,* pp. 1–12.

———. November 15, 1991. "Reasons Why *Final Exit* Ascended on the Best-Seller List." Lecture delivered at the Annual Meeting of the National Hemlock Society, Denver, Colo.,

———. "Final Exit Around the World." Spring 1992. *Hemlock Quarterly.*

Katz, Marvin. December 1991. "Critics Fear Misuse of Suicide Books." *AARP Bulletin,* pp. 4–5.

Logue, W. May 15, 1992. "Abandoned Alzheimer's Patient Off to New Home." *New York Times,* p. B1.

Marker, Rita. *See* Ames (op cit.).

Quindlen, Anna. August 14, 1991. "Death: The Best Seller." *New York Times,* p. A19.

*"Readers Fight Back." March 1991. *Vanity Fair* (response to McCrystal article), pp. 38–42.

Chapter 3: The Birth of the Hemlock Society

*Goetz, Harriet. January 1990, "Euthanasia: A Bedside View." *Hemlock Quarterly* (reprinted from the *Christian Century*), pp. 1–4.

Humphry, Derek. April 29, 1990. "A History of the Euthanasia Movement." Lecture before the Hemlock Society of the Delaware Valley, Beaver College, Glenside, Pa.

McCrystal, Cal. January 1992. "Ann Humphry's Final Exit." *Vanity Fair,* pp. 80f.

National Hemlock Society. March 1989. "Q and A on the Hemlock Society." National Hemlock Society, Eugene, Ore., pp. 4–7.

———. March 1988. "The 1988 Roper Poll on Attitudes Towards Euthanasia." National Hemlock Society, Eugene Ore.

*Nursing Life Editorial, ed. January–April 1984: "Does a Terminal Patient Have the Right to Die?" *Nursing Life,* pp. 81–85.

*Schmeck, Harold. September 11, 1987. "Guidelines Issued on Time Care." *New York Times,* p. 12.

*Sheff, David. August 1992. "Derek Humphry: A Playboy Interview." *Playboy,* pp. 49–144.

Chapter 4: The Flowering of Hemlock

*Allen, Charlotte. March 19, 1990. "A Deadly Mix of Power and Poison." *Insight,* pp. 52–53.

*Donaldson, Sam. March 26, 1992. "Derek Humphry and Hemlock." "Prime Time Live" (ABC-TV network).

*Forney, Robert. January 1989. "Scientists Tell How Drugs Take Effect." *Hemlock Quarterly,* pp. 9–12.

Gabriel, Trip. December 8, 1991. "A Fight to the Death." *New York Times Magazine,* pp. 44–88.

Goode, Erica. September 30, 1991. "Defending the Right to Die." *U.S. News and World Report,* pp. 38–39.

Humphry, Derek. 1989. *Let Me Die Before I Wake.* Eugene, Ore.: Hemlock Society.

———. *Final Exit.* 1991. New York: Carol Publishing Co.

McCrystal, Cal. January 1992. "Ann Humphry's Final Exit." *Vanity Fair,* pp. 80f.

Reinhold, Robert. February 8, 1990. "Right to Die Group is Shaken as Leader Leaves Wife Dying with Cancer." *New York Times,* p. 26A.

U.S. Centers for Disease Control. 1992. *1991 Stats.* Atlanta, Ga.

U.S. Department of Health. 1992. *1991 Stats.* Washington, D.C.

Chapter 5: The Origins of the Modern Right-to-Die Movement

Armstrong, Paul, et al. May 11, 1989. "Who Should Decide on Whether to Pull the Plug?" *New York Times,* p. 19.

Associated Press. January 2, 1991. "Another Right to Die Case Poses New Questions." *New York Times,* p. 5.

Clines, Francis. October 31, 1986. "Dutch Quietly Lead in Euthanasia Request." *New York Times,* p. 4.

Colt, George H. 1991. *The Enigma of Suicide.* New York: Summit Books.

Cranford, Ronald, Dr. September 1992. Speech before National Hemlock Society Annual Meeting, Long Beach, Calif.

Gibbs, Nancy. March 19, 1990. "Love and Let Die." *Time,* pp. 62–71.

Humphry, Derek. April 29, 1990. Lecture to Hemlock Society of the Delaware Valley. Beaver College, Glenside, Pa.

Mero, Ralph. May 15, 1991. Public Lecture to Hemlock Society of the Delaware Valley, Philadelphia, Pa.

Ministry of Justice, the Netherlands. September 1991. "Outline of Report of the Commission Inquiry into Medical Practices with Regard to Euthanasia." Gravenhage, Netherlands, pp. 1–7.

Chapter 6: Breakthrough on the Euthanasia Frontier

Associated Press. February 5, 1991. "State Makes Public Videotape in Right to Die Case." *New York Times,* p. 7.

*Freed, Roy. August 15, 1989. "Let's Take a Look at This Right to Die." Letter to the Editor, *New York Times,* p. 14.

Gibbs, Nancy. March 19, 1990. "Love and Let Die." *Time,* pp. 62–71.

Goodman, Ellen. December 13, 1989. "Cruzan Case Shows Need for a Living Will." *Philadelphia Inquirer,* p. 14.

Greenhouse, Linda. July 25, 1989. "Does Right to Privacy Include the Right to Die? Court to Decide." *New York Times,* pp. 1–15.

———. December 17, 1989. "Right to Die Case Gets First Hearing." *New York Times,* p. B26.

Malcolm, Andrew. December 3, 1989. "The Ultimate Decision." *New York Times Magazine,* pp. 38–46.

Chapter 7: The Right to Die Becomes the Law of the Land

Associated Press. January 7, 1992. "Jane Doe Dies." *Philadelphia Inquirer.*

Belkin, Lisa. January 10, 1991. "As Family Protests Hospital Seeks an End to Woman's Life Support." *New York Times,* pp. 1–10.

Greenhouse, Linda. June 26, 1990. "Justices Find a Right to Die, But a Majority Sees Need for Clear Proof of Intent." *New York Times,* pp. 1–19.

Goodman, Ellen. January 1, 1991. "The Legacy of Nancy Cruzan Touches Everyone." *Philadelphia Inquirer,* p. 14.

Lewis, Anthony. June 29, 1990. "Conscience and the Court." *New York Times,* p. 23.

Lewin, Tamar. December 27, 1990. "Nancy Cruzan Dies: Outlived by a Debate." *New York Times,* pp. 1–5.

Malcolm, Andrew. April 14, 1990. "Two Right to Die Groups Merging for Unified Voice." *New York Times,* p. 14.

———. December 23, 1990. "What Medical Science Can't Seem to Learn: When to Call it Quits." *New York Times,* p. 6E.

———. December 29, 1990. "Nancy Cruzan Dies: End to a Long Good-bye." *New York Times,* p. 15.

Nachtigal, Jerry. December 15, 1990. "Comatose Daughter Can Die, Court Rules." *Philadelphia Inquirer,* pp. 1–11.

Quindlen, Anna. June 3, 1990. "A Time to Die." *New York Times,* p. 27E.

Chapter 8: "Dr. Death" Concocts a Suicide Machine

Associated Press. June 8, 1990. "Opposition to Kevorkian," *Philadelphia Inquirer.*

Belkin, Lisa. June 6, 1990. "Dr. Tells of First Death Using Suicide Device." *New York Times,* pp. 1A–B6.

*Cameron, Mindy. June 10, 1990. "The Remarkable Death of Mindy Cameron." *Seattle Times,* editorial page.

Cassel, Andrew. May 19, 1989. "He Pulled the Plug, But It's Not Murder." *Philadelphia Inquirer,* p. 9.

Gibbs, Nancy. June 18, 1990. "Dr. D's Suicide Machine." *Time,* pp. 69–70.

"Good Morning America," ABC-TV, June 12, 1990.

Humphry, Derek. November 16, 1991. Interview by Donald Cox. Denver, Colo.

Smith, Cheryl, J. D. August 1990. "Change Laws in Michigan." *Hemlock Quarterly,* p. 3.

Chapter 9: The Double Deaths in Cabin 2

Associated Press. August 4, 1990. "Murder Trial is Ordered for Man Who Helped Wife Commit Suicide." *New York Times,* p. 6.

———. September 20, 1991. "Prosecutor Seeks Murder Charge Against Doctor." *New York Times,* p. A18.

———. November 21, 1991. "Michigan Board Suspends License of Doctor Who Aided Suicides." *New York Times,* p. 5.

———. December 16, 1991. "Michigan Judge Bars Doctor from Using Suicide Machine." *New York Times,* p. 4.

Colens, B. D. October 24, 1991. "Charges Against Dr. Death Are Weighed." *New York Times,* p. 3.

Irwain, Jim. December 14, 1990. "Judge Drops Charge in Doctor-Aided Suicide." *Philadelphia Inquirer,* pp. 1–12.

Kevorkian, Dr. Jack. October 12, 1992. National Press Club Talk, C-SPAN TV, Washington, D.C.

Kole, Bill. October 29, 1991. "On Videotape, Two Women Reveal Their Sufferings on the Eve of Their Suicides." *Philadelphia Inquirer,* p. 4.

Smith, Cheryl. October 1991. "Kevorkian Agenda is Experimentation in Organ Harvesting." *Hemlock Quarterly,* p. 6.

*Svoboda, Sandra. October 24, 1991. "Suicide Doc Helps 2 Kill Selves." *Philadelphia Daily News,* p. 17.

Treen, Joe, et al. October 25, 1991. "Opponents Weigh Action Against Doctor Who Aided Suicide." *People,* p. 10.

———. November 11, 1991. "Appointment in Cabin 2." *People,* pp. 85–86.

Wilkerson, Isabel. January 15, 1991, "Prosecution Seeks to Ban Doctor's Suicide Device." *New York Times,* p. 5.

Chapter 10: Was it Really Murder?

Anderson, Kelly. July 22, 1991. "Charges Dropped in Aided Suicide." *Philadelphia Inquirer,* p. 3.

Associated Press. May 16, 1992. "Michigan Dr. at Side of 4th Suicide." *New York Times,* p. 6.

———. May 17, 1992. "Kevorkian Provided Gas for Woman's Suicide." *New York Times,* p. 21.

———. July 22, 1992. "Murder Charges Against Kevorkian Dismissed." *New York Times,* p. 12.

Day, Brenda. May 16, 1992, "Kevorkian Present at Another Suicide." *Philadelphia Inquirer,* pp. 1–7.

Drummond, Steve. June 6, 1992. "Coroner: Kevorkian Aided in Suicide." *Philadelphia Inquirer,* p. 4.

Editorial. February 16, 1992. "Kevorkian Pays Unfortunate Price in Cause of Suicide Help." *Oakland* (Mich.) *Press,* editorial page.

Goodman, Ellen. May 14, 1992. "Kevorkian Should Be Stopped Before He Can Kill Again." *Philadelphia Inquirer,* p. 14.

———. August 5, 1992. "Suicide Can Be a Rational Course, But Not the Death Doctor's Way." *Philadelphia Inquirer,* p. 14.

Hoogterp, Edward. February 29, 1992. "Dr. Death to Trial." *Ann Arbor News,* p. 1.

*"Kevorkian Raps Doctors, AMA and Hippocratic Oath." April 1992. Book Review of *Prescription Medicide, Hemlock News* (Lee County, Fla.), pp. 3–4.

Reuters. June 6, 1992. "Death at Kevorkian's Side Is Ruled Suicide." *New York Times,* p. 7.

Chapter 11: Other Doctors Speak Out

Humphry, Derek. Spring 1989. "Lessons of the Rosier Trial," *Hemlock Quarterly.*

Rosenblatt, Stanley. 1992. *Murder of Mercy* (Buffalo, N.Y.: Prometheus Books).

Chapter 12: Of Living Wills and an Act of Congress

Berlin, Lisa. December 1, 1991. "Hospitals Will Now Ask Patients if They Wish to Make a Death Plan." *New York Times,* pp. 1–47.

*General Assembly of Pa. 1992. "Senate Bill #3, Session 91, *Living Wills,*" #2095.

Gleicher, Abigail. April 1992. "Four New Bills Demand Physicians Assist Dying." *Hemlock Quarterly,* p. 3.

Gutis, Philip. May 30, 1989. "Patient Proxy for Treatment Gains Backing." *New York Times,* p. 16.

Holmes, Kristin. December 12, 1991. "New Law Asks Hospital Patients to Prepare for the Worst." *Philadelphia Inquirer,* p. 1B.

King, Wayne. June 11, 1991. "Right to Die Is Approved by Assembly in Trenton." *New York Times,* p. 1B.

Kirkpatrick, Rich. June 13, 1991. "Living Will Bill Passes Senate." *Philadelphia Inquirer,* p. 13.

Lewin, Tamar. July 23, 1990. "With Court Leading the Way, Living Will Gaining New Life." *New York Times,* pp. 1–13.

Motley, Wanda. November 20, 1991. "Pa. House Approves 'Living Wills'." *Philadelphia Inquirer,* p. 2B.

Sack, Kevin. July 2, 1990. "Right to Die Is Approved in Legislature." *New York Times,* p. B1.

Seelye, Katherine. June 2, 1991. "Deal Clears Path for Pa. Living Wills." *Philadelphia Inquirer,* pp. 1B–4B.

Spears, Greg. November 8, 1990. "New York Law to Require Living Will Information." *Philadelphia Inquirer,* p. 3.

Weber, Bruce. December 2, 1990. "Positive Reaction Greets Living Will Law." *New York Times,* p. 8.

Chapter 13: The Coming of #119 and
Chapter 14: The Going of #119

Associated Press. November 4, 1991. "Euthanasia Favored in Poll." *New York Times,* p. 4.

Conklin, Ellis. November 9, 1991. "Support for Initiative #119 Slipped Away in Final Hours." *Seattle Post-Intelligencer,* p. 1.

Dority, Barbara. August 1992. "Attorney General Sues Initiative Opponents." *Hemlock News* (Hemlock Society of Washington, Seattle), p. 1.

Egan, Timothy. July 6, 1990. "Euthanasia Bid in Washington State." *New York Times,* p. 1.

———. October 14, 1991. "Washington Voters Weigh if There Is a Right to Die." *New York Times,* p. 1–20.

Goodman, Ellen. November 2, 1991. "Death With Dignity Goes to the Voters." *Philadelphia Inquirer,* p. 9A.

Humphry, Derek. January 1992. "Why Were They Beaten in Washington?" *Hemlock Quarterly,* p. 4.

Kamisar, Yale. November 15, 1991. "An Unraveling of Morality." *New York Times,* OpEd page.

Keller, Janelle. October 18, 1991. "Voter Groups Argue Both Sides of Death with Dignity." *The Evergreen* (Washington State University, Pullman, Wash.)

King, Warren. "Surprise Defeat for Aid-in-Dying." *Seattle Times,* p. 1.

Mero, Ralph. January 1991. "Doctor Assisted Death Initiative Qualifies." *Hemlock Quarterly.*

———. July–August 1991. "Death With Dignity." *The Unitarian Universalist World* (Beacon Press, UUA, Boston, Mass.), p. 38.

———. October 1991. "Washington Vote Gets Close." *Hemlock Quarterly,* pp. 1–10.

———. November 15, 1991. "Proposition #119." Lecture, Annual Meeting of the National Hemlock Society, Denver, Colo.

———. November 16, 1991. Interview with Donald Cox. Denver, Colo.

———. January 1992. "Fear Campaign Beneath the Washington Initiative." *Hemlock Quarterly,* p. 5.

Robinson, Herb. October 26, 1991. "Initiative #119: A Wise Plan." *Seattle Times,* p. 10.

Stemfels, Peter. October 28, 1991. "At Crossroads: U.S. Ponders Ethics of Helping Others Die." *New York Times,* pp. 1–B7.

Vorenburg, James. "The Limits of Mercy." *New York Times,* OpEd page.

Washington Citizens for Death With Dignity. October 1991. Flyer.

———. October 1991. "Vote YES on 119" (flyer).

Washington Hemlock PAC. October 1991. "Facts About Initiative #119" (flyer).

*Washington State Democratic Committee. October 1991. "What Initiative #119 Will Do"

*Watson, Joe. September 18, 1991. "Don't Legalize Suicide for the Selfish: Defeat 119." *Pullman* (Wash.) *Daily News,* p. 4A.

Woestendiek, John. November 4, 1991. "Doctors Role in Suicide Put to a Vote." *Philadelphia Inquirer,* pp. 1–5.

Chapter 15: California Here We Come and
Chapter 16: Death with Dignity Legislation in Other States

Allison, State Senator Bonnie, et al. November 16, 1991. "Panel Discussion on Active Euthanasia Bills in Other States." Annual Meeting of the Hemlock Society, Denver, Colo.

*Bereny, Gail. March 4, 1982. "Death With Dignity Bill Passes House." *Hemlock News* (Hemlock Society of Washington State, Seattle, Wash.)

*California Death With Dignity Act, California Civil Code, Title #105. 1991. Californians Against Human Suffering, Los Angeles, Calif., pp. 1–12 (See Appendix 7.)

Hendricks, Jane. Fall 1991. "Legislative Update." *Florida Hemlock Quarterly* (Sarasota, Fla.), p. 2.

Humphry, Derek. April 29, 1990. Lecture to Annual Meeting of the Hemlock Society of the Delaware Valley, Beaver College, Glenside, Pa.

———. November 16, 1991. "The Impact of *Final Exit*," Hemlock Annual Meeting, Denver, Colo.

———. January 1992. "Why Were They Beaten in Washington." *Hemlock Quarterly,* p. 4.

Mero, Ralph. January 1992. "California Campaign Off to Good Start." *Hemlock Quarterly,* p. 1.

———. March 25, 1992. Phone Interview by Donald Cox re: "Washington Feeding Tube Law."

Miles, Rufus. June 19, 1990. "Quick and Painless Death Should Be a Right." Letter to Editor, *New York Times,* p. 14.

White, Michael. September 1992. "California Campaign in Final Phase." *Hemlock Quarterly,* pp. 1–2.

Chapter 17: Abortion and Assisted Death

Altman, Lawrence. April 17, 1991. "U.S. Quizzes W.H.O. on Abortion Pill." *New York Times,* p. 6.

Associated Press. August 8, 1991. "U.S. Judge Strikes Down Louisiana Abortion Law." *New York Times,* p. 15.

Bates, Michael. August 7, 1981. "U.S. Backs Abortion Codes in Kansas." *Philadelphia Inquirer,* p. 3A.

———. August 9, 1991. "The Judge Who Kept the Clinics Open." *Philadelphia Inquirer,* pp. D1–D3.

Blood, Michael. August 3, 1990. "Arguments End Abortion Law Trial." *Philadelphia Inquirer,* p. 3B.

Cannon, Carl. January 26, 1992. "Abortion Issue May Hurt Bush." *Philadelphia Inquirer,* p. 9.

Chartrand, Sabra. March 29, 1992. "Baby Missing Part of Brain Challenges Legal Definition of Death." *New York Times,* p. 8.

Clymer, Adam. July 10, 1991. "White House Hints at Easing Prohibition on Abortion in Clinics." *New York Times,* p. 3.

*DeWitt, Karen. April 6, 1992. "Huge Crowd Backs Right to Abortion in Capital March." *New York Times,* pp. 1A–13A.

Epstein, Aaron. October 31, 1990. "Court Keeps Intact Ban on Promoting Abortions in Clinics Abroad." *Philadelphia Inquirer,* p. 16.

———. April 19, 1992. "Pa. Abortion Case Goes to High Court This Week." *Philadelphia Inquirer,* pp. 1–8.

———. April 23, 1992. "Supreme Court Hears Pa. Abortion Arguments." *Philadelphia Inquirer,* pp. 1–12, B1.

Goodman, Ellen. October 31, 1990. "Free Speech Limited to Abortion Issue." *Philadelphia Inquirer,* p. 16.

———. July 13, 1991. "The Catholic Bishops Have Put Abortion in Forefront." *Philadelphia Inquirer,* p. 13.

———. April 25, 1992. "Taking Abortion to the Court." *Philadelphia Inquirer,* p. 13.

Green, Charles. June 29, 1991. "Abortion Issue Looming Before a Reluctant President." *Philadelphia Inquirer,* p. 8A.

Greenhouse, Linda. May 24, 1991. "5 Justices Uphold U.S. Rule Curbing Abortion Advice." *New York Times,* pp. 1–18.

———. January 2, 1992. High Court Takes Pa. Case on Abortion Rights." *New York Times,* pp. 1–17.

Greenhouse, Linda. April 20, 1992. "Both Sides in Abortion Argument Look Beyond Court to Political Battle," *New York Times*, pp. 1A–B11.

———. April 23, 1992. "Court Gets Stark Arguments on Abortion." *New York Times*, pp. 1–B11.

———. April 25, 1992. "Abortion Rights Strategy: All or Nothing." *New York Times*, pp. 1–17.

Hentoff, Nat. February 16, 1991. "Abortion Gag Rule." *The Progressive* (Madison, Wisc.), pp. 16–17.

Hinds, Michael de Courcy. October 22, 1991. "Appeals Court Upholds Limits on Abortion." *New York Times*, pp. 1–16.

Klein, Julia. April 21, 1992. "The Abortion Face-Off." *Philadelphia Inquirer*, pp. C1–C4.

Kolata, Gina. January 5, 1992. "In Late Abortions, Decisions are Painful and Options are Few." *New York Times*, pp. 1–20.

*———. November 10, 1991. "Koop" (a book review of Dr. C. E. Koop's Autobiography). *New York Times Book Review*, p. 9.

Lewin, Tamar. June 20, 1991. "High Court Has Several Options for New Look on Abortion Rights." *New York Times*, pp. 1–18.

———. January 26, 1991. "Strict Anti-Abortion Law Signed in Utah." *New York Times*, p. 15.

———. August 2, 1991. "Quiet Hearing Could Lead to Resounding Decision on Abortions," *New York Times*, p. 10.

Quindlen, Anna. July 7, 1990. "Abortion: The Clash of Absolutes" (review of Prof. Lawrence Tribe's abortion book). *New York Times Book Review*, p. 7.

———. November 1, 1990. "Banning the 'A' Word." *New York Times*, p. A29.

———. March 26, 1991. "Indictment." *New York Times*, p. 25.

———. July 17, 1991. "Rust, Roe and Reality." *New York Times*, p. 21A.

———. April 22, 1992. "Hearts and Minds." *New York Times*, p. 25A.

Schneider, Karen. April 12, 1992. "High Court Ruling May Make Abortion Major Election Issue." *Philadelphia Inquirer*, p. E3.

Slobodzian, Joe. July 31, 1990. "Federal Judge Begins Hearing New Challenge to Pa. Abortion Law." *Philadelphia Inquirer*, p. 3.

———. August 5, 1990. "A Pa. Abortion Case with Wider Implications." *Philadelphia Inquirer*, pp. 1C–8C.

Slobodzian, Joe. October 27, 1991. "Abortion Law Ruling Is a Surprise to Many." *Philadelphia Inquirer,* pp. F1, F2.

———. October 28, 1991. "Pa. to Appeal Abortion Decision." *Philadelphia Inquirer,* pp. 1B–2B.

Suro, Roberto. July 28, 1990. "La. Abortion Bill Vetoed: Governor Calls Too Restrictive." *New York Times,* pp. 1–9.

———. June 19, 1991. "Nation's Strictest Abortion Law Enacted in La. Over Veto." *New York Times,* pp. 1–18.

*Terry, Don. August 8, 1991. "U.S. Judge in Abortion Case Target of Death Threats." *New York Times,* pp. 1–9.

Tribe, Lawrence. July 6, 1990. "U.S. A Nation Held Hostage." *New York Times* (reprint in the *Philadelphia Daily News*), p. 6.

Vrazo, Fawn. August 25, 1991. "Preparing for an End of Roe." *Philadelphia Inquirer,* pp. 1–4.

———. April 13, 1992. "Abortion Views from 'A to Z'." *Philadelphia Inquirer,* pp. 1B–2B.

*———. April 22, 1992. "A Clinic Braces for Ruling on Abortion." *Philadelphia Inquirer,* pp. 1–10.

———. "Warriors in a Cave: On Both Sides of Abortion." *Philadelphia Inquirer,* pp. 1–12.

Chapter 18: The AIDS Factor

*AIDS Action Network. March 1, 1987. "AIDS Education and Service Providing Organizations Updated." Washington, D.C., pp. 1–35.

Biddle, Larry. November 21, 1991. Interview by Donald Cox. AIDS Task Force, Philadelphia, Pa.

Burns, Kevin. November 27, 1991. Interview by Donald Cox. Action AIDS, Philadelphia, Pa

Eckholm, Erik. November 17, 1991. "Facts of Life: More than Inspiration Is Needed to Fight AIDS." *New York Times,* p. E1.

———. November 18, 1990. "Journal of the Plague" (review of *A History of AIDS,* by Mirro Grmek). *New York Times Book Review,* p. 5.

*Estes, Dan. Nov. 9, 1991. "AIDS and Society." *Philadelphia City Paper.*

Jamison, Stephen. July 1992. "AIDS and Assisted Suicide." *Hemlock Quarterly,* pp. 4–5.

Kolata, Gina. June 18, 1991. "Experts Debate if AIDS Epidemic Has at Last Crested in U.S." *New York Times,* pp. C1–C9.

Levine, Stephen. 1986. *Healing into Life and Death.* New York.

Schmitt, Eric. December 10, 1991. "Citing AIDS, Judge Backs Service Ban on Gays." *New York Times,* p. 13.

Schilts, Randy. December 10, 1991. "Good AIDS, Bad AIDS." *New York Times,* p. 13.

"September AIDS and Self-Deliverance Meeting Draws Record Crowds." October–November 1991. *San Diego Hemlock News,* p. 2.

Verdile, Dr. Ben. March 10, 1992. Interview by Donald Cox. Philadelphia Gay and Lesbian Task Force, Philadelphia, Pa.

Chapter 19: The Ethical-Medical Issue

Armstrong, Paul, et al. May 11, 1989. "Who Should Decide on Whether to Pull the Plug?" *Philadelphia Inquirer,* p. 19A.

Abrams, Dr. Fred. November 1991. "Reforming the Law." Lecture Delivered at the Annual Meeting of the National Hemlock Society.

Altman, Dr. Lawrence. March 12, 1991. "More Physicians Broach Forbidden Subject of Euthanasia." *New York Times,* p. 14.

———. April 7, 1992. "Alzheimers Dilemma, Whether to Tell People They Have the Disease." *New York Times,* p. C3.

*Belkin, Lisa. March 2, 1992. "Choosing Death at Home." *New York Times,* p. 1–B4.

Billings, Nan. July 1992. Interview by Donald Cox.

Bouton, Katherine. August 5, 1990. "Painful Decisions: The Role of the Medical Ethicist." *New York Times Magazine,* pp. 32–65.

Brody, Dr. Sam. September 7, 1992. "We Have Lost Our Humanity." *Newsweek.*

Cassell, Eric, MD. 1973. "Learning to Die: Problems of Older People." New York Health Conference, New York Academy of Medicine, p. 1110.

Colt, George Howe. November 15, 1991. "Is There Such a Thing as Rational Suicide?" Lecture at Eighth Annual Conference of National Hemlock Society.

*Eckholm, Erik. December 22, 1991. "Costs and Hope Battle in Intensive Care Units." *New York Times,* pp. 1–24.

Egan, Timothy. March 25, 1992. "Cast Away." *New York Times,* pp. 1–B12.

Ferris, Timothy. December 15, 1991. "A Cosmological Event." *New York Times Sunday Magazine,* pp. 44–54.

Goodman, Ellen. March 21, 1990. "Bettelheim's Death Puts Focus on Suicide." *Philadelphia Inquirer,* p. 15.

Lewin, Tamar. March 28, 1980. "Strategies to Let Elderly Keep Some Control." *New York Times,* pp. 1–22.

Locke, Michelle. November 29, 1991. "Granny Dumping; A Sign of the Times." *Philadelphia Inquirer,* pp. 12–13.

Nichols, Stephanie. September 29, 1991. "Death With Dignity." A Sermon delivered at the First Unitarian Church, Philadelphia, Pa.

Rich, Spencer. August 24, 1991. "Catastrophic Care Costs Soar." *Washington Post,* p. 1.

*Rothman, David. Spring 1992. "Strangers at the Bedside." *Columbia Quarterly,* pp. 20–24.

Schuchman, Miriam. November 15, 1990. "Depression Hidden in Deadly Disease." *New York Times,* pp. B1–3.

*Schuster, Evelyn. October 1990. "The Suicide Machine: The Ethics of Suicide and Euthanasia." *Philadelphia Medicine,* pp. 461–63.

"Sounding Board" (letters). March 1989. *New England Journal of Medicine.*

*Tolchin, Martin. July 19, 1989. "When Long Life Is Too Much: Suicide Rises, Among the Elderly." *New York Times,* pp. 1–15.

Uffelmann, Hans. November 15, 1991. "Euthanasia: The Ethical Issue." Lecture to the Eighth Annual National Hemlock Society Conference, Denver, Colo.

Chapter 20: Where Do We Go from Here?

Benrubi, Guy. August 16, 1991. "Euthanasia: The Need for Procedural Safeguards." *New England Journal of Medicine,* pp. 34–35.

Cassell, Christian, et al. September 13, 1990. "Morals and Moralism in the Debate Over Euthanasia and Assisted Suicide." *New England Journal of Medicine,* pp. 45–47.

Delaman, William. February 6, 1963. Interview with author.

Humphry, Derek. November 15, 1991. "Reasons Why *Final Exit* Ascended on the Best-Seller List." Lecture delivered at the Annual Meeting of the National Hemlock Society, Denver, Colo.

Misbin, Robert. October 31, 1991. "Physicians Aid in Dying." *New England Journal of Medicine,* pp. 37–91.

Simons, Marlise. February 9, 1993. "Dutch Move to Enact Law Making Euthanasia Easier." *New York Times,* pp. 1–9.

Singer, Peter. June 28, 1990. "Euthanasia: A Critique." *New England Journal of Medicine,* pp. 42–45.

Glossary*

ACTIVE EUTHANASIA Actively accelerating death by use of drugs, etc., whether by oneself or with the aid of a doctor.

ADVANCE DIRECTIVE, ADVANCE HEALTH CARE DIRECTIVE, ADVANCE DECLARATION or LIVING WILL Document enabling you to express your wishes with respect to conditions where no treatment is desired in the event of becoming incompetent.

ASSISTED SUICIDE Assisting another person to end his or her life at that person's express wish. The legal definition of what constitutes "assisting" varies from country to country.

ATTENTION STICKER Adhesive labels for a person's medical records to indicate the inclusion of an advance declaration or living will.

AUTO-EUTHANASIA, AUTO-DELIVERANCE Ending one's life without any direct assistance; rational suicide.

AUTONOMY See *SELF-DETERMINATION*

BIOETHICS A new offshoot of the medical profession (since 1971) combining sociology, psychology, philosophy, and medicine.

DOUBLE EFFECT When drugs are administered to relieve pain but have the secondary effect of shortening life.

---

*Adapted with permission from the Voluntary Euthanasia Society of Scotland, Edinburgh (1992) and the World Federation of Right-to-Die Societies.

DURABLE POWER OF ATTORNEY A formal way of empowering another person to represent you legally even if you later become incapacitated.

EMERGENCY CARD Personal plastic card, the size of a credit card, stating health care wishes briefly. Complements a living will declaration.

EUTHANASIA Dying well—a good and easy death. Does not include irrational or emotional suicides or the forced killing of another person.

EUTHANASIC (*adjective*) That which can facilitate euthanasia; (*noun*) a drug suitable for euthanasia.

EXIT Former name of the Voluntary Euthanasia Society (VESS) of England.

FINAL EXIT Book by the founder of the Hemlock Society (America) detailing methods of self-deliverance.

FORCE-FEEDING Forcibly making someone ingest food against his or her wishes in order to prolong life.

GUIDE TO SELF-DELIVERANCE Manual detailing methods of self-deliverance published by EXIT in 1980/81, but withdrawn after repeated litigation.

HEALTH CARE PROXY Person appointed to look after your affairs in the event that you are unable to do so.

HOSPICES Experimental group of hospitals, nursing homes, religious-orientated, set up to research methods of pain control and transmit their findings to ordinary hospitals.

HOW TO DIE WITH DIGNITY Manual published by VESS and detailing methods of self-deliverance. The first book of its kind anywhere in the world.

JOINT SUICIDE When two people commit suicide together.

LIVING WILL See *ADVANCE DIRECTIVE.*

MERCY KILLING Ending another person's suffering by ending his or her life. Different from voluntary euthanasia (where the dying person has been able to clearly state his or her wishes).

PALLIATIVE CARE Care that provides comfort and relief from pain, but does not aim to cure the condition.

PARASUICIDE Suicide "gesture" or cry for help. A self-mutilating act which may or may not be motivated by a genuine desire to die. It is common in young people who are distressed but not mentally ill.

PASSIVE EUTHANASIA Euthanasia without active intervention relying on nontreatment.

PERSISTENT VEGETATIVE STATE Nonterminal state characterized by irreversible brain damage, and with brain metabolism equivalent to that in deep surgical anaesthesia, yet breathing without mechanical assistance, a sort of living death.

PROPHYLACTIC TREATMENT Treatment used to prevent a disease developing, rather than attempting to cure.

SELF-DELIVERANCE See *AUTO-EUTHANASIA*.

SELF-DETERMINATION The ability to decide one's own actions and their result on oneself, including auto-euthanasia if one so desires.

SLIPPERY-SLOPE The "slippery-slope" argument says that once legislation were to be obtained, abuse would gradually landslide. In spite of claims to the contrary, this has not happened in other countries, where the laws have been reformed; the slippery-slope argument implies an alarming and quite unfounded distrust of our medical professionals.

SUICIDE Ending one's own life.

SUICIDE CLAUSE Clause in certain life insurance policies that disqualifies beneficiaries in the event of suicide; note: it usually only applies to the physically fit who have recently taken out life insurance.

SUICIDE PACT A promise, usually between two people, for assisted suicide if one or the other becomes incapable of auto-euthanasia. Sometimes used to refer to joint suicides.

UPDATE STICKER Method of updating your living will to indicate that you have not had a change of mind since the time you signed it.

VOLUNTARY EUTHANASIA Euthanasia; the word voluntary emphasizes the express intent of the person wanting to die and distinguishes it from mercy killing or any other form of killing.

WORLD FEDERATION OF RIGHT TO DIE SOCIETIES (WFRTDS) Member societies advocate passive or active euthanasia or both.

Select Bibliography

A Sampling of Recent Significant Books
on the Subject of Euthanasia

Colt, George H. *The Enigma of Suicide*. New York: Summit Books, 1991.

Downing, A. B., and Barbara Smoker, eds. *Voluntary Euthanasia* (Peter Owen-Imprint). London: Humanities Press International, 1986.

Gomez, Carlos, M.D. *Regulated Death: The Case of the Netherlands*. New York: Free Press Inc., 1991.

Humphry, Derek. *Jean's Way: A Love Story*. New York: Harper and Row, 1978.

———. *Let Me Die Before I Wake*. Eugene, Ore.: Hemlock, 1991.

———. *Final Exit*. New York: Carol Publishing, 1991.

Humphry, Derek, with Ann Wickett. *The Right to Die*. New York: Harper and Row, 1990.

Johnson, Gretchen. *Voluntary Euthanasia: A Comprehensive Bibliography*. Eugene, Ore.: Hemlock, 1990.

Kevorkian, Jack, M.D. *Prescription: Medicide: The Goodness of Planned Death*. Buffalo, N.Y.: Prometheus Books, 1991.

Larue, Gerald. *Euthanasia and Religion: A Survey of the Attitudes of World Religions to the Right to Die*. Eugene, Ore.: Hemlock, 1990.

McCuen, G. E., and Therese Boucher. *Terminating Life: Conflicting Values in Health Care.* Hudson, Wis.: Gem Publications, 1985.

Morgan, Ernest. *Dealing Creatively with Death: A Manual of Death Education and Simple Burial.* 12th ed. Celo, N.C.: Celo Press, 1990.

Pence, Gregory. *Classic Cases in Medical Ethics.* New York: McGraw-Hill Inc., 1990.

Portwood, Doris. *Common Sense Suicide: The Final Right.* Eugene, Ore.: Hemlock, 1990.

Rachels, James. *The End of Life: Euthanasia and Morality.* New York: Oxford University Press, 1986.

Risley, Robert, J. D. *Death With Dignity: A New Law Permitting Physician Aid-in-Dying.* Eugene, Ore.: Hemlock, 1991.

Rollin, Betty. *Last Wish: The Controversial and Courageous True Story of a Mother's Dark Victory and a Daughter's Love.* New York: Warner Books, 1990.

Rosenblatt, Stanley. *Murder of Mercy: Euthanasia on Trial.* Buffalo, N.Y.: Prometheus Books, 1992.

Sloan, Irving J. *The Right to Die: Ethical and Legal Problems.* New York: Oceana Publications, 1988.

Spohr, Betty Baker, with Jean Vallens Bullard. *To Hold a Falling Star: Living at Home with Alzheimers.* Carbondale, Colo.: Sirpos Press, 1991.

Index

303